D1257930

The Story of Naples

Mus. Naz.] [*Alinari*

PAUL III, CARDINAL A. FARNESE, AND OTTAVIO FARNESE

(*Titian*)

The Story of Naples

by Cecil Headlam Illustrated

by Major Benton Fletcher

London: J. M. Dent & Sons, Ltd.
Aldine House ❦ ❦ *Bedford Street*
Covent Garden, W.C. ❦ ❦ 1927
New York: E. P. Dutton & Co. ❦

First Published 1927

PRINTED IN GREAT BRITAIN

TO

C. I. E.

NAPLES

Γράφε τὰς πόλεις τὸ πρῶτον
ἱλαράς τε καὶ γελώσας

ANACREON

(Write first of gay and smiling cities)

PREFACE

THE chief authorities for the history of Naples after the fall of the Roman Empire are two eminent Neapolitans, Pietro Giannone and Pietro Colletta. The *Istoria civile del regno di Napoli*, published by the former in 1723, takes the story of Naples down to the end of the Spanish dominion; it was continued by the latter in his *Storia del reame di Napoli dal* 1734 *al* 1825, a brilliantly written history, especially valuable for events in which he shared. Both historians require to be read in the light of modern criticism, such as that of Benedetto Croce in the critical essays collected under the title of *Storia del regno di Napoli* (1925), and *Uomini e cose della vecchia Italia* (1927). The former volume has a useful bibliography of writers on Neapolitan history. New light has been thrown upon the Masaniello rebellion by Michelangelo Schipa, *Masaniello* (1925), and upon the Parthenopean Republic by Niccolo Rodolico, *Il popolo agli inizi del Risorgimento* (1926). Much invaluable topographical research is enshrined in B. Capasso's *Napoli Greco-Romana*. Mr R. W. Gunther's *Bibliography of Topographical and Geological Works on the Phlegræan Fields* (1908) enumerates the chief treatises upon the topography, meteorology, and mineralogy of Naples and its environs. *Pausilypon* (1913) and *The Submerged Greek and Roman Foreshore near Naples* (1903), by the same learned author, have practically settled the vexed questions of the sites of Palæopolis and Vergil's tomb.

Since the lines on future excavations at Herculaneum were printed (p. 176), it is announced that the Italian Government has sanctioned a large scheme for that purpose (January 1927).

In the same month it was reported that the tomb of the elder Pliny (p. 166) had been discovered near Miseno.

C. H.

SUGGESTIONS FOR THE SHORT-TIME VISITOR

Those who have only *one day* to spend in Naples will probably do best to drive up to St Elmo and S. Martino in the morning (Chap. XII.), and afterwards to visit the Museo Nazionale (App. II.), Sta Chiara (Chap. X.), and Castel Nuovo (Chap. XII.).

Given *three or four more days*, spend them

(1) On Herculaneum, Pompeii, and Vesuvius (Chaps. VII. and VIII.).

(2) On the Phlegræan Fields (Posilipo, Pozzuoli, Solfatara, Baia, Averno, Cuma (Chaps. II.–VI.).

(3) On Naples proper, Sta Lucia, etc. (Chap. I.), Anticaglia (pp. 10, 125), Duomo (Chap. V.), and the Churches and Castles, and again the Museums (App. I., II.).

(4) Capri, etc. (App. III.).

IN LINE

LIST OF ILLUSTRATIONS

IN HALF-TONE

CONTENTS

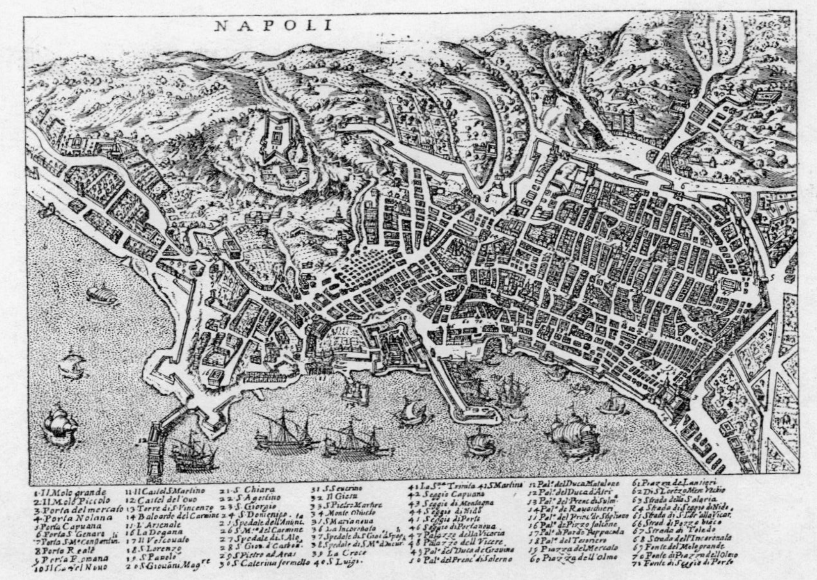

XVIITH CENTURY MAP OF NAPLES

The Story of Naples

Illustrations

The Story of Naples

CHAPTER I

Modern Naples

"Naples! thou Heart of men which ever pantest
Naked, beneath the lidless eye of Heaven!
Elysian City, which to calm enchantest
The mutinous air and sea: they round thee, even
As Sleep round Love, are driven."

SHELLEY, *Ode to Naples.*

"Un pezzo di cielo caduto in terra" (*A piece of Heaven fallen upon earth*).—SANNAZARO.

Naples modernised—Its developments and attractions—The Siren City and modern industry—Sta Lucia to-day—Outlines of the City—Old Naples—The approach by sea—The Bay of Naples—Approach by land—Vesuvius—Climate—The people and their characteristics—Fascismo and the modern spirit—Old customs—Præsepi, Pulcinella and the Neapolitan Theatre—Macaroni—Street scenes and street cries—Bassi—The Tarantella—Via Caracciolo, Via Toledo and Via dei Tribunali—Old Palaces—Styles of architecture—S. Paolo Maggiore—S. Lorenzo—Sta Maria Maggiore—S. Pietro a Maiella—College of Music—Via S. Biagio—SS. Sosio e Severino—Vico di Nilo and the Corpo di Napoli—Neapolitan carts—Charms and the Evil Eye—Gambling and lotteries—Festivals—SS. Giuseppe e Cristoforo—Sma Annunziata—The Bagpipers—Sta Maria di Piedigrotta—Neapolitan wines.

NAPLES as a mediæval city lasted well into the nineteenth century. Before the Risorgimento it was mediæval in government, or misgovernment; mediæval in sanitation, or the lack of it; mediæval in the individuality of the costumes and characteristics of its population ; mediæval in the picturesqueness and the squalor of its narrow, crowded streets ; mediæval in its social and political inequality ; mediæval in its crime and its passions, in its superstitions, in its queer, light-hearted abandonment. Within the last fifty years, inwardly and outwardly, it has been modernised out of all recognition. Since the Great War the change has been continued and quickened. Outwardly, Naples is being rapidly extended and rebuilt. So rapid, indeed, has been the process, and so determined and unchecked is its course, that much that has been written and re-written about Naples and the Neapolitans—much that one might quite recently have written—is now completely out of date. A change, too, has come over the spirit and circumstances of the people. Naples is no longer the mere city of leisure and pleasure for which Ovid declared it was made—*in otia natam Parthenopen*, and which earned it the title of *Città dei piaceri* in later times. It retains its gaiety. It provides, like all large ports, opportunities of amusement, relaxation, debauchery, if you will, but mainly for the foreigner. The low haunts of the quays and the side-shows of the Galleria Umberto I. are there for his delectation. Artistic and historic Naples has its theatre, its music, its famous opera house, its vast tourist business, its glorious scenery, its unique treasures of art, the marvels of Baiæ, Herculaneum and Pompeii, its architectural illustrations of an extraordinary history, the beauty of the Bay, the exquisite aloofness of Capri, Ischia and the other islands, glittering in an azure sea. It has the terror and the fascination of Vesuvius and Solfatara. All these are there for the delight and wonder of the visitor. They draw him irresistibly to the Siren City. But the Naples of the native and its suburbs are no longer mere scenes of pleasure, or the haunts of bandits, of beggars and parasites living on blackmail and the curiosity of travellers, or starving on the largesse of an impoverished nobility. It is no longer the city of the Lazzaroni, no longer the city of the Camorra. Naples is now not only a great port, the chief port of Southern Italy, but is also becoming industrialised. Open to the sea, at the junction of roads from north and south, and with communication with the east through a pass in the Apennines, and surrounded by a most fertile district, it has always been magnificently situated for commerce. Apart from the old industries of wine-making, coral and tortoise-shell *objets d'art*, glass, fruit, flowers and vegetables, factories have sprung up in and around the city, from Sorrento to Nocera. The leading manufactures are ships, paper, cars, wool, cotton, and silk. The cotton and silk mills, indeed, have attained an enormous output. On the other hand, the port has suffered recently from the curtailment of emigration to the United States. The quota of emigrants still allowed is now largely assigned to Italian ships, with the result that the great English liners have restricted their calls at the port.

As if to harmonise with this new outlook and development, Naples is being rebuilt in a new style, just as Pompeii was rebuilt after the earthquake, and Paris under the Empire, and London is being rebuilt to-day. The distinctive features of the modern style are lofty buildings of ferro-concrete, faced with stone,—and sanitation. Slums have been, and are being cleared away. Broad new streets have been, and are being driven through the narrow, fever-stricken alleys which formerly rendered Naples one of the most picturesque and one of the most unhealthy cities of Europe. This process began after the last terrible outbreak of cholera visited the filthy, crowded city in 1884. In a striking phrase, De Pretis, the Italian Prime Minister, declared that Naples must be disembowelled, "*Bisogna sventrare Napoli.*" Matilde Serao, the famous Neapolitan novelist, described the horrors of the slum area, the *Ventre di Napoli*, which needed to be cleaned and opened up. It embraced the four oldest parts of the city, Porto, Mercato, Vicaria, Pendino. It was a serious operation, but it was undertaken, and, in spite of very great difficulties, material and topographical, is now nearly completed. Light, air, and good water are the chief enemies of pestilence, poverty and crime. Naples needed them all. Good water was the first necessity. A plentiful and wholesome supply, as good as that of any city in the world, has been provided by the Acqua del Serino, drawn from an underground lake in the Apennines, beyond reach of pollution. The effect upon the health of the inhabitants has been quite magical. A great drainage scheme, completed in 1895, by which the sewerage is carried into the sea near Cumæ, has relieved the poisonous and offensive pollution of the Bay. "See Naples and die," we used to be told by the ecstatic lovers of her beauty. "Smell Naples and die," the disillusioned traveller would often exclaim. The jest has lost most of its savour as the result of these improvements. Most, but not all. In the residential quarters it is really out of date. There are slums enough left, where garbage rots and generates an aroma fit for the nostrils of any lover of the antique. When the dog-days return, or the sirocco blows, there are smells indeed remaining, neither rich nor rare, but fierce, strong odours compounded of every conceivable abomination of rotting filth. But those who remember the miasma of disgusting stenches which pervaded the whole city a generation since, the fine old Neapolitan reeks of forty years ago, now find comparatively little cause for offence.

Light and air were introduced by destroying the slums and constructing broad new thoroughfares in place of the old narrow streets. For the typical, stifling old *vichi* were blinded by tall houses supported by archways overhead, called *supportici*, and suffocated by overhanging balconies. The Corso Umberto Primo, or Rettifilo as it is popularly termed, supplanted and ventilated the old region of Porto and Sellaria. The Via del Duomo and Corso Garibaldi were driven at right angles to it. The ancient Via Mezzocannone was broadened and rebuilt, so that it is hard to realise that it was the highway of the primitive Greek city of Neapolis. An embankment, a row of fashionable hotels along the sea-front (the Via Parthenope), and a splendid thoroughfare lined by modern shops (the Via Sta Lucia) have replaced the most characteristic, and the most ancient, the most picturesque, and perhaps the most squalid part of old Naples, the famous fishermen's quarter, rendered doubly famous by the Neapolitan song :

> " O dolce Napoli,
> O suol beato
> Ore sorridere
> Volle il creato ;
> Tu sei l'impero
> Dell' armonia
> Santa Lucia, Santa Lucia ! "

This old picturesque quarter of Santa Lucia, with its fish-stalls, its filth, and its teeming, half-clad population—long one of the sights and sores of Italy—has entirely disappeared, and given place to the broad streets of a modern city. The narrow, fetid, overpopulated alleys have almost disappeared, only a few cut-off ends of high, narrow streets climbing up the

Pizzofalcone remain to suggest the babel, the squalor and the colour of old days. Seawards, the famous old fish-market has been replaced by the Via Nazario Sauro. Nobody but an artist regrets these things, and an artist nowadays is—nobody.

The process of aeration and enlightenment has been accelerated since the War. In order to deal with the shortage of houses after the Great War, the Italian Government took measures to induce capital to flow into the building trade. Exemption from taxation was granted for twenty-five years on all new buildings and additions to buildings. The result has been a positive riot of masonry all over the country. Naples to-day is being rebuilt and extended up the hills and along the Bay from Posilipo and Vomero to Torre del Greco and Resina at a speed and in a style which are wholly modern.

Sad, then, as her history of strife and bloodshed has been, and savage as was the treatment she was subjected to by her successive conquerors, Naples is no Niobe. She has always been quick to wipe the tears from her eyes. The sun soon dissipates the heaviest clouds. Laughter and smiles, gaiety and song, the offspring of sunshine and of race, have always helped this fair city to banish ere long the memory of her hardships and her sorrows. The Naples of to-day shows few of the scars or wrinkles of age. Ruins have been rebuilt, landmarks somewhat too ruthlessly destroyed, or their destruction disguised by new ornamentation. Here is no " nameless column with a buried base " in the Forum. Modern Naples, whatever else it is, is not a dead town. There is nothing about it of the atmosphere of Aigues Mortes, or the haunting melancholy charm of an obsolete or obsolescent mediæval town. Whilst retaining the fascination of a curious history and mementoes of former civilisations of extreme interest, the place to-day is vibrant with the energy of healthy civic and industrial occupations and aspirations. It is not without significance that it was from Naples that the post-war era of discipline, endeavour, and social unity was inaugurated under Signore Mussolini. For it was from Naples that the Black-shirts, the Fascisti, led by Il Duce, started upon their historic march to Rome. . . .

Modernised as it is, Naples yet remains one of the cities of the world most eminently worth seeing. It

CASTLE OF ST ELMO

is as true now as ever it was that you should see Naples before you die. For it is unique in the beauty of its site, unique in its individuality and history, unique in the marvels of nature which surround it, and in the treasures of art which it preserves.

The city lies at the base and on the slopes of an amphitheatre of volcanic hills which run down to the Bay. Crowned by the Castle on the height of St Elmo, it is divided into two crescent-shaped sections by a sharp ridge of rock which descends from St Elmo to the sea. This ridge, which boasts the name of Monte Echia, but is more familiarly known as Pizzofalcone (the Falcon's beard), ends in a promontory beyond which, and connected with the mainland by a causeway, is the historic little egg-shaped island of Castel dell' Ovo (*see* Chap. VI.). Pizzofalcone divides old Naples from the new, and dominates them both. The chief means of communication between the two is the Via Chiaia, which winds along a depression in the ridge and connects the Piazza S. Ferdinando (rechristened Trieste e Trentino since the War) with the Via Amedeo, the fashionable quarter of the Chiaia and the Rione Amedeo. South and east of the Pizzofalcone ridge the Rione di Sta Lucia stretches along the shore, resplendent in its new garb of quays and hotels and the old and new moles and lighthouses of the military and commercial harbours (Porto Beverello, Porto Militare and Porto Mercantile). Westwards, from the Piazza Vittoria to Mergellina, the great marine promenade of the Via Carácciolo borders the sea. Behind it, and parallel to it, stretches the charming public park and " rotten row " of the Villa Nazionale, behind which again, and beneath the hill of Vomero, is the broad street and tramway line of the Riviera di Chiaia, heading for Piedigrotta and Posilipo.

On the eastern side of the Pizzofalcone ridge three main routes—running, roughly speaking, from south to north—connect the harbour with the centre of the town. The Via Roma (the old Via Toledo), continued by the Via Sta Lucia to the sea, is the main fashionable thoroughfare and connects the Piazza del Plebiscito and Piazza Trieste e Trentino at its southern extremity with the Piazza Dante and Porta Alba to the north. The Via Sta Lucia bends eastward and upwards. Houses crowd and climb the steep sides of Pizzofalcone on the left above it. Only here and there on this side can a peep of the old Neapolitan slum life be glimpsed. Passing the Museum of Industrial Arts on the left, the new thoroughfare merges into the Via Cæsario Console, which, leaving the old Naval Arsenal below on the right, leads northwards into the magnificent open space known as the Piazza del Plebiscito. This is the finest creation of the Baroque period in Naples. It is surrounded by some remarkable buildings. On the left, in the centre of a Doric colonnade forming the circumference of a grand semicircle, rises the Church of San Francesco di Paola, an imitation of the Roman Pantheon by Pietro Bianchi (1817). Equestrian statues of Charles III. of Bourbon and Ferdinand IV., by Canova and Calì, remind us that it was founded by the latter king. Official buildings, the Preffetura and Palazzo Salerno, occupy the north and south sides. On the right, or eastern side, is the vast red pile of the *Palazzo Reale*, the fine façade of which, over 500 feet in length, is broken by niches in which are gigantic statues of representatives of the eight successive dynasties of Naples. This Royal Palace, designed by Domenico Fontana in 1600, was burnt down in 1837, and re-built in 1841. It is at present in a state of transition. Presented to the State, it is being converted into a National Museum, and several scattered collections of works of art and libraries are being transferred to it. It is therefore at present closed to the public. This is the new home of the Biblioteca Nazionale, which was founded in 1734 and consists of 420,000 volumes, 225,000 pamphlets, 8000 MSS. and 4000 incunabula. It has been transferred from the overburdened *Museo Nazionale*. Here, too, is housed the Lucchesi-Palli Library, which comprises 41,000 volumes of music and dramatic literature, as well as the famous Herculaneum papyri (*see* Chap. VII.). The entrance to the garden and the Palazzo is on the left-hand side of the *Teatro San Carlo* (facing the main entrance) in the adjacent Piazza Trieste e Trentino. This famous

Opera House, which for music-lovers recalls memories from Rossini to Caruso, was designed by Giovanni Medrano in 1737, the courtyard and loggia by Antonio Niccolini. Opposite to it is the new arcade of the Galleria Umberto I., which is lined with shops and has already recovered from the devastation caused by a fire two years ago. Further down, to the right, the Castel Nuovo (*see* Chap. XII.). East of the Via Roma, the Via del Duomo runs from the Strada Nuova della Marina through the Piazza Niccolo Amore and past the Cathedral to the Porta S. Gennaro. Parallel to the Via del Duomo and on the eastern side of it, the Corso Garibaldi leads from the sea and the Via Marinella, past the Castel del Carmine, the Piazza Pepe and Piazza del Mercato, to the Porta Nolana and the Central Railway Station (Stazione Centrale), and onwards to the neighbourhood of the Porta Capuana. Within the eastern and western boundaries, marked roughly by the Corso Garibaldi and the Via Roma, lay the old Greek and Roman cities of Neapolis. Three parallel streets, narrow and ancient, running from east to west, are clearly original Decuman ways, the cross streets of a Roman town. These are the Via Anticaglia, with the Porta Romana at the west end, the Via dei Tribunali, its eastern gate leading to Capua, and the Via Biagio, with gates leading to Nola and Cumæ. The modernised Via Mezzocannone was one of the streets at right angles to them which originally connected them with the sea. Probably it marks the line of the western wall of old Greek Neapolis, running by way of S. Domenico and S. Pietro a Maiella to the neighbourhood of the Porta Constantinopoli.

These are the main outlines of the lower part of the city. It is well to bear them in mind, for they are obscured by an enormous tangle of narrow and winding streets, intersecting them and each other, and spread over a vast area. But these indications, combined with a free use of an exceedingly good tram-service with a very cheap and universal fare of 60 centesimi, and an underground railway service, will render the task of the traveller comparatively light.[1] All the same, Naples and its treasures cannot be seen in a day. Owing to its variety and extent it is really more difficult to "do" Naples than it is to do Rome in three days. A fortnight at least, and preferably three weeks are needed to appreciate its treasures. It is in and about the old Decuman ways, especially the Via Anticaglia, with its remains of the theatre where Nero sang, and the Tribunali, which connects the very modern Piazza Dante and the Porta Alba with the Castel Capuano and the characteristic street scenes about the Porta Capuana, and again in the neighbourhood of the old Forum or Market Place, Mercato Vecchio, that one finds most of the fascinating bits of old Naples. Crowded with stalls and shops that embouch upon the uneven flag-stones of the roadway —there are no side walks—and filled with jostling passengers and pedlars, cars, carriages, and donkey-carts, these narrow streets present all that familiar yet surprising scene of busy, noisy, cheerful life which is one of the attractions of an old Italian town. It was down these streets that Nero drove on his way to perform in the neighbouring theatre; it was down these streets that all the conquering kings rode in the splendid pageantry of their state entries through the Porta Capuana; it was of these streets that Boccaccio wrote in the *Decameron*; and it is in these streets that now throbs the full tide of modern Neapolitan life, laughing, loving, singing, bartering, jostling.

[1] The chief tramway centres are the Piazza Dante, Piazza Trieste et Trentino (S. Ferdinando) and the Piazza Vittoria.

Fortunate is the traveller who obtains his first view of Naples from the sea. Approaching the city by land one sees little of its setting before one is engulfed in the turmoil of its streets. But before the eyes of the seafarer, if the weather be fine, there is slowly unfolded the most wonderful panorama in Europe, a panorama of blue sea and glistering isles and smoking volcano, of a city climbing from a curving shore to the crest of hills which sink again into a distant, fertile plain.

The islands of Ischia (north-west) and Capri (south-east) stand as sentinels over the entrance to the Bay, guarding the fifty miles of crescent-shaped coast and jutting promontories within it, and the vast white city which spreads fanwise up the slopes of the encircling amphitheatre of mountains. They rise, those rocky islets, sheer, silent, forbidding almost, through the diaphanous blue haze that lightly veils the azure loveliness of the sea. But to those who know their history they seem to whisper the romance of all those seafarers who have followed in the wake of Odysseus and Æneas, and come to these haunted shores in search of wealth or sunshine, of beauty, love, repose. Greeks, Romans, Normans, Saracens, French, and Spaniards, successive waves of foreigners have swept into this lovely Bay before us; have come and gone; and leave it now—Italy!

These volcanic islands guard, or herald, the approach to the Capes which form the horns of the crescent of the Bay. Ischia, with the island of Procida behind it, points the way to the Cape of Miseno; Capri to the Punta della Campanella. This bold headland of Campanella, which forms the eastern extremity of the Bay and faces Miseno across some thirty-five miles of sea, took its name of old from the goddess Minerva. *Promontorium Minervæ* it was called. It is separated from Capri by a strait four miles wide. Island and promontory alike are, geologically, but the continuation of a mountain range, an offshoot of the Apennines, which, stretching from the parent range near Cava to the sea, frames and enfolds the eastern half of the Bay. Among the cliffs of its southern coast lies exquisite Amalfi, by no means destroyed by the earthquake of a few years ago, and the Bay of Salerno, Sinus Pæstinus as it used to be called, taking its name from Pæstum. On the

ISCHIA

Neapolitan shore of the Punta della Campanella is beautiful Sorrento with the giant hills behind it, the Monti Lattari which were for so long the homes of the *Lazzaroni* and brigands. At the foot of Monte Sant' Angelo, which rises sheer from the sea to a height of 4722 feet, is the industrial town of Castellamare di Stabia, by the site of that Roman Stabiæ which shared the doom of Herculaneum and Pompeii. Famous for the beauty of the woods on the mountain slopes in the background, Castellamare was long a favourite resort of Bourbon kings. They inherited the villa of Quisisana from Pier Luigi Farnese, Duke of Parma and heir of Pope Paul III., evil of life and evil of face, whose features live for us in Titian's portrait in the *Museo Nazionale*. The villa is now an hotel, very popular as a summer resort. Westwards along the coast glitters the continuous series of villages at the base of Vesuvius which form, as it were, one long suburb of Naples—Torre Annunziata, by Pompeii, Torre del Greco, Resina, Portici, San Giovanni a Teduccio, Pazzigno—the names of these ever resurgent victims of the Volcano's wrath recall the recurrent tragedies of ages, forming, as it has been said, an unbroken chain of tragic horror, of smiling grace.

Within these Capes of Miseno and Punta della Campanella is outspread the sinuous beauty of the Bay of Naples. On the right rises Vesuvius, a column of vapour streaming lazily from its cone into the blue sky; on the left lie Baia, Posilipo, and the Phlegræan Fields, and in the centre Naples spreads fanwise upon the breasts of the encircling hills. The palms, oleanders, and holm-oaks of the Park of the Villa Nazionale contribute a welcome splash of green, contrasting with the white vista of quays and houses, otherwise only broken by the red façade of the eighteenth century barracks above Castel dell' Ovo. Earth, sky and sea mingle in a rapture of physical delight. In this natural picture, form, colour, atmosphere, composition, grouping of detail, shade, balance of parts, relation of the centre to the whole design, all the points which the critic has learned to look for in the masterpieces of painting, are observed and exemplified. Here, it might be thought, the Great Landscape Painter has thrown down a challenge to all those lesser artists whom He created in His own image, drawing the outlines of His design in elemental sea and rock, and washing them over with colours that are for ever

[*Alinari*

THE CAPUAN GATE

changing and for ever lovely, even as the sunshine, sea and air of which they are composed.

Much the larger proportion, however, of the travellers who have time to see Naples intelligently must come by train from Rome or Reggio and Palermo. For the brief visit of a liner is all too short for that purpose. Happily for them, there is no finer view of Vesuvius than that provided by the road from Rome. The train swings down from the snow-capped Apennines, beneath the famous Benedictine monastery of Monte Cassino, with its great library, crossing the river of Liris, which waters the fields Horace loved and sang, and passing the gates of Capua, where Hannibal wintered his army and where a great amphitheatre bears witness to the triumph of Rome. So it winds its way into the rich Campanian plain, that Campania Felix which is, as it has ever been, a very garden of fruit and flowers and vegetables and vineyards. Then, on the right, appear the twin peaks of Vesuvius, whose beauty is so great and whose history is so horrible, that the least emotional must feel a thrill when for the first time they see it outlined against the sky, " the terror and the pride " of Naples. A column of vapour curls placidly upwards from the crater and drifts away in a cloud across the Bay. Flushed by rays of the setting sun, it has, close at hand, a sombre and lurid effect, contrasting vividly with the transparent sky, blue and egg-green, in which it floats. But as it dissipates in the distance, it bathes the bare tops of the neighbouring mountains in a delicate amethystine haze. Amidst green gardens and vineyards, tiny houses climb daringly up the threatening, heavily-scarred sides of the volcano, playing as it were a game of Tom Tiddler's Ground with the ogre of the mountain, regardless of the streams of molten lava and stifling ash with which he may overwhelm them. At night the lights of Messrs Cook's funicular railway glitter like a diamond brooch pinned along the shoulder of the hill.

It is a fortunate circumstance, from the point of view of the dweller in Naples and the western half of the Bay, that the sun rises behind Vesuvius. Unforgettable is the vision of the dawn flushing with flame colour the tongues and edges of the vapour column and tingeing with saffron and coral the long streak of diaphanous white cloud which has drifted across from the cone, drawn across the pure blue sky as a painter with his brush might draw a muslin scarf. The azure water below is flecked with tiny waves and dotted with painted boats, oared by fishermen working their nets; a schooner with the full picturesque Mediterranean rig crosses the middle distance, and in the mouth of the Bay a liner or big cargo boat is riding at anchor between the guardian isles of Capri and Ischia.

So long as that column of vapour rises steadily from the volcano it produces a cloud and haze which give colour and atmosphere to the surroundings and soften the glare of the sun. It is also a sign of fair weather. As a general rule, when the clouds cover the peaks of Vesuvius, they are precursors of rain. For Naples, of course, is not always bathed in sunshine.[1] No daughter of the mountains and the sea can ever be monotonously placid and smiling. There are grey

[1] Naples enjoys what is known as the Mediterranean climate. The average annual rainfall is 26½ inches. From June to August it is practically negligible, but the autumn and winter rains are fairly heavy. October to December are the wettest months (4.3, 4.9, 4.2), July the driest (.08). Though snow is rare in Naples it often whitens the surrounding mountains. The average number of perfectly fine days in the year is 90, cloudy 70, variable, 120, and 80 wet. Of the latter 30 occur in the autumn, 24 in the winter months, 18 in the spring, and only 8 in the summer.

days when the sky is overcast and the sea of leaden hue—when the *Sirocco* is blowing from beyond Capri, or *Libecchio*, the enervating, pestilent south-west wind from over the African deserts. There are days of bitter, blustering north-easters, when the *Tramontano* whips down from the snow-covered Apennines, cutting and exasperating with its biting gusts and choking dust storms. But these and the heavy rain-storms are soon over. Naples soon wears her smile again, and the rain-swept skies are more pellucid than before, and the transparent sea breaks in tiny wavelets on the shore, smiling like a child the more sweetly after a brief outburst of ill-temper. Then more than ever one appreciates the purely physical charm of Naples and the curious luminosity of the Neapolitan sunlight which renders distance oddly deceptive and makes it hard to realise how great is the stretch of sea across the Bay. Clear but not hard, brilliant but not blinding; softened but unshaded it shines through an atmosphere rendered iridescent by the unnumbered particles of volcanic dust and vapour, and the moisture of the sea.

Naples, "*il desiderio eterno dei stranieri*," as an old chronicler terms her, became the unwilling mistress of many foreigners. To Greek and Roman, Norman and Saracen has been added not only the blood of French and Spanish conquerors, but also of all the drift of a seaport town on the high road to the East—Maltese, Arabs, Levantines, Jews, and a sprinkling of all the European races. Jews, however, do not flourish here any more than at Genoa; native shrewdness, it is said, is too much for them. The immense increase of population in recent years has rendered Naples the second city of Italy and one of the largest cities in the world. Since 1850 it has more than doubled its numbers, which are now in the neighbourhood of a million. This increase, due to the development of the place both as a port and an industrial centre, has left its mark noticeably upon the physique of the people, not for the better so far as size and looks are concerned. The successive waves of invaders have left marks of their civilisations on the land. Many traces, for instance, survive in the common parlance, such as the use of the Spanish Don and Donna for Signore and Signora, and the term Minzu, which is applied to cooks and is an obvious corruption of Monsieur. A writer in the seventeenth century collected a large number of words which he thought were derived from the ancient Greek.[1]

From this great mixture of peoples it cannot be said that there has emerged a new and dominant race. But the Neapolitans are a peculiar and very interesting people. They are as distinct from other Italians as their language is unintelligible to them.

Everybody has observed the sunny, mercurial temperament of these people. Excitable and roguish, they balance a childlike curiosity with childlike confidences. Quick to laughter and eager for a smile, they have a ready and often Rabelaisian wit. A smile, be it said, will take you far in Naples while a cross word may land you in difficulties. For, in accordance with their passionate natures, the Neapolitans pass with surprising readiness into outbursts of fierce resentment and uncontrolled anger. You must take them as they come. These characteristics are all parts of a sunny temperament, woven, to put it nicely, out of the very beams of light which rise, like Aphrodite herself, reflected from their dazzling seas. As an accompaniment to these changing moods one notices

[1] Capaccio, *Descrizione di Napoli.*

A STREET IN NAPLES

the changing tones of voice, which pass with startling rapidity from the soft and musical notes of their ordinary conversation to shrill cries of protest or hoarse, raucous barks of anger, threats or fear, sounds hardly human. A more attractive accompaniment of all conversation is the extraordinarily expressive language of gestures, the silent eloquence of fingers and hands which illumine and illustrate each sentence, each idea. It is fascinating to watch. After a little observation you see that many of these gestures are stereotyped. It might, indeed, be possible to carry on conversation by their means without uttering a word.

Since the War there is observable a certain change of tone and spirit in the people. Something of the old-time gaiety and light-heartedness has gone. The causes are not far to seek. A valiant effort is being made by Italy to pay her war bills and to reconstitute her finances on a sound basis. Immense new enterprises are being started in every direction. But in the meantime taxation is heavy and living is dear—terribly dear compared with pre-war days. Rents have been increased, and the cost of such necessities as wine, bread and tobacco has risen and keeps rising. Increased demands, increased taxes, increased prices, pursuing one another in a vicious circle, involve an increased struggle for existence which does not tend to lightness of spirit or buoyancy of demeanour.

Politically, too, there is a new spirit. "Fascismo" preaches, deliberately and self-consciously, the doctrine of discipline, of serious work, of self-control, of national effort, as against self-indulgence, abandonment to the whim or fortune of the moment, against idleness, corruption, talk. In the Naples of to-day there is much less of that helpless, fatalistic attitude summed up in the phrase, *Non c'e che fa* (there is no help for it), which Di Giacomo described as comprising the people's whole philosophy. And no one can deny that in manners and conduct Naples has left the days of a ruined nobility and rapacious *Lazzaroni* happily far behind. If the influences we have mentioned have noticeably sobered the excesses of the Neapolitan temperament, it is equally noticeable that the people have rapidly outgrown the evil effects of the generations of tyrannical oppression which these pages will have to record.

A new civic consciousness is developing, growing from an awakened municipal pride and responsibility and embracing a sense of national unity and national endeavour. It is typified in one small way by that notice in the gardens, "*Cittadini, Protegete i vostri giardini*"—Imagine Bomba putting up such a notice! It is typified, too, by modernisation of Naples to which we have referred, and by the frequent statues to local politicians and municipal workers; typified again by the cotton factories, the Italian steamship lines, the taking over of all dock and steel works.

Some, indeed, may think that they have gone too far in modernisation and have sacrificed too ruthlessly the things of the past, whether in the destruction of old buildings, or the abolition of old customs, even though they be but old superstitions. Among the good things of the past which have been discarded must be reckoned the old national costumes. The drab round coat, the soft hat or cap, and the uniform Paris fashions are but a poor substitute for the brilliant and picturesque and varied dress of old Naples. A very good idea of what these costumes were like can be obtained from the remarkable *Præsepe* which is preserved in the museum of S. Martino. A *præsepe* was a representation of the Nativity, and it was the custom to portray the figures about the Manger in contemporary dress. Large sums were spent and good artists employed in their production. They were produced at Christmas time, often upon the flat garden roofs which used to be such a striking feature of Naples. Yielding to the influence of cars, trams, and education, the last public letter-writer has disappeared from the archways of San Carlo. The reciters of Tasso no longer declaim on the Molo. But the *præsepe* still appears at Christmas-tide, though not in such numbers as in the eighteenth century, when each household prided itself on the possession of one more magnificent than the rest. It is a striking demonstration of the popularity of Pulcinella that his figure was frequently exhibited in close proximity to the Manger.

Pulcinella, or Policinella, was the stock comic character evolved by the Neapolitan Mask Comedy and brought to fame and perfection, if not invented, by Silvio Fiorillo in the seventeenth century. Another popular " mask " of the same type was that of a Spanish braggadocio, Captain Matamoros. Pulcinella, with his companion Piripicchio, is always getting into difficulties through his naive extravagances—the Charlie Chaplin of a former stage and art—but manages to extricate himself from every embarrassment by his native wit and bland air of innocence. Greedy, cowardly, awkward, he is endowed with the mingled cunning and stupidity of the peasant. He is a more human and genial creature than our Mr Punch, who is his direct descendant. There was no limit to his outspokenness, and indeed the value of the character was that in the hands of a capable actor it gave scope for the coarse wit and buffoonery, enlivened by gestures and grimaces typical of Neapolitan comedy, *lazzi*

Napoletani.[1] Pulcinella's make-up consisted of a black mask and white domino, a peaked cap above a large hooked nose, and he uttered his jests in a high squeaky voice—all features familiar in Mr Punch. Croce thinks that his name was derived from *pulcino* (a chicken), suggested by the appearance of the mask. The coarse comedies in which he was the leading character used to be played in the Largo del Castello, and afterwards in the famous little theatre of S. Carlino, which disappeared when the Piazza Municipio was widened in 1884. Policinella, however, still keeps the boards in the dialect comedies which may be seen in the little house nearly opposite the Piazza Cavour station. The Marionettes, too, still flourish in a tiny theatre near the Stazione Centrale (Via Foria, Via A. Poerio), in spite of the competition of the Cinema. Probably the scene and the audience will prove more interesting than the story of the *Reali di Francia*, which the dolls, still arrayed in their gorgeous traditional costumes, perform so well. Your visit to this house —it is just a room with two low galleries built into it—will probably be a short one. For you will find it crowded with fellow-creatures—and others—and the atmosphere is unendurable.

Such conditions do not, apparently, inconvenience a populace accustomed to the dark and airless slums which have been described in such lurid detail by Matilde Serao. Those who wish to know how the lower classes live, eat, labour, and sleep in Naples should read her *Paese di Cuccagna*, or Stamer's *Dolce Napoli*, or Mario's *Miseria in Napoli*. They will

[1] The subject of the Neapolitan Theatre may be pursued in Benedetto Croce's *Teatri di Napoli*, and Di Giacomo's account of the S. Carlino Theatre. Guappo was another stock character of Neapolitan comedy, a fine dashing fellow, a "whopper" in fact.

be appalled by the revelations of sordid poverty, and the more amazed when they observe the careless gaiety and the overflowing animal spirits with which it is borne. For it remains true, in spite of the post-war changes we have noticed above, that something perhaps of the blood of the old Greek race, something tonic in the air and sunshine of their wonderful Bay, something exhilarating in the blending of the mountains with the sea, has filled the inhabitants of this old afflicted city with a perennial frivolity of spirit. Some reaction, too, of the human mind may be there, born of the immense and ever-present terror of Vesuvius, of towering volcano, recurrent earthquakes, of racing tides. Whatever its origin, it is here, here in the blood of every true Neapolitan, enabling him to rise superior to the oppression of slums and politics, superstition, poverty, ignorance, stupidity, fecklessness, and all the darkening and depressing influences to which mankind is heir. Their songs, their gesticulations, the very exaggerations of phrase bear witness to it. Naples and Capri have always been to Rome—and therefore to the world—as Paris used to be to the dreary, repressed London of a hundred years ago. The one thought of the Roman proconsul, hurrying home after wringing a million from his province, was to build a villa and share in the gaiety of the Bay. And to-day the joyous Neapolitan airs insist on being sung in spite of the political and industrial seriousness characteristic of the age.

The standard of living has been raised all over the world since the War. It is perhaps no longer so true as it was of the Neapolitan poor, when Dumas wrote his *Le Corricolo*, that they only demand a stone for a pillow and a *pizza*—a piece of sweetened bread often spread with garlic and crushed tomato—and a slice of *cocomero* (water-melon) for a meal, content to contemplate the stars in the velvet firmament, each one of which, in their belief, is a lamp which burns at the feet of the Virgin. But even so, the Neapolitan is content with a diet which an Englishman would consider unsubstantial as the stuff that dreams are made of. Fruit in summer, in winter bread, garlic, and mussel and other shell fish (*vongole*), snail or vegetable soup suffice him. For macaroni, like meat, is beyond the reach of the very poor. Those who can afford it are connoisseurs both of the manufacture and the cooking thereof. It must be "green," that is newly made, and cooked just so, with tomato sauce or *vongole*. The Neapolitan would not touch the sodden over-boiled mess of stale macaroni which is the English notion of the dish.

Matilde Serao, in her *Leggende Napoletane*, has rescued from oblivion a lively legend of the discovery of this national dish. In the narrow and wretched Vico dei Cortellasi, which has now disappeared, there dwelt in the reign of the Emperor Frederick II. a mysterious old man. People passed his house with a sign and a shudder, for it was rumoured that Cicho was a magician. Night and day he toiled behind barred doors at his crucibles and alembics, his pots and pans, decocting none could tell what deadly potion or magic elixir of life from the herbs he collected in the fields. In reality, Cicho, who had once been rich and courted, and was now poor and lonely, was devoting himself to discovering one of the secrets which render mankind happy. In the same house there dwelt a woman, whose curiosity at length overcame her superstitious dread. For one day she heard Cicho cry, like Archimedes, Eureka! Eureka! and rush excitedly into the street. Seizing the moment and darting into his room, Jovannella, for that was the woman's name, beheld nothing there that savoured of black magic. What she saw was a smoking dish, a divine stew, cooking upon a charcoal stove. She took it and tasted of it, and knew that her fortune was made. She bade her husband go straight to the Palace and submit this savoury wonder to the Emperor's palate. Frederick tasted and fell into an ecstasy of delight, for this was macaroni as it should be made, with grated cheese and tomato sauce and all the ingredients which render it the food of the blessed—*μακαρῶν*—macaroni. Jovannella's fortune was made. But Cicho il Mago, returning to his house and finding the dish gone and his secret stolen, fled from it and was never seen again. But in after years those who passed the *Casa del Mago* at midnight would often see the ghostly figure of the magician bending over his stove or cutting his macaroni in lengths, as you may see the macaroni makers do in the streets on the way to Herculaneum to-day. And by his side stood Jovannella making tomato sauce, whilst the Devil himself grated the cheese and blew up the fire.

It will have been gathered that those who remember the disreputable, noisy, fever-stricken city of forty years ago, with its crowds of laughing, shrieking, gesticulating, quarrelsome, and sometimes threatening inhabitants, the din of touts and beggars and whip-cracking cabmen, lashing their wickedly ill-used, cruelly bitted horses, and the shameless dirt and squalor of the narrow alleys and fetid slums, will hardly recognise Naples if they revisit it now. Yet for those in search of the picturesque, narrow tortuous streets enough survive, some climbing up the several hills by means of steps and ramps; streets lined by lofty tottering houses upheld by arches which join the upper stories, and, spanning the road, combine, with the overhanging balconies and the day's washing hung across from house to house, to block out the narrow slit of sky above.[1] Incredibly noisy, insanitary and picturesque.

Though a good deal of poultry still pick up a living in the by-streets, the cows and goats which used to add to the gaiety of scenes by taking their milk from door to door, and even climbing the stairs of tenements, are now only allowed in the streets before 9 a.m.

These conditions of life, added to carts and cobblestones, involve a vast amount of noise. Whilst centuries of sunshine would seem to have filled this people with an excess of energy which must find its vent in a wonderful output of talk and vehemence of gesticulation, centuries of their own din would seem to have rendered them impervious to noise. One notices the same tolerance among the inhabitants of the noisier streets in London. They almost seem to like the din which is distressing to more sensitive and less accustomed ears.

The great height of the old houses and of many of the new ones has led to the custom of shopping by basket. The occupant of an upper story, in order to avoid the journey up and down the steep and dirty stairs of a tenement house, lowers a basket by a string from the window when a barrow of fish or vegetables, or whatever it may be, appears in the road below. This custom adds considerably to the permanent babel of the streets. For the vendor must first make his

[1] The high narrow by-streets of Naples, called *Vichi* or *Vicoletti* or *Strettole*, are frequently connected and supported by arches aloft, and in that case are sometimes termed *Supportici*. The steep flagged lanes leading into the country are known as *Salite* or *Calate*, or *Gradoni*, if they are provided with steps or *rampe*. *Fondaco* is the name of a closed courtyard, or *largo*, the Neapolitan word for *piazza*. But the more general Roman word *Via* is rapidly superseding both these specific Neapolitan terms and the word *Strada* for street.

presence known, then the housekeeper her needs, and bargaining must be carried on—and Neapolitan bargaining is a life's work in itself.[1] All these processes are conducted by the respective parties at the top of their voices, in order to carry the distance and to overcome the surrounding din of bawling neighbours, passing traffic, and the cries of other pedlars. It is little wonder if the voice of the average Neapolitan, by nature soft and musical, is often hoarse and raucous to a degree.

The cries of the street-vendors, like the gestures of the people, are an amusing study in themselves. Among these hawkers (*bociatori*) you will hear a woman with a basket on her head crying up her fruit, or a man displaying his fish with the exclamation, "*Che belle cose, che belle cose!*" or "*Ma guardate, come sono!*" There is a *mellonaro*, a seller of water-melons, praising his wares in a frenzy of admiration, extolling their coolness or their beauty, for they come from Castellamare, or likening them to the sun, the moon, Vesuvius itself, on account of the redness of their flesh. Or in the winter there is the seller of roasted chestnuts (*bruciate*) crying "*Le caldarroste!*" and the seller of *pizze* and *franfellichi* (pastry and gingerbread); and of course there is the *maccaronaro*, the macaroni man. Sitting by his glowing stove from which rise strong odours of hot oil, tomatoes, onions and cheese, he announces that his macaroni is fresh made, *Avvi cca* (*a cotta deli verdi!*). Then there are sellers of roast Indian corn (*vendi-spighe*)

[1] In the larger shops the practice of charging fixed prices (*prezzi fissi*) has recently to a great extent superseded the old custom of oriental bargaining by which the seller asked about three times as much as he expected to get. The haggling that ensued used to involve a marvellous waste of time and energy, but was amusing if you had the leisure for it, and very good for your Italian.

who announce their wares as fine, tender and young turkey-cocks, all hot! (*Gallinacettin teneri*, *bellicaldi*), and the sellers of herbs, "*Centerbe! Centerbe!*" Most common and striking of all is the *acquaiolo*, or water-seller, whose gaily-painted stall brightens every other street corner, and who dispenses *acqua fresca, acqua fresca e sugo di limone!* (fresh water and lemon juice and other flavourings), or *acqua acetosa*, the sulphurous medicinal water drawn from the famous spring of Sta Lucia. The two-eared water-pots (*mummarelle*) of these lemonade sellers suggest a direct descent from the amphoræ of classical times, some very fine specimens of which lie in the gardens of the Museo Nazionale. These itinerant and other *bociatori* add very much to the vivacity as well as to the noise of the streets.

The stabilised shops in the poorer quarters, which are also the homes of the tradesmen, consist of one ground-floor room, and are known as *bassi*. They are closed at night by huge sliding doors, and have neither window nor chimney. At the back of these dark and tiny shops and work-sheds there is always visible a vast bed. This was the dowry which the mother of the establishment brought when she came thither as a bride. Always too, within the tiny living-room, and at the back of every shop counter, a picture or figure of the Madonna hangs upon the wall, and before it a lamp or candle is kept burning night and day. As years go by and the occupants of the family bed increase, the father of the establishment takes to sleeping in summer for the most part in the street. The Neapolitan, according to the saying, lives in the street. There, too, his cooking is largely done, upon a low charcoal pot which is roused by fanning or by lighting fragments of wood from the top. But to a great extent he relies upon purchasing a dainty morsel from one of the innumerable cookshops which dispense fried fish or savoury soups.

There is a wall painting found at Pompeii which depicts very much the same scene. It represents a cook with his pot in the open air—one of those large

BASSO (S. AGOSTINO)

bronze vessels we see in the museum. He is surrounded by people attracted by the good smell of his cookery. He holds at the end of the stick a little copper cup, with which he is about to fish out from the pot the savoury morsels as he sells them to the crowd.

People accustomed to live so much in the open air are naturally affected by the cold and wet of winter and spring. For the rainfall as measured by inches is heavy in Naples from October to March, and the snow often lies low upon Vesuvius and the surrounding mountains. The cold winds and rain depress the volatile temperament of the Neapolitans, who become in those seasons comparatively quiet and sluggish. But as the heat of summer advances, and the broom and oleanders break into flower, they recover their vitality. It reveals its presence by an access of song and laughter, breaking through the din of trams and street cries. This is the case not only among the musicians who sing before the *caffe*, but among the people, the children, the workers. They take to song as they take to the sea, young and old spending more and more hours in the refreshing waters along the shores of Mergellina and of Posilipo. Then the bathing stations (*stabilimenti*) and villas along the shore begin to open their windows after the long sleep of winter. And from *caffe* to *stabilimento*, from *trattoria* to *hôtel de luxe*, mandoline, guitar, and fiddle accompany the Neapolitan tremolo to the tunes of which they never tire—*Marechiaro*, *Sole Mio*, *Santa Lucia*, or *Addio*, *Mia Bella Napoli*. Or the dance, the native *Tarantella*:

> " When cooler shadows fall,
> And the mild moon her fairy network weaves,
> The lute or mandoline accompanied
> By many a voice yet sweeter than their own,
> Kindles nor slowly; and the dance displays
> The gentle arts and witcheries of love,
> Its hopes and fears and feigning, till the youth
> Drops on his knee as vanquished, and the maid,
> Her tambourine uplifting with a grace,
> Nature's and Nature's only, bids him rise."
>
> ROGERS, *Italy*.

This graceful, expressive dance is well worth seeing when performed at an hotel in Naples by professional

PORTA NOLANA

dancers dressed up for the occasion. But it is still more attractive when rendered by the peasants themselves in holiday mood in some unsophisticated spot, on the occasion of some local *festa*, such as that of San Michele in the island of Procida. Mr Vaughan, in his *Riviera of Naples*, describes the instruments of the primitive orchestra which accompanies the dancers. The idea of the dance is the representation of all the moods of courtship. The lover and his lass perform in a dramatic and wonderfully vivacious manner all the incidents of ardent love-making, supplication, rejection, acceptance, quarrels, forgiveness, coyness, surrender, jealousy, and the final delirium of kisses, confidence and joy. It is danced with the utmost spirit but also with grace and elegance, and there is nothing of the Corybantic frenzy about it, which the popular derivation of its name might lead one to expect. For it is said to be derived from the *tarantula*, a poisonous spider, whose bite renders a man stupid and comatose. The cure for the bite was violent exertion, which the affected person was most easily induced to take by music which roused him to frantic capering. More probably the word is derived from a bacchanalian dance introduced by the citizens of the old Greek city of Taranto, which has now lost its more aggressive characteristics.

The hot nights, the stir of song and sentiment, the gentle splash of the cooling sea, the blue darkness of the curving shores lit by a myriad lights, the white moonlight outlining the mighty, ominous mass of Vesuvius and the rock of Capri, couched like a guardian sphinx at the approach to the Bay—all contribute to form a picture delightful to the eye and senses, unforgettable in the memory. Along the Riviera di Chiaia and the Via Caracciolo the car and the motor-bicycle continue the traditions of the famous *trottata*, where in the evening every Neapolitan, high and low, would turn out to "eat the air," as they say in India, in little trotting carriages (*carrozzele*), which are by no means yet extinct. Apart from these drives and the Rotten Row of the Villa Nazionale, the Via Toledo is the chief fashionable thoroughfare. Via Toledo, one says, for although it has been re-christened Via Roma, it is still to the Neapolitan "Toledo." For all that, it is very different from the street that Dumas and even recent guide-book writers have described. Crowded indeed it usually is, and noisy, and it is still a broad thoroughfare of shops and *caffe*, and the main artery of the town's traffic and the resort and promenade of all classes. But it is no longer conspicuous as the first step made by Naples towards civilisation. The construction of the Via Sta Lucia and the driving of other and ever newer broad thoroughfares through former slums render it no longer unique. It was built by the great Viceroy, Don Pedro de Toledo, at the beginning of the sixteenth century, and was long one of the finest streets in Europe, remarkable for its broad pavements for pedestrians.

When we have had our fill of such things, we turn again to those narrow streets which offer so vivid a contrast to the garish, brilliantly lit thoroughfares of modern Europe. "Sir," as Dr Johnson ought to have said, "let us take a walk down the Via dei Tribunali." For here are your pictures of characteristic Naples. The street is lined by shops of the primitive type, and bunkered at every step by cooking vessels or stalls of *vongole* or *pizze* in the middle of the roadway. Horses and carts, donkeys and motor-cars, which nearly fill the width of the street, push their way past whilst you flatten yourself against the walls of the houses. On either side, the ruins of old Renaissance palaces, with their balustrades and arcades, now used as shop and warehouse, interrupt the line of tall balconied old houses. This is true also of most of the neighbouring streets.

The history of these old palaces may be summed up as follows. Fashionable Naples has tended to move northwards and westwards, leaving the old princely palaces stranded in the centre and east of the city. When their aristocratic inmates no longer wished to dwell in them, and found the burden of keeping them up too heavy, they were sold to speculators, who cut them up into small tenements and let them out room by room. Huddled up between wretched houses, with their old Renaissance doorways and courtyards with fine *portici* and balustrades, these palaces have been absorbed into the slums by which they were surrounded. A striking example of this is the Palazzo Laurino, by Vanvitelli, on the south side of the Tribunali, not far from the Vico Cinquesanti. The walls of the circular courtyard are decorated with elaborate lunettes and statuary, and there is a fine stairway in the corner. The whole place is now used as a wine store.

To the investigator of old streets and the inquirer after archæological remains Naples presents some curious and baffling features. The city has been rebuilt piecemeal a score of times since the Greek colonists from Cumæ first settled here. Original buildings have been used as quarries for, or incorporated in, their successors. These processes, and the steady deposit of soil and debris throughout the ages—amounting, it is calculated, roughly to one foot per century—have buried the remains of Grecian Naples many yards beneath the modern city. As to later work, houses have been built upon and around Roman remains and in the very arches and entrances of the Roman theatre. Renaissance porches and stucco plaster have cut into or overlaid Roman substructures. Houses have been built both around and upon churches, and workshops inserted beneath them, as you may see, for instance, in the case of S. Eligio, or SS. Ascenzione in Chiaia, and the huge round towers of the Angevin fortifications and gateways have suffered the same treatment, as at Porta Gennaro and Porta Nolana, or been cleared away altogether. Streets, again, have been cut through, or been tunnelled and burrowed under older streets and buildings. The very names of the streets which remain have been altered again and again, and continue to be altered.

These various processes have been going on for centuries. Change has been the only continuity of style, under each succeeding dynasty and in each succeeding age. Norman Sicilian supplanted Roman, as Roman supplanted Greek; Angevin and French Gothic were followed by Renaissance, and Renaissance by the Aragonese and Spanish baroque. The process is being continued, as we have seen, at the present time. The modern buildings are constructed for the most part on the Parisian model, huge blocks of houses built around a courtyard. This dull and uninspired type of architecture has entirely superseded that of those splendid old palaces of the great families and rich merchants with which the centre of Naples especially was once filled, and of which deplorably dilapidated remains still rouse our curiosity and regret.

Pursuing our way westwards from the Via del Duomo down the Tribunali, we pass between the churches of S. Paolo Maggiore (north), rebuilt by Francesco Grimaldi in 1690, with its Corinthian columns, relics of a Temple of the Dioscuri, and S. Lorenzo (south), the Angevin Gothic church, largely restored by Ferdinando Felice after the earthquake of 1732, where Boccaccio first beheld Fiammetta. It replaced a fifth-century basilica. Presently we come to the old campanile of Sta Maria Maggiore on our right. This campanile has a curious, conical-shaped top. Its base abuts upon the street; and built into the brickwork of it are fragments of a Roman building—a marble cornice, an engaged pillar, and a lion halfway up the wall. If rightly attributed to the eleventh century, it is the only surviving bit of Lombard architecture in Naples. The church was a basilica erected in the fifth or sixth century upon the site, it is said, of a Temple of the Sun. Hence the name of the *Vico del Sole* which skirts its western side and runs past the Policlinico of the University, and from which a good view of the campanile is obtained. Inside the church an archway of the old basilica is visible; the rest was gutted and modernised by Fansaga in the seventeenth century. Without, in the *Piazza Pietrasanta*, stands the charming Tuscan Renaissance tomb of the poet and humanist, Giovanni Pontano (1426–1503). An inscription inset in the walls gives the date of the foundation of the church as 453.

CAMPANILE S. MARIA MAGGIORE

At the end of the Tribunali (L.) is the fourteenth-century church of S. Pietro a Maiella, with a pyramidal belfry over the door like that of the Cathedral of Lucera. A high blank wall skirting the Vico

S. Pietro a Maiella encloses the cloisters, in which is the College of Music founded in 1637 by Alessandro Scarlatti, whose first opera was produced in Naples in 1585. It is the oldest in existence. One of its most famous pupils—Vincenzo Bellini (1806–35)—the composer of *Norma* and other popular operas, is commemorated by a statue in the Piazza to the right. The College possesses an exceedingly interesting and valuable collection of antique musical instruments and records.

The street which runs parallel to the Via dei Tribunali on the south, the Via Guiseppe de Blasiis, or San Biagio, is equally crowded and equally full of characteristic Neapolitan scenes. Even more so is the continuation of it east of the Via del Duomo, the Via Vicaria Vecchia (whose name recalls the old Court of Justice held here until it was removed to the Castel Capuano), and the Via Forcella.

West of the Via del Duomo, the Vico San Severino leads out of the Via S. Biagio to the fifteenth century church of SS. Sosio e Severino (*v.* Ch. XI.).

Further down the Via S. Biagio we pass the fine Renaissance Palazzo Sant' Angelo (No. 121), beyond which are the Piazzetta di Nilo and Vico Nilo. These take their names from a statue of the Nile, the Corpo di Napoli, as it is called, in the Piazzetta. The gigantic figure of the River God reclines with his elbow resting on the Sphinx and a crocodile's head beneath his feet. Children symbolise his fertility. It was brought from Alexandria in Nero's day by the merchants of that time, whose ships bringing corn from Egypt for Rome, enjoyed the distinction of carrying a purple topsail as they entered the Bay, making for Puteoli. This was the quarter in which they dwelt. Hard by is the little church of Sant' Angelo a Nilo (*v.* Chap. X.). In traversing this

Nilense quarter of old Naples we have now reached the Vico Mezzocannone on the site of the western boundary of the ancient Greek city. It leads us to the Piazza S. Domenico Maggiore, with its baroque Guglia di San Domenico, and thence to the great Gothic church of San Domenico Maggiore (*v*. Chap. X.).

You will not have proceeded far along any of these narrow streets before you are arrested by the presence of one of the most constant impediments to traffic except trams. It is a long, narrow, two-wheeled cart, bringing in perhaps from the country barrels of wine or the charcoal which is the staple fuel for cooking. Three horses are struggling abreast, one between shafts and in loose traces, slipping and staggering about the uneven, greasy flagstones of lava, and guided by a noseband pressing upon the nostrils, a form of bit which is of great antiquity and which is said not to be so cruel as it looks. The cart is composed of two high wheels, between which two long poles are slung. The heavy load is balanced to a nicety. It is a standing marvel why, in case of a sudden jerk or a hole in the road, it does not lift the little shaft horse off its feet and hold it suspended in the air by its belly-band. The most striking feature of the turn-out, however, is the saddle of the centre horse. It carries a lofty pommel of brass, bedecked with metal studs, and a guardian Madonna and local saint at the base. Two flags of shining brass revolve about the pommel. They are said to represent the flaming sword which turned every way and expelled Adam and Eve from Paradise. On his head the horse wears flags and feathers and bells and a horn, not to mention a bag of sea-sand or a piece of wolf's skin, which is mentioned by Pliny as rendering a horse proof against all fatigue. Unfortunately the horse does not always know that.[1] All these devices are intended to protect the animal from baleful influences, but especially as charms to attract and intercept the glance of the Evil Eye which some passer-by may cast upon it. The brass ornaments upon the harness of our own cart-horses are very possibly survivals of the same preventive magic.

In spite of industrial and political developments and the advance of education, woven into the warp of modern life run strong threads of old customs and superstitions. Belief in the fatal influence of the Evil Eye is still almost universal in Naples. It is a belief which has existed in most countries and in all ages. It is supposed that certain people are gifted with the power of casting a baleful spell (*jettatura*) upon others. They convey their disastrous influence through the first glance which they may happen to cast upon any particular person. It is not the cross-eyed who are endowed with this sinister power, as is often supposed, but, happily, you can usually tell a *jettatore* by his sallow countenance, melancholy aspect, and thin habit of body. He has a piercing gaze and protruding eyes, usually disguised behind pince-nez. The *jettatore* is born a *jettatore* and dies a *jettatore*, but is very often quite unaware of his singularity, until it is brought home to him by the way in which people begin to avoid him. He has looked perhaps with eager interest upon a pretty child, and the child falls ill, or dies. He makes some casual, innocent remark, and his words prove to have been of ill-omen. So he becomes known, and his life is rendered a misery to himself and all with whom he comes in

[1] The frightful cruelty to horses which used to spoil a visit to Naples for any lover of animals has been enormously ameliorated by the efforts of the Società Napoletana per la protezione degli animali (Via Vittoria 8; telephone, 992).

contact. It is an uncomfortable superstition. Many are the stories told in ancient and modern times of the exercise of this unhappy gift in Neapolitan society.[1] The trend of these stories is that the evil-eyed one looks pointedly at his hostess at a garden-party, let us say, and remarks how fortunate it is that it is a fine day. Thereupon a thunderstorm rushes up and everybody's frock is ruined, and so forth, with tragic variations of the same theme. Granted the existence of the power in a stranger or an acquaintance to cast a *jettatura* upon you, should you meet him unawares, it is obvious that some form of protection must be devised. There is a reply to every form of the offensive. That is the doctrine of the British Navy, and it is the practice of all superstitions. Against the Evil Eye which Vergil's shepherd complained had been cast upon his sheep, against the Evil Eye which the modern Neapolitan blames for every misfortune that may befall him or his, preventive magic has been called into play by the wisdom of the ages. It provides to-day a comfortable livelihood for many Neapolitan jewellers.

Should you recognise a *jettatore* as he approaches, it will suffice to point the middle finger of your hand at him whilst closing the others. "*Digitum porrigito medium*," says Martial. An alternative gesture is to extend the first and little fingers, closing the two centre ones. This, also, is an ancient gesture. It is shown in the mural paintings of Pompeii (Museo Nazionale, No. 9257). So the malevolent glance will be avoided. But it is not always possible to recognise the advent of the owner of the Evil Eye. Should the *jettatore* see

[1] The curious will find them delightfully told in Dumas' *Le Corricolo* (I. xv.-xviii.); in the appendix to Lord Lytton's *Last Days of Pompeii*; and in Mr Neville Rolfe's *Naples in the Nineties*; and in Mr Ellworthy's study of the subject, *The Evil Eye*.

you first, or first utter some ill-omened remark before you are aware of him, the harm is irretrievably done. To guard against so horrid a contingency and to ward off the ruinous effect of such an unexpected encounter, you must wear a charm, an amulet. Since the object of the charm is to distract that first evil penetrating glance and to divert from the wearer the sinister influence which flows from it in an unguarded encounter, when the victim has not had time to protect himself by a sign, the charm to be worn must have some startling and attractive quality. It must, by its unusual character, distract and fascinate the attention of the Evil Eye and absorb as it were its poison. *Fascinum* was the old Latin word for it. Nothing could be more startling or likely to attract attention than the display of that distinctive feature of a man which modesty normally conceals. This emblem was therefore chosen. You find it erected upon the thresholds of the houses at Pompeii, and, in a slightly disguised form, in the ornaments universally worn in Naples to-day. It is not the only one. Sometimes the charm, made of coral or silver, takes the form of a pair of horns, sometimes of a sprig of rue, sometimes of a serpent, sometimes of a crescent moon, sometimes of the hand with the index and little fingers extended, sometimes of a key with a heart in its handle. One very popular type of amulet, worn especially by children, and known as the *cimaruta*, combines all these various charms against ill-luck. Most if not all of these symbols are connected with the ancient worship of Diana—the presiding deity of magic—in one or other of her threefold forms, *tria virginis ora Dianæ*. As Latona, the goddess of prolific maternity, the horns of plenty and the medicinal properties of rue are related to her; as Hecate, the queen of hell, the serpent, whose sign is found also upon the painted walls of Pompeii; as the Virgin Queen of Heaven, the Chaste Huntress, Diana Virgo, the half-moon, the keys of heaven, and the emblem of the virgin heart belong to her. Pagan, as Mr Pecksniff said, "Pagan, I regret to say."

It is customary to be supercilious when writing of these childish ancient beliefs and superstitious practices of the Neapolitans. But it is very probable that those who scoff most readily at them have their own pet superstitions at home. All superstitions are bad, and all belief in magic is bad; because superstition is the greatest enemy of intellectual freedom and knowledge, and because belief in magic plays into the hands of those whose interest it is to encourage superstition and to prey upon the credulity of the ignorant. But before we sneer at the Neapolitans let us be sure of ourselves. It is so easy to compound for sins we are inclined to by damning those we have no mind to. The superstition of the Evil Eye may not appeal to us; it is not a general northern superstition, though I have often seen the signs of preventive magic against this dreaded influence raised even in London. But, granted that we do not generally bother about the Evil Eye in England, let us be sure, before we scoff at those who do, that we have entirely discarded all belief in lucky numbers and lucky stars and lucky days and lucky colours; that we do not sneakingly prefer blue to green, or Tuesdays to Fridays, or sevens to thirteens; and let us be quite sure that we never throw salt over our left shoulders if we spill it; or invoke a fox's brush if we pass under a ladder, or touch wood if we mention our immunity from some misfortune. Let us be honest. Do you never turn your money at the first sight of the new moon? Have you not a mascot on your car?

Like most Italians, the Neapolitans are fond of

gambling. Cards are produced on every possible occasion, and still as hundreds of years ago men play *mora* at the taverns and street corners, crying the *Uno! cinque! sette! tre! ah!* and *io!* and swiftly jerking their deft brown fingers, too swiftly for the stranger to follow. But the gamble which exerts the greatest influence on their lives is the *Lotto*, the State Lottery. This takes the place with them that betting on horse races occupies with us, and appeals to the same instinct, the desire to get something for nothing. And just as those who follow horses and jockeys and stables and form and tipsters soon persuade themselves that their play is based upon knowledge, so in the case of the lotteries a pseudo-science of numbers has arisen, and a whole encyclopædia of interpretation of omens which are supposed to lead to the selection of the winning number. *Smorfia* is the title of this extraordinary book, which is consulted by the faithful as though it were a racing expert. Or if further help is needed in "spotting the winner," recourse is had to a professional tipster, the *cabalista*, who is sometimes a monk. At Naples the drawing of the lottery takes place in public every Saturday, near Sta Chiara. The crowd of expectant onlookers presents a typical Neapolitan scene, as well as a curious study in psychology.[1]

The other occasions on which Neapolitan crowds are seen at their liveliest, not to say noisiest, are undoubtedly the numerous *festas*. Religious festivals are innumerable, each quarter celebrating not only the usual feasts of the Christian year, but also those of their own particular tutelary saint. We refer

[1] Those who wish to be introduced to the details of this subject should read the chapter in Mr Neville Rolfe's *Naples in the Nineties*. The social evils arising from it are portrayed with painful intensity in Matilde Serao's *Il Paese di Cuccagna*.

elsewhere to the feasts of St Anthony, Piedigrotta, Monte Vergine, S. Giovanni, and S. Gennaro. These *festas* are celebrated with an incredible amount of noise, to which the explosion of crackers, fireworks, and bombs contributes considerably, though efforts have been made by the municipal authorities to restrain this form of religious enthusiasm. The effigy of the Saint in gorgeous raiment is taken from his particular church and paraded in procession through the streets, where he is received with explosions of bombs and fireworks (*botte*) in his honour. One such occasion, and a very pretty one, is the Feast of San Giuseppe and Santa Josephina on 19th March. St Joseph, amongst other virtues, was the patron saint of robbers, but this is essentially the children's *festa*, on which a toy must be bought for every child. A vast bazaar of little wooden stalls (*bancarelle*), crowded with cheap toys, books and sweetmeats, fills the Via Depretis and the streets about the Piazza Municipio, in the neighbourhood of SS. Giuseppe e Cristoforo, a crudely decorated baroque church, and all the world and his wife turn out to do their duty by their children and Joseph, their guardian Saint, who lends his name to so many. Special *pizze* are made with cream tops for this occasion, which are intended to represent the shavings from the Carpenter's bench.

Another popular festival connected with children is the Feast of the Annunciation. On that day, too, the streets about the church of the Santissima Annunziata (*see* Chap. X.) are crowded with gay throngs and stalls loaded with toys and *pizze*, whose merits are proclaimed by the excited vendors at the tops of their raucous voices. In the church itself, draped in curtains of azure blue, ablaze with lights and flowers, Mass is conducted to the strains of an orchestra, whilst crowds of all classes file through it. Outside is the *Asilo Infante*, the Foundling Hospital, where the babies are decked in their best clothes and blue ribbons awaiting the chance of adoption by some Christian soul, just as, when they reached marriageable age, they used, not so long ago, to be dressed up for selection by likely husbands. The hole in the wall of the Hospital, through which foundlings used to be pushed by their wretched mothers, has been closed long since.

Christmas, as with us, is a season of good cheer, when the delicacies especially favoured by Neapolitans are exhibited decked with greenery and rosettes, in the shops and market-places of the Porta Capuana and the Piazza del Mercato, whilst *bancarelle* invade even Toledo itself. A full ration of noise is contributed by fireworks and bombs, to which is added the shrill pipings of the *Zampognari*. These rough bagpipers from the wilds of the Basilicata or Calabrian Mountains invade the town about the time of the Feast of the Immaculate Conception (8th December), and play and sing Christmas hymns before the shrines in the streets or in houses to which they are invited, something after the fashions of our waits and carol-singers. If their patron can afford it, they perform this function on nine separate days, thus completing the number of the *Novena*. There is a charming dialect poem by Salvatore di Giacomo upon this subject (*Nuttata 'e Natale*). Nothing could be more picturesque than the appearance of these shaggy mountaineers, with their long hair tumbling over their shoulders and gold-ringed ears and coloured ribands hanging from their tall, steeple-hats. They wear sandals on their feet, rough goatskin trousers, and blue cloaks over crimson velvet waistcoats. They look, in fact, like brigands who have just stepped off the operatic stage. The skirling pipes are sometimes accompanied by a shrill flute. Both instruments are very primitive and of great antiquity. Shakespeare's allusion to their musical quality in Othello is no libel. "Why, Masters, have your instruments been in Naples, that they speak i' the nose thus? . . . Then put up your pipes in your bag, for I'll away."

The arrival of the *Zampognari* is connected with the December harvest of oranges, of which the second and best crop is gathered at Easter. In anticipation of their coming, the little sanctuaries of the Madonna in the orange groves of the Piano di Sorrento and the surrounding districts are decorated with garlands of the ripening fruit and the green leaves of laurel and bay.

Easter Day is celebrated by the slaughter of lambs which have been nurtured or purchased for the occasion. Thursday and Friday have previously been observed by visits to the *Sepolchri* in the various churches, and in the case of the more worldly minded, by an examination and display of new fashions and frocks. The combination of these pursuits, and an outburst of *bancarelle* in the streets, produces a wonderful crowd in the Via Toledo. The swish and *frou-frou* of their silk garments in the street on this occasion have earned the title of *Il struscio* for this festival. The Feast of Piedigrotta (7th to 8th September, *see* Chap. VI.), apart from the worship of the wooden image and miracle-working Madonna much cultivated by the people, is the occasion for new songs being "tried out," as the modern *impresario* would say. The Grotta of Posilipo is then filled all night with a merry crowd, who blow trumpets and play every kind of musical instrument to the utmost of their capacity. Amidst this fearful din the popular song of the year is chosen, which may or may not be one which achieves such world-wide and lasting popularity as *Funiculi, Funicula*, or *Santa Lucia*, or *O Sole Mio*. This festival is not the great *tamasha* it once was, for it is no longer graced by official splendour as in the time of Ferdinand, and as a scene of pilgrimage the shrine of Sta Maria di Piedigrotta has recently been supplanted by the Madonna di Pompeii (*see* Chap. VII.).

The hills on the northern side of Naples, Antignano and Conocchia, were famous for their fruits and delicate vintages in the seventeenth century. In classical times Horace, we know, was never tired of singing the praises of the wine of Falernus. The best wine on the mainland to-day is produced by the vineyards on the slopes of Vesuvius (*Vesuvio*), though the wine of the Falernian district, between Pozzuoli and Baia, if obtained in its virgin state, is by no means to be despised. *Lagrima Christi*, grown in the neighbourhood of the Observatory on Vesuvius, is perhaps the most delicate of the local wines and possesses the most fragrant aroma. As a rule the white wines are the best, the red varieties being too rough for ordinary palates. The *Asprino* of Aversa is a light and pleasing beverage. The mountains of Castellamare produce the grateful wine of Gragnano, whilst the white wines of Ischia now vie in excellence with the vintage of Capri. For the most part, however, the wines of the district have been "commercialised," that is, a standard type and quality have been achieved on which the consumer can rely. They are quite pleasant to drink, but by no means likely to excite the palate of a connoisseur. Even in Capri itself it is difficult to obtain the really good wine which is grown there. None of these wines, it must be confessed, has the distinction of the best Sicilian vintages.

CHAPTER II

The Siren City

The Siren City—Naples and its Greek Founders—Legend of Parthenope—The Siren—S. Giovanni Maggiore—S. Giovanni a Mare—S. Eligio—The colonisation of Cumæ—Palæopolis and Neapolis—Struggle with Etruscans—Characteristics of Greek civilisation—Oscans and Samnites.—Neapolis retains its Greek individuality under the Romans—S. Paolo Maggiore—Greek artists at Naples and Pompeii—Site of Greek Neapolis.

ACCORDING to legend, Naples, land of youth and love, owed its first peopling to the escapade of two lovers, who fled from Greece and landed on these shores.

One version of this dim legend runs that Cimon, the Greek, loved a beautiful Greek maiden named Parthenope (the Virgin). Her father forbade their union. When they learned that he was about to give her in marriage to another, they quitted their Ionian home. They made their way in their skiff across the wine-dark seas until they reached the loveliest shore ever beheld by the eyes of man, where the land was carpeted with flowers and fruits and the heat of the sun was tempered by soft sea-breezes. Here the fugitives brought their voyage to an end, and on the wave-kissed strand beneath the star-lit summer skies lived their life of love and kisses. But not for long were they destined to "live in Paradise alone." Their father and family followed in pursuit. They came to seize the runaways, but remained to bless their choice of an abode so kindly and so beautiful. The rumour of their beatitude and the riches of the country was carried back to Greece, whence there soon began to flow increasing numbers of colonists. The settlement was named Parthenope after the Greek maiden who thus founded it. Some twenty-five centuries later she stood sponsor to the short-lived "Parthenopean Republic" of Masaniello, and again to that which was set up by the French Republican invaders in 1799. To-day the name is borne proudly by the Via Parthenope, the street which continues the Marine Parade of the Via Caracciolo beyond the Castel dell' Ovo, and of which we have already spoken. According to another and better known legend, the city of Parthenope was named after the Siren of that name. Odysseus, on his perilous voyage 'twixt Scylla and Charybdis, by binding himself to the mast and stopping his comrades' ears with wax, succeeded in passing the rocky island homes of the Sirens—the Galli islands in the Bay of Salerno—without succumbing to the seductive songs of the enchantresses. Thereupon Parthenope, it was said, and her two sisters flung themselves into the sea, in despair at the failure of their spells. The dead body of Parthenope was washed up on this shore.

Some declare that the tomb of Parthenope is by Sant' Aniello, under Capodimonte; others that she was buried where now stands the church of San Giovanni Maggiore, which was once upon the seashore. A Greek inscription discovered amongst the foundations doubtfully confirms this view. Certainly the Corinthian columns and a *pluteus* in this church (at the foot of the Via Sta Chiara) bear witness to the existence of a former temple, reputed to have been dedicated by Hadrian to Antinous. The present

[*Brunner & Co.*

BAGPIPERS (*Zampognari*)

church was designed by Dionisio Lazarri in 1685. The church contains a good Baptism of Christ, by Giovanni da Nola, and an early Byzantine representation of the Baptist.

Parthenope is not the only legendary person who has given a name to a site in these regions. Each hill, indeed, each island-rock or river is the local habitation of some pretty Neapolitan legend of unhappy lovers, whom they personify and after whom they are named. Vesuvius, for instance, it is said, is the ardent lover of Capri, sighing and heaving with passionate desire for the lips of the lady-love he can never reach. The heights of Capodimonte, Poggioreale, San Martino, and Vomero are four brothers who loved one girl. She fled from them and left them all faithful, all disconsolate. Posilipo, again, personifies a gallant youth who flung himself into the sea when his passionate love for Nisida was not returned, and the gods, staying the hands of both, turned them into hill-crest and rocky island. Mergellina was a sea-nymph, a mermaid who swept a handsome fisher-lad into her toils, as she sat one day combing her long golden hair upon the rocks off that point. Hercules, too, visited these shores, and the island at the foot of Naples, now known as Castel dell' Ovo, was called Megaris after his wife.

According to more prosaic historians, the settlement of Parthenope was an offshoot from the prosperous neighbouring community of Cumæ. At a time when the dawn of Italian civilisation had hardly begun to break, the sun of other nations on the eastern shores of the Mediterranean was already high in the heavens. The Egyptians were not a seafaring people, and therefore exercised no influence upon Italy. The civilisation of Greece could scarcely reach her by land. But the hardy Hellenic mariners learned at a very early period to set at nought the dangers of the Tyrrhenian Sea and the Ionian Gulf, as the Adriatic was named by them. Setting out from the Æolian and Ionian coasts of Asia Minor and the islands of the Ægean, they explored the Italian seaboard. Their first settlements of importance in this direction were made first on the island of Ischia, and then at Cumæ. They were guided in their choice, the legend runs, by the god Apollo, who sent a dove to lead them over the sea.

When these earliest voyagers to the West reached the coasts and islands of South-western Italy, it seemed to them that they had arrived at a fabled land whose wonders were already familiar to them in story. For just as, in later times, the fabulous East inspired the imagination of Western romancers, so the West, as long as it remained unknown, was largely used by the story-tellers of the East for the scene of their tales of wonder and adventure. Before the geographical outlines of Italy and Sicily became familiar to the Greeks, some hints of the swirling currents of the Straits of Lipari or Messina, and of mountains vomiting fire had doubtless reached them from the lips of terrified mariners driven by storms into the uncharted Western seas. Such stories were seized upon and amplified by the poets, and became through the Homeric poems the universal heritage of the Greek people. As the navigation of the Tyrrhenian sea became more familiar to the seafarers of Ionia, and Hellenic traders began to erect factories on the promontories and islands upon its shores, the legend of Odysseus was ever in their minds. They beheld in the flaming terrors of Etna, Stromboli or Vesuvius, in the cliffs and currents of the capes and islands, or in the fierce storms of the Straits a physical demonstration of the truth of the national story of his wanderings. They seemed to recognise the Homeric Isle of Æolus in the Lipari Islands, the Isle of Calypso at the Lacinian Cape, the Isle of Circe at the Cape of Circeii, and Scylla and Charybdis at the Straits of Messina. And when they first sighted the rocky islands off Salerno, they thought that they had come to those haunted scenes where the Sirens lure men to their doom with fatal fascination. Thrilling with pleasure, shuddering with dread, they drew near to the rocks where, as Homer had sung to them, "the Sirens dwell, the sweet deluders, whose song is death, yet makes destruction please." In Avernus they beheld the sombre lake which led to the nether world, and upon its shores the cave where dwelt the Sibyl.

Whilst the natural beauty of the country suggested the paradise of the Elysian Fields in other directions, the subterranean murmurs and upheavals, the sulphurous fumes and bubbling lava of extinct craters seemed to proclaim the horrors of Tartarus and the abodes of the Cimmerians (Odyssey, XI.). The legend of the voyages of Odysseus, for which the Ionian mariners thus found a local habitation about Cumæ and its neighbourhood, lives on in the nomenclature and traditions of Naples and its Riviera.

The Siren, to whom Naples owes her romantic name, the Siren City, and whose image was stamped upon her coins, still keeps her place in the hearts of the people. If you leave the Corso Umberto I., at the Piazza Nicolo Amore, and turn seawards down the Via Duomo, you will find the Via Giovanni a Mare on your left. Between the church of that name and the church of St Eligio, the large battered head of a Siren stands on a pedestal in the street. It was found in the amphitheatre, and is known as the head of Naples, *Testa di Napoli*, or *'a Cap e' Napule* in Neapolitan language. It holds a peculiar place in the affections and superstitions of the populace. It is believed that were it to be removed or to fall, the end of the city would be at hand. The people, therefore, set themselves resolutely against any suggestion of removing it to a museum.

As we are in this neighbourhood, it will not be out of place to visit the curious old church of S. Giovanni a Mare, for it is full of suggestion of the days when the early seafarers landed close to its walls. Even in the Middle Ages the sea used to cover the whole of the foreshore here. Indeed, it was an old custom for people to assemble here in the summer-time, to divest themselves of their clothing and plunge into the adjacent sea. The church is shut in by houses which have been built about it, and its Gothic portal is reached through an archway under a house. The exterior, therefore, in no way prepares one for the curious scene within. A tessellated pavement green with damp reminds us at once of our proximity to the sea. Six round marble pillars of older date—possibly remains of a Roman temple where fishermen and seafarers worshipped the Dioscuri and hung their votive offerings to the gods of the sea—carry Gothic vaulting. The boldly carved capitals are all of different designs. The whole of the roof is painted with a mouldering remnant of rich blue fresco-work, depicting the stars and firmament, and symbols of the Knights of Malta, with whom this church was specially connected. The sojourn of St John at

CAPO DI NAPOLI

Malta, where he is supposed to have written his Revelations, naturally suggested him as the patron saint of that order.

Behind the high altar is preserved an ancient carriage formerly used to convey the last Sacrament to the dying. In the chapel on the north side of the high altar are the charred remains of the Cross of St Bridget. On her pilgrimage to the Holy Places of Palestine, the Swedish saint visited the famous cities of Italy. Naples she scolded particularly for its sins (1372). When asked to intercede on behalf of the people who were stricken with the plague, she declared that it was due to their pride and wickedness. The luxury of women's dress and their shocking habit of painting their faces she particularly denounced. It is said that the house in which she lived was burned down and this cross alone saved from the conflagration. Another shrine is that of a wooden black Madonna. But perhaps the most interesting feature of this curious church is the ceremony which takes place every Monday morning (the Feast of Souls in Purgatory) in the chapel on the south side of the high altar. At eleven o'clock, after Mass has been said, the priest retires and leaves the people to sing their own litanies. The centre of their devotions is a

DETAIL OF PORCH
S. GIOVANNI A MARE

small hole in the ground, in which lies a group of three or four skulls upon a blue mat. One of them is crowned with a chaplet of roses. It is said that this skull was found in the street some 300 years ago, and, there being no particular person to pray for the release of its owner from Purgatory, it became the subject of the people's intercessions. The prayers of the multitude were needed for a certain number of years before he or she could reach Paradise. That number has now been completed, and in gratitude the blessed owner now intercedes for all who pray to the skull.

On entering the church one is startled by the wild and discordant cries of prayer and adoration which proceed from the shrine. They blend into a sort of litany, which is led by a woman in charge of a collecting bag. Across the dark aisle a group of women is seen to be huddled round the hole in which lie the skulls. Their forms are lit fitfully by rows of candles above the hole, the light of which falls upon their faces as they throw back their heads in an ecstasy of prayer and hope. Each worshipper names aloud the disease for which he or she craves a cure, lights a candle, contributes a coin, and then, led by the high priestess of the ceremony, the congregation raise again the litany through which resounds the name of their illness or diseased member. Having finished their prayer, the worshippers blow out their candles and take them home. There they relight them every evening, repeat their prayer, and extinguish them again.

A similar custom, I am told, is growing up around heaps of nameless bones which are collected as the result of the Neapolitan system of burial.

The Via S. Eligio, a continuation of Via Giovanni a Mare, ends with a Norman-Sicilian clock tower over an archway adjoining the church of S. Eligio, the first ecclesiastical monument of Angevin architecture in Naples. There are remains of a rich Gothic doorway on the left, with bold grotesques and gargoyles. The whole exterior is in a crumbling condition. S. Eligio de' Chiavettieri was erected on the site of a temple of Hercules, the remains of which were observed among the foundations by Celano in 1650. Its old dedication was Sta Maria ad Herculem. Around this church are little shops installed in archways, which are closed by heavy folding doors of great age. These shops and similar ones round the *Piazza del Mercato*, which now lies ahead of us, and which some think to be the site of the original Neapolis, remind one forcibly of the shops which surrounded the Forum at Rome or Pompeii in ancient days.

It was, as Thucydides tells us, the city of Chalcis, one of the two principal towns on the island of Eubœa, which was the pioneer of Greek colonisation in the western Mediterranean. Whilst other settlements were made in Sicily and the south of Italy, the Chalcidians planted at Ischia the northern outpost of the Hellenic nation. The exposed and volcanic nature of Pithecusa, the Monkey Island, as they termed Ischia,[1] presently induced the settlers to transfer themselves to the mainland. They chose a strong position about eleven miles from modern Naples, and named the new city they built there Cumæ, calling it after a little town on the east coast of Eubœa, which no doubt contributed a contingent of settlers. The city of Cumæ on the Anatolian coast, which Strabo names as the mother city, was probably the parent town of the Eubœan city of that name, and therefore the grandparent of the Italian town. Here the land-

[1] The present name is derived from the Latin word for island —Insula. The Romans called it Œnaria.

hungry colonists from the Ægean found a rich and volcanic soil to cultivate, as full of promise and wonder as later a new Western world was to prove to the adventurers of Genoa and Bristol. From this station, too, they began to push a trade in Greek and Eastern wares with the tribes of the interior. How successful the Greek traders were in these parts is demonstrated by the prevalence of Hellenic arts throughout the lowlands of Campania, and the absence of any imports of their Phœnician trade rivals.

Other Greeks from other towns followed in their wake. From Naxos, Corinth, Rhodes, Sparta flowed a stream of settlers, who founded towns in Sicily and upon the southern shores of Italy, bidding fair to eclipse the old in size and prosperity alike, until the new land earned the title of a greater Greece—Magna Græcia. The date of their coming cannot be precisely determined. It was probably some time, possibly a long time, before the legendary date of the foundation of Rome, 753 B.C. The proto-geometric ornamentation of the earliest type of vase found at Cumæ—the *lecythus Talaie*—is certain proof that the first settlement was at least as early as the year 800 B.C. But the ancient tombs discovered there seem to point to a considerably earlier date and to confirm the tradition which puts it back as far as 1050 B.C.

One has, then, to think of the south of Italy in these early times as forming an integral part of the Hellenic world. The occupation of this coast was the result of a colonising movement of the Greek race westward. The Doric temples at Pæstum are the supreme abiding witnesses of it in architecture, unique only in their survival, and the introduction of alphabetical writing to the Italic races by the Cumæans in literature. For the alphabet of Cumæ became the foundation of the Latin and therefore of our own alphabet.[1] And this foundation of Cumæ was not only the source from which Greek culture was introduced to Rome, but also the occasion of the name of Greeks (Grai) being applied to the Hellenes by the Romans and thence by the world at large, Grai being the name of a small tribe of Bœotian settlers there.

Of the Greek colonies with which Sicily and the southern coast of Italy were studded from before the eighth century B.C., we have seen that this on the Bay of Naples was not only the first but also the most northerly. The choice of this site by the Greeks for their earliest settlement of any importance in the West may at first sight seem a curious one. There were suitable landing-places nearer to their starting-point which might rather have been expected to prove more tempting to the Greek mariner and trader. But further reflection shows that the island of Ischia was well chosen. Protection for such a colony and trading station was needed not only from storms, but also from the raids of the natives on the land side and of pirates from the open sea. The steep and rocky cliffs of Ischia afforded such protection. These necessary conditions were repeated at the site to which they soon removed their settlement on the mainland, the steep but well protected cliff, which bears to the present day the venerable name of their mother city.

From Cumæ, their second home upon this Italian, or as they called it, Opican (Oscan), shore, they presently made extensions eastward. Increasing in wealth and numbers, and reinforced by some colonists from Rhodes, they founded the seaport of Dikæarchia (afterwards Puteoli, and now Pozzuoli), and then the settlements of Parthenope and Neapolis. When

[1] On the difficult subject of deciphering the Cumæan inscriptions *see* Dr R. S. Conway, *Cambridge Ancient History*, vol. iv.

Neapolis, "the new city," came into being, Parthenope was naturally referred to as Palæopolis, "the old city." Its vanished site is probably off the Point of Posilipo (*see* Chap. III.). This new foundation was made about the year 600 B.C. The tradition that there was a subsequent wave of emigration from Athens which helped to develop Neapolis, is perhaps confirmed by the adoption of Thurian coin-types by that city (*circa* 400 B.C.[1]). Similarly, the old name of Megaris given to the island of Castel dell' Ovo, referred to in the legend we have quoted, may indicate a later influx of colonists from Megara who made their home upon that island, just as settlers from Megara supplemented the colonies in Sicily founded there by Chalcis and by Corinth.

The spread of Greek settlements northwards was checked by the opposition of the Etruscans. Though they were insatiable buyers of the Greek and Oriental wares imported by the Cumæans, they would brook no rivals in the Tyrrhenian sea. From Liguria to Sicily they held that for their own. They pounced upon every Greek vessel that dared to show a prow in the sea to which they had given their name; and ere long, as the flourishing condition of the Greek settlements tempted them south, they advanced by a series of wars and established an Etruscan dynasty in Rome and Campania. Their advance was stopped at the very gates of Cumæ. Attracted by the wealth and trade of the place, the Etruscans combined with other inhabitants of Campania to attack Cumæ. Their privateers scoured the sea. They seized and occupied the high promontory of Sorrento and the precipitous cliffs of Capri, whence their corsairs could keep a lookout for prizes sailing between the bays of Salerno and Naples. But in their onslaught upon

[1] *See* the great collection of coins in the *Museo Nazionale.*

Cumæ itself they were repulsed, largely owing to the heroic exploits of one Aristodemus (524 B.C.). Increasing, by his eloquence and generosity to the people, the popularity he had thus gained, Aristodemus established himself as despot. Afterwards he is said to have disgusted his admirers by forcing them to manual labour on a large scale. It was at the Court of this despot that the Tarquins found refuge when they were banished from Rome.

Baulked in their endeavour to destroy Cumæ, the Etruscans joined with those other rivals of the Hellenes, the Phœnicians, to curb their intrusion into the commerce and colonisation of the Mediterranean, entering into a definite alliance of arms with Carthage for that purpose. Thus held in check, the settlers about Vesuvius were able to do little more than hold their own. Rendered incapable of aggression, their relations with the natives of the interior, Campania and Latium, were those of peaceful traders. And through such peaceful trade, they brought to Italy the torch of Greek civilisation.

These Greeks brought to Italy the qualities, but also the defects of a rich and highly developed and varied, yet alien civilisation. Apart from a common zest for trade, the Greek outlook upon life differed very materially from that which was afterwards to become the characteristic of the Romans. The difference was fundamental. It became more marked as each nation developed, and degenerated into different forms of licence as each nation began to show signs of decay. It was the tendency of Hellenism to sacrifice the whole to its individual elements, or as Mommsen has summarised it, the nation to the single State, and the single State to the citizen. The Hellenic ideal of life was the beautiful and the good, and only too often the pleasure of idleness. Political development, for the Greeks, consisted in intensifying the original individualism of the several centres, and subsequently led to the internal dissolution of the authority of the State. Their view of religion first invested the gods with human attributes, and then denied their existence. They gave full play to the limbs in the sports of the naked youth, and gave free scope to thought in all its grandeur and in all its awfulness. Very different was that Roman ideal, of virtue and piety, of manliness and duty to the family and the State, which solemnly bound the son to reverence the father, the citizen to reverence the ruler, and all to reverence the gods; which required nothing and honoured nothing but the useful act, and compelled every citizen to fill up every moment of his life with unceasing work; which made it a duty even in the boy modestly to cover his body; which deemed every one a bad citizen who wished to be different from his fellows; which viewed the State as all in all, and a desire for the State's extension as the only aspiration not liable to censure.

Differences in national outlook so radical as these were naturally marked by corresponding differences in the art and private lives of the individuals of each nation. The art of the citizens of the more practical and disciplined State found its most natural expression in the creation of works useful to that State, of roads, aqueducts, or buildings with leanings towards the grandiose, of temples or triumphal arches intended to typify and bear witness to the greatness of Rome. The art of the more sensitive and individualistic Hellene was more concerned with making something, whether a building or a statue, which should minister to the delight of the eye and be informed with the beauty of proportion. It aimed at the perfect adjustment of the parts to the whole, as being not only an end but the end of achievement, whether in the case of a building in its relation to itself and its environment, or of the reproduction in plastic form of that lovely masterpiece of gods and men, the human body. Beautiful themselves, they worshipped the physical beauty of which they were the supreme examples. So worshipping it, they loved to endeavour to reproduce it, in its most graceful aspects, its most characteristic attitudes of life and action, whether of young men riding in a procession, of women performing their household duties, of gods as men made perfect in strength, in line, in poise. In so doing, they approached their task as a whole. Their problem being the perfect adjustment of parts to the whole, they studied, not in parts but in whole, the beautiful nude forms of youth which they were accustomed to see in daily life, in the gymnasium, the bath, or the street. They did not emphasise a head, and leave the body or the limbs for guessing. If they wished to represent a draped figure, they reproduced the curves and folds of drapery about the body as things in themselves beautiful and worthy of portrayal, not as a cloak for impropriety. The indecent devices of sacerdotal prudery, the tin fig-leaf or the suggestive hand as screens for modesty, would have been to them nothing but the most outrageous and incredible exhibition of bad taste. And bad taste was in their eyes the worst of all sins.

In the Greek ideal of liberty of thought and individual life, guided and restrained only by the canons of good taste, there lurked, of course, as in other more ascetic ideals, the seeds of degeneration. In art the tendency is indicated by a descent from the cult of pure beauty to that of mere grace and charm or cleverness, and thence to effeminacy, exaggeration, *bravura*, corruption, straining after effect or the unusual, culminating even in the cultivation of the ugly. In life, the liberty of individualism easily degenerates into selfishness and licence, just as the discipline of the State quickly develops into tyranny. The devotee of beauty is tempted to become the slave of the senses, and the senses through over-indulgence soon begin to demand the stimulus of strange joys and artificial delights. Nature is outraged by excess as much as by asceticism. Inexorably she exacts the penalty. There is the same *facilis descensus Averni*, through charm, innovation, effeminacy, to debauchery and corruption. Something of all that is visible in the art as in the life of the Græco-Roman inhabitants of Pompeii, as we have it caught and immortalised for us to-day, preserved in the dust of Vesuvius.

If such, in broad outline, are the natural differences between the ancient Greek and Roman civilisations, and such their divergences in decay, it is not surprising if we find not only at Pompeii, but in Naples throughout her history and even in a slight degree to-day, a touch of the exotic, of something foreign to Italy, a persistent savour, as it were, of ancient Greece, and a faint aroma of the East.

The Greek settlements on the fringe of the southern coast of Italy retained and developed their natural characteristics, their vices as well as their charms, their failings as well as their virtues. This was due to several causes, geographical and historical; but chiefly because at the beginning Italian civilisation was not sufficiently developed to absorb an alien immigration. The Greeks who settled in the Bay of Naples had at first nothing to learn but everything to teach to the people of the Peninsula, with whom they came in contact. The riches which came to them from their Mediterranean trade kept them with their faces to the sea. Their minds were ever turned to the East. The Hellenic Colonists of the West always retained the closest connection with their original homes, and long continued to participate in the national festivals and rights of their motherland. But the delicious climate, the easy prosperity arising from a fruitful soil, and the beauty, the very earthly beauty, of the Western land in which they delighted, tended by degrees to enervate them. The forms of life which they had brought from Asia Minor and the isles of Greece persisted. Their physical beauty and excitable temperaments remained part of an undying heritage. But they were never inoculated with the virtues of the Roman character. They never learned the *pietas* of the Roman citizen, his creed of subordination of the individual to the State, his constancy in adversity, or his concentration upon success. Thus they were destined to fall an easy victim to the foreign invader, and never were people more cruelly punished for their weaknesses.

The Greek colonies in Italy retained, as was natural, the language, the social customs, the religious rites and festivals, the alphabet and the forms of government of the cities from which they were sent forth. These in the case of Naples continued long after it might have been expected that they would be absorbed into the Roman system. Those colonies which were planted in the neighbourhood of Vesuvius lived still under the laws of Charondas of Catana, enjoying a democratic constitution so modified that it was really a disguised plutocracy. For all real power lay in a Council drawn from the richest merchants of the city. This constitution had the merit of stability. It endured for many centuries and it kept the city free from tyranny, whether of usurpers or of the mob.

For a while Rome acted as a bulwark against the landward advance of the Etruscan power in the direction of the Greek cities of Campania. But when Rome fell before Lars Porsena, King of Clusium, it was the Greeks of Cumæ who gave the first check to their victorious advance (506 B.C.). It was the Hellenic nation which broke up the Etruscan and Carthaginian coalition. The Syracusans overwhelmed the Carthaginian army at Himera on the same day as the battle of Salamis was won (480 B.C.), and ten years later, Hiero of Syracuse, in combination with the Cumæans, shattered the Etruscan fleet off Cumæ. He occupied Ischia, thereby cutting off the Campanian Etruscans from communication with those of the north. The Hellenes of Sicily, Marseilles and Tarentum succeeded to the dominion of the Italian seas. At the same time the Etruscan power on land was weakened by furious conflicts with Rome. By the force of these circumstances, whether in direct alliance with Rome or not, and by their own efforts, the inhabitants of Neapolis were relieved from the pressure of Etruscan pirates by sea, and the presence of Etruscan armies by land.

But the removal of these dangers only opened the door to others. The rulers of Syracuse were now fired with the ambition to obtain dominion not only over all Sicily but also over Lower Italy and the Tyrrhenian and Adriatic seas. The collapse of the Etruscan power permitted the advance of the Samnites and Lucanians upon Campania and Magna Græcia. The Samnites seized and sacked Cumæ (421 B.C.), dealing it its death-blow. They drove out the native Oscans,[1] a pastoral people. By degrees

[1] The most important remains of the Oscans (Greek, Opici) are to be seen in the *Museo Campano* at Capua. After the conquest of Campania by the Samnites (438 B.C.) the tongue of the Samnite tribes came into general use there, and was termed by the Romans Osca lingua. Inscriptions at Pompeii show that this Oscan tongue was the language used by the peasants down to the end of the reign of Augustus.

S. ELIGIO

they settled in the country and built strongholds. They continued to do so up to the second century B.C. These strongholds they built of huge blocks of stone fitted without mortar, such as may now be seen at Pompeii, which was one of their forts, and where some of the Samnite tombs have been discovered.

The Greeks formed a league to combat the Lucanians. But Dionysius of Syracuse, whilst wresting from Magna Græcia the supremacy of the seas, allied himself with the Italian hordes against his countrymen. One Greek city after another was captured and annihilated. In an incredibly short time the circle of flourishing cities was destroyed. Only a few Greek settlements succeeded with difficulty, more by means of treaties than by force of arms, in preserving their existence and their nationality. Neapolis—which, being better and more securely situated than Cumæ, had succeeded to the former prosperity of her mother city—was one of these. She took her revenge by humanising the barbarian immigrants and subjugating the conquering invaders by means of the softening charms of Hellenic culture. In these quarters the rough and turbulent Samnite nation was rapidly absorbed into the Greek civilisation. This is shown by the objects found in the Samnite tombs at Pompeii. For they closely resemble in style those of the later Greek period (*cf.* Mommsen, I. p. 362).

Whilst the Samnites were engaged in hostilities with the Italian Greeks, the Romans had made themselves masters of the rich province of Campania and the chief power in the Peninsula. It remained for them to reduce Palæopolis and Neapolis to subjection. These twin cities enjoyed the same form of government and ruled over the Greek islands in the Bay. In anticipation of such a move on the part of Rome, the Samnites threw a garrison into Palæopolis. The Romans immediately declared war, and laid siege to the city. Negotiations were soon opened, and the Romans offered the Neapolitans very favourable terms. These were accepted and exercised a profound influence on the future of the Neapolitans. They were granted full equality of rights, exemption from military service, equal alliance and perpetual peace (326 B.C.). They thus retained their Greek communal constitution. So favourable were these conditions that Neapolis remained faithful to the Roman Confederacy even after the disaster of Cannæ (216 B.C.). Whilst Capua and numerous other important towns and tribes among the non-Latin allies of Rome passed over to the side of the Carthaginian conqueror, the Neapolitans, in common with the other Greeks of southern Italy, courageously resisted the attack of Hannibal in person. The possession of a southern seaport would have been invaluable to the Carthaginian general for the purpose of landing reinforcements. But the determined defence of the citizens gave the Romans time to throw a garrison into Neapolis and so prevent the port from falling into his hands. More than a hundred years later the Neapolitans showed that they were still satisfied with their institutions and the status they had obtained in 326. For when in 89 B.C. the Italian allies of Rome were admitted to Roman citizenship, the Neapolitans were by no means anxious to be swept into the fold. Some bargaining occurred, as the result of which they retained their Greek constitution and the use of Greek as their official language, even after they were admitted to the Roman franchise.

Whilst, then, Naples was drawn into the orb of the Roman Empire, it retained all the freedom and self-government of an allied city. It paid tribute to Rome

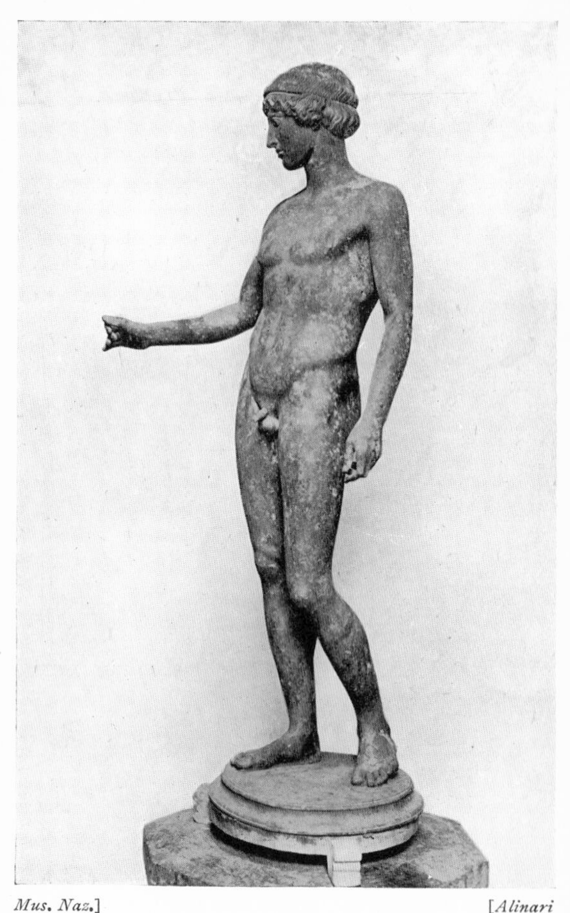

Mus. Naz.] [*Alinari*

YOUTHFUL GREEK ATHLETE

(Discovered at Pompeii, 1926)

as a confederate city, but in common with other cities of Magna Græcia, it retained its own form of government, made its own laws, and elected its own magistrates. The latter bore the Greek titles of archons and demarchs, as at Athens, even down to the time of Hadrian. In customs, as in costume and in language, in fact, Naples long remained essentially Greek.[1] The citizens, for instance, appear to have been divided into groups, called Phratriæ, after the Athenian model, who devoted themselves more especially to the cult of some particular deity. Of such a sort were the gods Eumolo and Ebone, Ceres and the Dioscuri.

Naples endeavoured to oppose the domination of Sulla. The city, however, was betrayed to him. He sacked it and deprived it of its fleet and the possession of Ischia. Sulla died in his villa there. Under the Empire Naples became a *municipium* and later a Roman colony.

Little by little, Greek ways and titles were discarded as the influence of Rome grew stronger and stronger, and Roman society came down in force to seek rest or dissipation by the waters of this delicious shore, to bathe at Baiæ or to build themselves luxurious villas along the Bay, whose charms their poets loved to celebrate. Then Neapolitan magistrates dropped their Greek titles and, ceasing to be archons, became ordinary Roman quæstors and ædiles. Their very gods were adopted and absorbed by the Romans, and reappeared under new names and often with new and rather contradictory attributes. For among the items of civilisation which Rome borrowed from the Greek settlers in Campania were many details of their religion. They learned to consult the oracles of

[1] Both Varro and Strabo, writing about the time of Augustus, note the survival of Greek institutions at Naples, such as the *phratriæ and gymnasia.*

Apollo at Delphi and to treasure the counsels of his soothsaying priestess, the Cumæan Sibyl, who was one day to inspire the verse of Vergil, and again the brush of Domenichino (Borghese Gallery), of Michelangelo (Sistine Chapel), and of Raphael (Sta Maria della Pace at Rome) (*see* Chap. III.). They early admitted into the holy company of their deities the gods of the Greek mariner, the Dioscuri, whom they named Castor and Pollux; Hermes, the god of traffic, whom they called Mercurius; and the god of healing, Æsculapius. Diana absorbed the attributes of both Artemis, the chaste huntress, and Hecate, the goddess of prolific maternity.

Of old Greek Naples there survives just one fragment of a temple. In the centre of the façade at the top of the steps of the church of San Paolo Maggiore, two Corinthian columns and part of an architrave can be clearly discerned. This is all that remains of the temple of the Dioscuri. Castor and Pollux have their temple also in the Forum at Rome. For did not the Romans have good cause to worship the twin gods who saved their army and nation at the battle of Lake Regillus? Castor and Pollux were also the tutelary deities of sailors, and it was rather perhaps in their marine aspect that their temple was raised here by the sea-going Greeks. The little Renaissance cloister of the monastery, now used for the *Archivio Provinciale*, provides a charming, unexpected peep from the Strada di S. Paolo. There is much old brick, covered with stucco, and some Renaissance porches in the grimy houses now used as workshops, in this street.

It is not altogether easy now, in view of the dense population of the shore from Posilipo to Castellamare, to imagine the scene which greeted the first Greek settlers on the Bay of Naples, or the buildings which they erected there. But by a visit to the desolate world of Pæstum,[1] where, amidst the ruined streets of the old Greek town, the majestic Doric temples of Neptune and Ceres look out upon the unharvested sea, one is enabled to form a pretty clear idea of the scene when Neapolis came first into being. The houses, too, in the suburb of Torre del Greco seem to recall by their oriental character the story of their ancient parentage. But apart from the temples at Pæstum and the temple of Hercules at Pompeii there are no true Italo-Greek buildings left. Only a few fragments of buildings and walls survive here and there, and tombs in the ancient Greek cemeteries, as at Capua and Cumæ. These tombs have yielded to archæologists a rich harvest of gold ornaments and vases buried with the dead in the streets of tombs outside the old Greek cities. The supreme beauty of these Italo-Greek vases in their best period, beauty of form, material, and painted design, may best be studied in the section devoted to them at the *Museo Nazionale*. Many of these were not the work of the Greek colonists themselves, but were imported direct from Greece. Such, for instance, were the " Pan-Athenaic " vases, which were brought back as prizes by colonists who proved successful in the Pan-Athenaic games, or the " Corinthian Lecythoi," vases painted with black figures on a white ground. But by the time that the Roman conquest of Campania was complete, Greek art in Italy was in its decadence, and the paintings and statues which Pompeii and Herculaneum have restored to the modern world, and which render the *Museo Nazionale* a treasure-house of unique delight, owe nothing to the Greeks who

[1] *See* Appendix. Founded by Sybaris about 600 B.C., Pæstum marked the extreme limit of the territory on the west coast controlled by that great and flourishing Greek city.

settled at Neapolis in these early days. They were the outcome of a Roman conquest and a new Roman fashion of imported art and artists.

From the time when Mummius carried off the masterpieces of Corinth to Rome in 149 B.C. down to the Augustan age, the cult of Greek art was the prevailing fashion at Rome. The Greek language was learned and even spoken by all men of refinement. Greek artists swarming into Rome received commissions in plenty, and proudly signed their names upon their vases, paintings and statues.[1] Greece and the Greek islands were ransacked for famous works of art. With these, or with copies of them by Greek sculptors, wealthy Romans adorned the halls and gardens of their villas. *Græcia capta ferum victorem cepit* (captive Greece led her rude victor captive), and the new race of invading Greek artists beautified the walls of Pompeii and Herculaneum with paintings and mosaics, and bedecked with carved gems and jewellery the persons of the Roman ladies. But if the works of art which we shall see in Naples are the works of a later generation of Greek artists, only indirectly connected with the Siren City, Naples itself may claim a large influence on the development of civilisation. For it was from this old Greek city that Emperor Frederick (King Frederick I. of the Two Sicilies) drew the cult of ancient art which led him to make his Court the home of a first *Renaissance*, and so to prepare the way for the later rebirth of things beautiful and intellectual.

[1] It will be seen in the *Museo Nazionale* that Salpion of Athens put his name to that wonderful Vase of Gaeta upon which he had so exquisitely carved scenes from the birth of Bacchus; Glycon signed the Farnese Hercules; Apollonius of Athens the bronze Doryphorus; the signature of Alexander the Athenian was attached to the picture of the daughters of Niobe playing at knuckle-bones, and that of Dioscorides of Samos to some mosaics, found at Pompeii.

The limits of the old Greek city of Neapolis cannot be definitely ascertained. But one may think of it as lying within the parallelogram of which the Via Mezzocannone formed the western boundary. Southwards, this street gave access to the sea, and somewhere in a prominent position by the shore, possibly upon the point of Pizzofalcone, so that all seafarers might behold it from afar, rose the Temple of Aphrodite Euploia, the giver of good voyages.

CHAPTER III

Posilipo and the Site of Palæopolis

The site of Palæopolis—Subsidence of the coast—Roman villas beneath the waves—The Romans and Baiæ—The old Roads and the new—Villa Rosebery—Capo di Posilipo—La Gaiola—Villa of Pausilypum—Vergil and Marcellus—Scoglio di Virgilio—Nisida—Grotta di Seiano—Augustus, Tiberius and Sejanus—Tiberius at Capri—Fall of Sejanus.

THE new settlement, as we have seen, was called Neapolis, as opposed to Parthenope, which was now naturally spoken of as the Old City—Palæopolis. The latter, like Cumæ itself, fell into gradual decadence, and finally disappeared so completely that the very memory of its site was lost. The question as to what was the situation of Palæopolis has therefore been a fruitful source of conjecture and dispute. It is not yet determined. Some have placed it at Castel dell' Ovo, others as far east as Torre del Greco. Salvatore di Giacomo would have it that Palæopolis was on the hill which rises from San Giovanni Maggiore towards the Duomo, and that Neapolis was built close at hand, where the old market-place, Mercato Vecchio, now is. According to this view, Palæopolis was defended by a deep ditch, or fosse, which is now indicated by the Strada di Chiaia.

The one definite statement we have about it by old and reliable historians is to be found in Livy. Palæopolis, he says, was not far from the place where

Naples is now situated. He adds that both cities were inhabited by the same people, who came from Cumæ.[1] That remark would hardly have been worth making if it referred to two settlements separated only by the few yards which divide Chiaia or Castel dell' Ovo from the Mercato Vecchio. We look more naturally for a site closer to Cumæ, a site east of Cumæ, which will fulfil the condition of being the first step in that eastward movement nearer to Sorrento and Pæstum, of which the founding of Neapolis was the second. We look more naturally for a site at least two or three miles removed from the city which was founded after it, "not far from the place where Naples is now situated." Such a site is the promontory of Posilipo, the natural half-way house between Cumæ andPæstum. This bold headland derives its modern appellation (though now usually spelt with two *l*'s, and with the accent on the *i*) from the old Greek name of Pausilypon (free from care—*Sans souci*). It is the one important promontory in the Bay of Naples—the Sinus Cumanus of Roman days—between the Capes of Miseno and Sorrento.

The long slope of the verdant hill of Posilipo (Collina di Posilipo), ending in grey sands and miniature bays framed by masses of tufa rock, forms the western boundary of Naples. Completing the horseshoe frame of heights which enfolds the city, it constitutes a definite line of division between the western, or Neapolitan side of the Bay, and the eastern—a division so definite that, landwards, it completely screens from view the section wherein Pozzuoli and Baiæ lie. This line of demarcation is emphasised by the changed character of the soil. For beyond the ridge of Posilipo is that haunted region of burnt rocks,

[1] "Palæopolis fuit haud procul inde, ubi nunc Neapolis sita est; duabus urbibus populus idem habitabat" (Livy, VIII. 22).

of sulphurous volcanic hills and haunted lakes, known as the Phlegræan Fields (*Campi Flegrei*).[1]

The site of Palæopolis, however, was probably not upon any part of the promontory of Posilipo as we see it to-day, but upon an extension of it, where a low tongue of land once ran out to sea beyond the group of little islands off its extreme point of La Gaiola (*Caveola*). This tongue of land is now hidden beneath the waves.

It is an accepted fact that, owing to earthquakes and volcanic upheavals, the whole level of the coast in this neighbourhood has sunk some 20 feet since the first century A.D. It is believed that at one time the subsidence was as much as 40 feet, but that a subsequent rise has reduced the total to 20.[2] Evidence of such post-Roman land-movements is found in the marks of the erosion line on the rocks and grottoes of Capri. The columns of the Macellum, or so-called Temple of Serapis, at Pozzuoli furnish another proof. For Babbage and others have demonstrated that the burrowings of marine shell-fish, clearly discernible in those columns at a height of about 19 feet *above sea-level*, bear witness to a subsidence followed by an elevation of the land. I think the same thing happened at Pæstum.

We have an instance of a similar process nearer home. For it is held on good geological and archæo-

[1] The geology of the Phlegræan Fields was the subject of Sir William Hamilton's epoch-making work. Students may like to be reminded that there is in London a whole library devoted to this subject, which is outside the scope of this book. The Johnstone Lavis collection of books about Naples is mainly concerned with the literature of Vesuvius and Etna, though it includes many old guide books and books of travel. It belongs to the Geological Department of University College, London, and is housed in Gower Street.

[2] R. W. Günther, *Earth Movements in the Bay of Naples.*

logical grounds that there has been a general subsidence of perhaps as much as a dozen feet in the level of the land between London and the mouth of the Thames since Cæsar first fought his way across the river nearly two thousand years ago.

If, then, we may accept the view which the researches of Mr Günther make more than probable, that the site of Palæopolis was on the low promontory which at that time stretched to seaward of the Gaiola

DUOMO, POZZUOLI

Islands, it is not to be wondered at if the memory of it was lost. For it was first obliterated by the Romans who built their magnificent villas above its ruins, and with them it was afterwards submerged owing to the subsidence of the whole coast-line. Nor can we be astonished if, among the remains of the sunken Roman buildings still visible beneath the waves, no recognisable traces have been discovered of the early Greek settlement.

The subsidence of the foreshore, then, submerged both the remains of the old Greek settlement of Parthenope or Palæopolis and the luxurious seaside residences which the Roman magnates had erected upon its foundations. For with the coming of the Augustan age a change came over the whole aspect and circumstances of the Neapolitan Riviera. Cumæ had been devastated with malaria and was abandoned. But now Baiæ and Neapolis were discovered by Roman Society and developed as fashionable seaside resorts. And all along the Campanian coast, from Misenum and Baiæ to Puteoli and Pausilypum, and from Neapolis and Megaris (Castel dell' Ovo) to Herculaneum, wealthy Romans began to crowd to the watering-places on this favoured shore. Escaping from the noisy crowded streets, the feverish heat or bitter winds of Rome, they found here a land where the heat of the sun was tempered by the sea and mountain breezes, where the steep cliffs of the shore afforded protection from the cold winds that blow across the snow-tipped Apennines, and baths whose salubrious waters might cure their town-bred ills. They made of it a veritable Roman Paradise. Here they built their villas and laid out their gardens and fishponds, or constructed even miniature lakes to ensure the greater delicacy of the cultivated fish and oysters which they loved. Here, on the Siren's shore, the Roman proconsul, retiring from his province with the fortune of a nabob, would raise him marble palaces. Baths were built at Baiæ and Pausilypum. Theatres and amphitheatres were erected at Cumæ, at Baiæ, at Puteoli and Neapolis to beguile the leisure of the visitors in the intervals of bathing; theatres in which the greatest actors and singers of the age performed, amphitheatres in which men fought for the amusement of their patrons, and in which sailors took part in sham sea-fights. Baiæ became a miniature Rome, where all the luxury and even more than all the wantonness of the capital reigned unchecked. So demoralising was the tone of the place that, as Propertius declares, no woman's reputation could survive a week amidst its manifold temptations. Beautiful Baiæ! the Lido or the Deauville of the day, evidently. Every one denounced it, and every one, poets, satirists, and moralists, went there. A pretty Greek epigram explained its influence. The God of Love, it says, whilst bathing here one day, dropped his torch in the waters of Baiæ, and ever since, whoever comes in contact with them straightway catches fire. As the sheltering cliffs narrowed the foreshore, the ever-increasing demand for villas soon compelled the Roman architects to devise means to secure more room. Landwards they quarried and levelled and terraced the close-sheltering cliffs and raised tier upon tier of dwellings resting upon vaults of concrete and thick retaining walls. Seawards, enticed by an almost tideless sea and the protection of rocks and headlands, they built out upon foundations of rock villas that encroached upon the water. These were protected too by the sea-walls and moles and piers constructed for harbour purposes. Traces of both these systems of building are plainly to be seen all along the coast from the Villa Rosebery to Baiæ. Vergil, in the *Æneid* (IX. 711), likens the fall of the stricken giant Bitas to the crashing into the sea of rocks hewn to construct the Baian mole, " raised on the seas the surges to control. . . ."

> " Prone to the deep the stones disjointed fall
> Off the vast pile; the scattered ocean flies;
> Black sands, discoloured froth, and mingled mud arise."

Horace, too, moralising in the intervals of indulging in the dissipations of dissolute Baiæ, bethinks himself of the death's head at the feast, and warns the multi-millionaire that death awaits him even whilst he is eagerly contracting for marble to build his palaces. " Unmindful of the grave," he cries, " you rear mansions and are eager to thrust back the shores of the sea which surges up to Baiæ, since the limits of the mainland fail to content you." Not that the scene was altogether one of mere pleasure-seeking and indulgence. If Baiæ was a corrupt bathing station, and Herculaneum a city of pleasure and repose, Neapolis and Pompeii were places of business, Pozzuoli was a huge commercial port, and Misenum the strongly protected harbour of the Roman fleet. If Augustus sought rest and distraction, and Pollio new forms of gluttony in his luxurious villa at Pausilypum; if the epicure Lucullus devised new dishes for the gourmet in his superb country seat on Nisida; if Calpurnius Piso was soon to be building him a new and yet more sumptuous retreat at Herculaneum; yet there were also serious men of commanding intellect, practised in affairs, who were busy, like Augustus himself, in working out the great problems of Rome's destiny, and bearing the burden of her prodigious Empire. Already Marcus Vipsanius Agrippa, Augustus' trusted general and adviser, had seen in the Lucrine Lake the shelter for the Roman fleets, which were to be manned and trained before they could hope to deal with Sextus Pompeius, the bold corsair chief, who swept the seas and threatened Rome with famine. There he constructed a military harbour of perfect security, the *Portus Julius*. He cut down the forest about Lake Avernus and connected it by means of a canal with the Lucrine Lake and the sea on the one side of Cape Miseno, and with Cumæ and the sea on the other by means of a tunnel, which he bored beneath the hill. The Tyrrhenian fleet could thus be passed from north to south of Misenum without being obliged to double that stormy Cape. And whilst these operations were being executed, he had constructed at Misenum a temporary harbour of

Mus. Naz.] [*Alinari*

VENUS

(Holding a Mirror)

refuge consisting of an inner and an outer basin. In the presence of works so typical of Roman energy Vergil, "landscape lover, lord of language," wandering along the shores of Posilipo, was fashioning those immortal verses in which he enshrined the doctrine of Roman piety and duty and the high destiny of the imperial race. Cicero, the great advocate, was busy with his books and politics and writings even whilst he was building himself first one villa at Puteoli, and then another by Pompeii.

The villas which were built out to sea have suffered from the subsidence of the coast-line even more than those which climbed the hill. Yet on a clear day you have but to row along the shore from the Villa Rosebery to La Gaiola, and, leaning over the gunwale, you will see the foundations of a whole town of those Roman seaside buildings. Seeing them, it is not difficult to imagine the scene which this Cape once presented when the Valley of Gaiola was faced with stone buildings peeping from green gardens, and from the sea below rose villas and colonnades and temples and quays bedecked with statuary. It was such a scene, in fact, as was often painted by the mural artists at Pompeii in those frescoes that you may see to-day in the *Museo Nazionale*.

When a Roman plutocrat left the torrid streets of the capital for the Campanian coast, to rest or amuse himself at the Brighton or Deauville of the day, he would drive down the Appian Way. That Queen of Roads (*Regina Viarum*) was constructed by the Consul Appius Claudius in the year 312 B.C., and afterwards extended to Beneventum and Brindisi. Our traveller's chariot would bear him swiftly southwards from the Forum, rattling over pavement of massive polygonal slabs of stone lined on either side with tower or tumulus, tombs and monuments to the Roman dead, past the spot where Christ was soon to meet St Peter and turn him back in answer to his question, "*Domine, Quo Vadis?*" and past the caves and catacombs where His followers were to seek refuge in life and death from the hands of the persecutor. But our Roman cared for none of these things. He held that a man might believe what he liked and do very much what he liked, so long as he served the State and worshipped the gods of the State, and did nothing to involve the anger of the gods against the State. With frequent relays of good post horses he sped along this corridor of the tombs of his ancestors, and rapidly reached the open country. Leaving the Appian Way at Capua, he turned right-handed by the road which ran due south through Atella and entered Neapolis by the Porta Capuana. Here he entered upon the *Decumanus major*—the central thoroughfare of the city, which is now the Strada dei Tribunali.

If our traveller was making his way from Neapolis to Puteoli or Baiæ, he might follow the old Roman road which scaled the steep ridge of Posilipo at the northern end. There alone the gradient would permit the construction of a carriage road. This was the Via Antiniana. Leaving Naples on the north-west, it ascended behind the *Museo Nazionale* to the plateau of Antignano, and passed by Soccavo and Lago Agnano to Pozzuoli, where a fragment of it is plainly visible outside the amphitheatre.

Later, as the attractions of Baiæ, the commerce of Puteoli (Pozzuoli), and the naval and military importance of Misenum made the question of communications with Rome more urgent, the Via Domitiana was constructed along the coast by Cumæ. By this route the distance from Rome to Neapolis was lessened by four miles. To-day, with the same intention of shortening the journey from Rome to

Naples, a new line of electric railway is being constructed, the *Ferrovia direttissima,* which will reach Naples from the same direction and pass through Fuorigrotta and the new tunnel under Posilipo.

Subsequently two other roads were made. But, so steep was the remainder of the Posilipo ridge that it was deemed easier, then as now, to burrow under than to carry a road over it. Two tunnels were therefore driven through the hill. The first, or more northern of them, was that now known as the Grotta Vecchia di Posilipo on the road to Bagnoli; the second, the Grotta di Seiano, in the vicinity of the Villa Pausilypum, probably connected with a road which ran along the coast from Mergellina to Pozzuoli. This road, as Mr Günther thinks, has been submerged along with the rest of the foreshore. His theory is confirmed by the discovery of *columbaria* in the rocks just above the present sea-level, since it was the Roman custom to bury their dead along a street of tombs just outside the city gates.[1] If we would follow our Roman traveller along his submerged coast-road, a boat may be chartered from the little strand where the fishermen congregate at Mergellina, at the end of the Via Caracciolo. Delicious are the hours spent in drifting through the gently lapping wavelets and marking the clear pools along the rocky shore, where fishermen haul their nets, or fish for octopus, or dive for *frutti di mare* among the ruins of Roman villas; where the water is more transparent than the scarves that Botticelli drew about his Graces, and the photograph of a bather will give the impression that he is swimming in air, above rocks where

[1] A *columbarium,* "pigeon-hole," was the word used to describe a hole cut in the rock in which the urn containing the ashes of the deceased was stored.

once the Siren may have sat and sung prophetically, "*Napoli! Bella Napoli!*"

The modern landward route, by the Strada Nuova di Posilipo, by way of Capo di Posilipo to Bagnoli, is a lovely marine drive.[1] The Strada Nuova, which joins the Via Caracciolo and Riviera di Chiaia by the Rotonda of Mergellina and passes through a cutting below the crest of Coroglio to the village of Posilipo, is a finely engineered road. It was begun by the French during their occupation and continued by the Austrians (1812–23), supplanting the mediæval Strada sulla Collina, which, starting from Vomero, and passing along the crest of the hill of Posilipo, comes down to Santo Strato.

The district we are now to visit is one of the most romantic, one of the most beautiful, and archæologically one of the most fascinating in this wide land of interest and beauty. From Mergellina to far Miseno and Cumæ both sea and shore of this venerable coast are strewn with fragments of Roman villas and Roman works.

Above the point of Mergellina a steep winding stone-way on the right leads up to the church of Santa Maria del Parto or del Sannazaro. In the apse is the tomb of the Founder of the church, Jacopo Sannazaro, by the Tuscan artist, Fra Giovanni da Montórsoli (1537). In the first chapel on the right is a painting by Leonardo da Pistoia (1542), representing St Michael overthrowing Satan. Satan is painted as a black she-devil, the only one of that sex known, it is said. That is as may be. It has given rise to the legend of the Devil of Mergellina. According to one version the artist thus revenged himself upon a model who refused to comply with his desires.

[1] No. 2 Tram from Via Piedigrotta runs to the point of Posilipo; Tram No. 15 to Bagnoli.

According to another, which is told by Matilde Serao in her highly-coloured way in *Leggende Napoletane*, the painter was following the instructions of Diomede Caraffa, Bishop of Ariano. A chaste soul and a lover of art, Diomede in his youth had loved the Lady Isabella with a pure and passionate devotion. She, vain as she was beautiful, fickle as she was cruel, played with his passion and was faithless to his love. She said she loved him, then turned her eyes to fascinate other admirers; swore she was his, then gave herself to his friend. Maddened by jealousy and despair, the noble youth sought consolation in religion. Diomede forswore the sex, became an ideal priest, an exemplary Bishop. But the memory of what he had suffered was always with him. One day he commissioned Leonardo to paint St Michael overcoming Satan, and bade him take for a model of his portrait of Lucifer the fair face of Madonna Isabella.

Beyond the tiny beach and rotonda of Mergellina, which commands a famous view of Naples and Vesuvius, the first point seaward is crowned by the massive walls of the Palazzo di Donna Anna. The foundations of this unfinished palace by Cosimo Fanzaga are set upon a rock jutting out into the sea. Supplanting an older palace and a still more ancient Roman dwelling, it was begun, but never completed, as a pleasure house for Donna Anna Caraffa, wife of the Duke of Medina, Viceroy of Naples in the seventeenth century. Its huge façade, reared upon so magnificent a site, is singularly effective, especially in the shadow of the setting sun or when the pale moonlight silvers the silent sea.

A series of tree-shaded villas, gardens, and restaurants [1] overlooking the sea stretches down to the rocky

[1] Notably the well-known Trattoria Soglio di Frisio, extolled by Robert Hichens in his beautiful story, *A Spirit in Prison*.

shore on either side of the Asilo Tropeano. This is a sort of Dr Barnardo's institution for waifs and strays, who are here housed and trained under the most ideal conditions. Above, on the right, a strange-looking building rears a cone-shaped dome above a portico which conceals a building in the Egyptian style.

PALAZZO DONN' ANNA

Formerly the Schilizzi Mausoleum, this has now been taken over and enlarged as a naval War memorial.

We have now reached the entrance to the Villa Rosebery on Capo di Posilipo. This beautifully wooded property of seventeen acres was formerly in the possession of Prince Luigi of Bourbon. It was purchased and laid out by the Earl of Rosebery, who recently presented it to the British Government for the use of British Ambassadors at Rome. The tiled floors within and the tiled terraces without are a notable feature of the sumptuous palazzo. Surrounded by orange and lemon groves and magnificent gardens, and shaded by dark pine trees and holm-oaks, it overlooks the sea at the Capo di Posilipo. At its base in the sea are evident remains of Roman buildings. Outside the breakwater built by Prince Luigi, the remains of old houses are clearly marked by the boats of fishermen raking for shellfish and other *frutti di mare* in the crannies of submerged walls.

West of the Point of Posilipo, remote from any road, and standing in front of a *pozzolana* quarry on the waterline, is the *Casa degli Spiriti*, reputed to be haunted by a spectre robed in white. It is the best preserved Roman house on Posilipo. Further west are the baths, or so-called fish-tanks, of Pollio.

Many remains of Roman buildings may be traced in the village of Marechiaro on the summit of the cliff. At the top of the path leading up to it are some fragments of a temple of Fortune. Behind the village, the picturesque campanile of the little rococo church of S. Maria del Faro has succeeded to the site of a Roman lighthouse (*Pharus*), from which the church and local Virgin have taken their title.

On the western side, at the point known as La Gaiola, the character of the Posilipo promontory changes abruptly. Here are cliffs lofty and precipitous, dropping sheer into the rippling waters of the sea. Just at this point, it is thought, was the site of the buildings of the Imperial Villa of Augustus, sloping down to the sea on one side and dominating the cliff on the other. Certainly the beauty of the locality is equal to its fame. For whilst shorewards the soft and smiling valley of Gaiola contrasts with the stern forbidding cliffs of the bay of Trentaremi, seawards the vista of blue waters ranges from the heights of Sorrento and Vesuvius to Misenum, and from the island rocks of Nisida to Capri and Ischia beyond.

Augustus, we know, frequently stayed at or near Naples. An inscription shows that the Pausilypum property was in the hands of imperial procurators at this time, and a leaden water-pipe, stamped with the name and title of Hadrian, which was found in the upper baths, indicates that it was imperial property in the second century A.D.[1] Hadrian probably inherited it from Augustus, to whom it had passed by the will of Vedius Pollio. Pollio was a favourite courtier of Augustus, who was his guest at this luxurious villa of his at Pausilypum. It is described by Statius in the third book of his *Silvæ*. Pollio, like many other epicures of the day, was interested in the fashionable science of pisciculture. Like Lucullus, who, at his neighbouring villa, the *Neapolitanum*, made a cutting through a hillside to let in a supply of sea-water for his fish-pools, he spared no trouble or expense in the cultivation of fish. But he was thought to have exceeded the bounds of decency when he experimented in fattening fish upon living men, choosing this death as a punishment for slaves who had offended him. Much was forgiven to a gourmet; but it was said that he indulged in this practice because he also took pleasure in beholding a man being devoured alive, " which pleasant sight he could not see by any other beast upon the land " (Pliny, IX. 23). Augustus, staying with this monster at Pausilypum, is said to have saved from such a death a slave who had chanced to break a crystal goblet. The Emperor signified his distaste for his host's idiosyncrasy by commanding all his glasses to be broken and thrown into the fish-tanks instead of the slave.

[1] Günther, *Pausilypon*, pp. 8, 129.

Pollio bequeathed his villa to Augustus (15 B.C.). The *Neapolitanum* of Lucullus also came into his possession. The ruins which survive among the verdant vines and orchard-gardens upon the Gaiola ridge have been carefully examined and described, with maps and plans, by Mr Günther. They stand on private property and are not easily accessible. For that reason it will be sufficient for our present purpose to refer the reader who wishes to pursue the subject to Mr Günther's work. These ruins include a large dwelling-house, lying high above the road, which he believes to have been the house of Pollio. The mural paintings in it are exactly similar in style and design to those of the house of Diomede at Pompeii, and must therefore assuredly date from before A.D. 79. Close to this villa are the remains of a theatre—the private theatre of the imperial villa—and of the Odeon, for music and recitations; a dwelling-house adjoining the theatre, and behind it, a rectangular enclosure terminating in a raised hemicycle, described by Giordano as a Nymphæum (for the display of fountains). Close to the south-east corner of the theatre the remains of a temple were discovered in 1842. Massive fragments of baths are within a few minutes' walk of the theatre, and others are to be found at the water's edge on the Gaiola beach. The marbles which once adorned the Imperial Villa went the way of other treasures of Imperial Rome. Many, no doubt, were appropriated by Spanish viceroys, and, like others since, have found their way into private collections. One well-known statue, *The Bearded Dionysos*, a Græco-Roman replica of a fifth-century type, found near the Grotta di Seiano, is preserved in the British Museum. At the Museum at Naples is the *Nereid riding on a Pistrix* (restored by Cali), a lovely composition and an exquisite study in curves.

It was perhaps within the walls of this once sumptuous villa that Vergil recited to the bereaved Imperial pair that magnificent passage with which he closes the sixth book of the *Æneid*, wherein Æneas, visiting the underworld, sees the shade of young Marcellus; a passage of such transcendent power and poetic inspiration that later ages deemed the poet to have reached in it the heights of Messianic prophecy. The young Marcellus, the hope and darling of his uncle, Augustus, had been cut off in his youth, attacked by malaria at Baiæ, or poisoned, as some whispered, by his aunt, Livia. Æneas beholds "the godlike form of that youth divine," with whom Vergil himself had been wont to pace these shores and teach him all his lore, and learns from his guide the doom of early death that awaits him:

> "This youth, the blissful vision of a day,
> Shall just be shown on earth, and snatched away.
> The gods too high had raised the Roman state,
> Were but their gifts as permanent as great. . . .
> No youth shall equal hopes of glory give,
> No youth afford as great a cause to grieve.
> The Trojan honour, and the Roman boast,
> Admired when living and adored when lost!
> Mirror of ancient faith in early youth,
> Undaunted worth, inviolable truth. . . .
> Ah! couldst thou break through Fate's severe decree,
> A new Marcellus shall arise in thee!
> Full canisters of fragrant lilies bring,
> Mixed with the purple roses of the spring.
> Let me with funeral flowers his body strow,
> The gift which parents to their children owe,
> This unavailing gift at least I may bestow!"

Octavia, the mother of Marcellus, listened here to the poet reciting those wonderful verses, tremendous in their pathos and their beauty, and fainted as she listened. Augustus rewarded him with a gift so generous—ten thousand sesterces (£80) for each line

—that it enabled him to purchase a small farm and live contented and composing for the rest of his days.

The memory of Vergil is fittingly enshrined upon this coast in the overhanging crag off the Punta di Coroglio, known as the *Scoglio di Virgilio*—the rock on which, according to local legend, the great Magician would come and sit, weaving magic lines and circles upon the surrounding rocks, bringing with him, too, at times, the young Prince Marcellus, and teaching him the secrets of the spirit world.

A little to the west of Vergil's rock, and at the water's edge, are the architectural remains to which tradition gives the name of *Scuola di Virgilio*, for here, it is said, he held his school. They are rapidly disappearing. Only a few ruins remain of the buildings with which the Romans covered the heights about the *Scoglio di Virgilio*. For the greater part they have crumbled and fallen with the cliffs into the sea, and those that remain, undermined by quarry-caves, are like to follow their example.

The scene upon which Augustus looked down from his luxurious villa on the Gaiola hill was, indeed, very different from the succession of rocky headlands and vine-clad slopes running down to the silent beaches of tiny bays which we see to-day. Then groups of buildings clustered about the water's edge. "Instead of being an island," Mr Günther writes, "the Gaiola rock was a little hill, upon a promontory which extended a quarter of a mile beyond the present shore ; around and on it stood splendid villas, colonnaded temples, and the little pavilions by the sea, such as we see painted upon many a Pompeian wall ; under the lee of the promontory rising brown out of the blue water was a row of massive piers, the mole of the little harbour." The harbour was protected by a breakwater composed of piers connected by arches of concrete, which is still traceable some eighty yards from the shore and only a few feet beneath the level of the sea. Similar breakwaters were constructed at Pozzuoli, Miseno and off the adjacent island of Nisida. The ancient name of this island was Nesis. It has been formed by the crater of an extinct volcano. It belonged to Lucullus, and here Marcus Brutus bade farewell to his wife Portia, after having planned with Cassius the murder of Julius Cæsar. This island and the neighbouring shore are the scenes of Robert Hichens' novel, *A Spirit in Prison*.

Close to the imperial villa is the entrance to the great tunnel, known as the *Grotta di Seiano*, which connected it with the highway leading to Pozzuoli. This, no doubt, is the carriage-way beneath the mountains between Dikæarchia and Neapolis described by Strabo, who wrote in the time of Augustus (*Geographica*, V. 242). He says that, like that at Cumæ, the tunnel is lit by shafts pierced in the mountain. This description proves that it was the Grotta di Seiano to which he refers, and not the Grotta Vecchia di Posilipo, for that was not so lit. It was probably constructed before the Grotta Vecchia, and may have been begun about the same time as that near Cumæ in the time of Augustus. An inscription on a milestone found within it clearly indicates that it remained in use as a public thoroughfare at least as late as the time of Constantius Pius (*circa* A.D. 360). This inscription is headed by the numeral VII, which may denote the distance in Roman miles from the western end of the tunnel by the old road to Cumæ. By degrees the tunnel became blocked and fell into disuse. Its existence as a road was forgotten. For a thousand years and more it was regarded as merely a large cave. At length it was reopened by order of King Ferdinand II. in 1490, when the making of the new road from

Corogli to Bagnoli brought it again to light. The length of the tunnel was then given as 2526 feet. The interior has been carefully described by Mr Günther (*Pausilypon*, pp. 21–26). Its name is derived from L. Ælius Sejanus, the crafty and unscrupulous general and minister of Tiberius. What connection he had with it is unknown, but it may be hazarded that he was responsible for repairing and improving it.

In the year A.D. 14 the Emperor Augustus came down from Rome to the Campanian coast. Enchanted by the beauty of its position and the excellence of its climate, he had purchased the little island of Capreæ (Capri) from the people of Neapolis, who exchanged it for Ischia. There Augustus was hoping to obtain rest and to regain his health. For the air of Capri has always had the reputation of rejuvenating the aged and restoring to them the vigour of youth. Augustus, it is said, was led to purchase the island by observing on his first visit to it that the branches of an old ilex which hung drooping to the ground suddenly recovered. But this time he was attacked by dysentery, and was barely able to crawl to Naples, and thence to Nola, where he died. Summoning his friends to his death-bed he asked them, as he gazed across the fertile plain at the foot of Monte Somma, "What think ye of the comedy, my friends? Have I played my part in it fairly? If so, applaud!" They gave their applause, and he died, kissing Livia, bidding her be mindful of their long married life. And his stepson, Tiberius, reigned in his stead. A tall, handsome man of great physical strength, a good soldier, a good man of business and a crafty statesman, Tiberius was of a retiring disposition and studious habits. He preferred the society of scholars to the business of an empire or the plaudits of a crowd.

His naturally gloomy temperament and unpopular manners had been intensified by the career of self-effacement and dissimulation which had been imposed upon him by the sneers and snubs of Augustus, who disliked him intensely. As he became older he grew more gloomy and suspicious and cruel, finding that he was surrounded by traitors and conspirators who schemed to supplant him. Chief among these were members of his own household, Agrippina, and his daughter-in-law, and his trusted, crafty, and unscrupulous minister, Sejanus. The popular idea of Tiberius as merely a cruel tyrant and monstrous debauchee is far from just. It is a conception largely created by the brilliant pen of Tacitus. Misled by the Empress Agrippina's prejudiced memoirs of palace intrigues, the great historian painted the gloomy and suspicious old Emperor in the darkest colours, using his portrait as an artistic contrast to his picture of the young, the brilliant, the popular, and magnanimous prince Germanicus, whose untimely death, maliciously attributed to his uncle, was sadly recognised as one more instance of the saying that " brief and unfortunate are the loves of the Roman people." But though hated at Rome, where the people liked neither his reserved manners nor his reform of abuses, Tiberius was beloved in the provinces. There his wise and broad-minded administration helped to produce a period of tranquillity and prosperity. One instance of Tiberius' recognition of the claim of the Provinces to aid in emergencies from the Imperial Treasury is recorded on a pedestal now in the *Museo Nazionale*. It supported a statue of Tiberius erected at Puteoli by the grateful citizens of fourteen towns in Asia Minor, which had been destroyed by an earthquake, and which Tiberius had caused to be rebuilt.

If the Romans hated Tiberius as a kill-joy whom

they feared, Tiberius hated Rome. The pomp of the imperial city bored him; the noisy and turbulent crowds he despised. His reserved and sensitive nature rebelled against the constraints of a publicity which was not even tempered by popularity. Three years after the death of his only son Drusus (A.D. 23), he determined to withdraw from the capital for ever. He thought, we are told, that he could best administer the Empire from the Provinces. On the pretext of

CAPRI, FROM MERGELLINA

dedicating a temple of Jupiter at Capua and a temple of Augustus at Nola, he left Rome and proceeded to the Campanian coast. There he was attracted by the charms and privacy of Capreæ, which had passed to him among the possessions of Augustus. It was small — some eleven miles in circumference — and therefore easily guarded. Its precipitous limestone cliffs rendered it difficult to approach. It was thinly populated. Here, the privacy of Tiberius was secure. He amused his leisure by building him no fewer than twelve villas in different parts of the island, and occupied his business hours with the multifarious details of administration, or reading in his library and holding arguments with philosophers and astrologers, the

Chaldæan crowd, as Juvenal calls them,[1] with whom he surrounded himself. For he was both crudely superstitious, like most Romans, and intellectually interested in philosophy.

From this safe place of retreat Tiberius conducted the affairs of State. Whilst protecting himself by encouraging informers to denounce any attempt at treason, he promoted the servility of the Senate by writing long and obscure letters of instruction or advice. Senators by these means were kept in constant fear lest they should have to pay with their lives for some unguarded word or applause at the wrong moment. Rome, anxious and deserted, retaliated by inventing lubricious stories of filthy and degenerate orgies in which the retired giant was supposed to be indulging. Tiberius was doubtless no more of an ascetic than other Romans of his time. But that he was sixty-seven years of age when he left Rome, and after a life of prolonged military campaigns and strenuous labour, lived eleven years more at Capri, are physical facts which render such stories of exaggerated debauchery wildly improbable. Tiberius was encouraged to retire to Capri by his trusted but treacherous minister and confidant Sejanus, whom he had made Prefect of the Prætorian Guard, and who aspired to succeed him. In the absence of the Emperor the stage was left clear for his favourite to develop his authority and his schemes at Rome. Tiberius, suspicious of, and troubled by the claims and ambitions of his own family, never dreamed that a man of such comparatively low origin as Sejanus would dare to aim at wearing the imperial purple. He trusted him implicitly. The crafty favourite worked upon the

[1] Tutor haberi
Principis augusta Capræarum in rupe sedentis
Cum grege Chaldæo (*Sat.* X. 91).

Emperor's fears by pretending to discover conspiracies against him. Whilst earning his misplaced gratitude and confidence thereby, Sejanus added to his Master's unpopularity by the condemnation of many innocent nobles and officials unjustly sacrificed to his groundless fears. But it was Sejanus himself who was the dangerous conspirator. Whilst making himself almost indispensable to the Emperor by the tact and ability with which he helped him in the administration of the Empire, that wily and unscrupulous minister was daily adding to his own power. He had begun already to clear his way to the throne.

Drusus, the young son of Tiberius, struck Sejanus in the face in a drunken brawl. The minister bore the blow in silence, and gave no sign to rouse suspicion of the resentment he felt. But by wily words and the charm of his winning grace and personal beauty, he seduced Livilla, Drusus' wife. Drugged with passion and ambition, the weak woman sacrificed her husband to her lover. With her help, Sejanus secured the death of Drusus by poison and thus removed the heir-presumptive to the throne. Soon came the turn of Agrippina, the proud and ambitious wife of the beloved Germanicus, and her family. Sejanus seduced Lepida, the wife of the elder Drusus, Agrippina's second son, as he had seduced Livilla, and with the same intention. He persuaded her to denounce her husband to Tiberius. Agrippina and her two eldest sons were thrown into prison, there to perish miserably by starvation and the sword. Now that his power was reaching its zenith, the haughtiness and presumption of Sejanus increased. It was whispered that he boasted that he was the real autocrat of Rome, and sneered at Tiberius as the "Monarch of the Isle."

But the suspicions of the Emperor were at length aroused. He concealed them by heaping honours upon his favourite, but even as he did so, he began to contrive his downfall. He betrothed Sejanus to his grand-daughter Julia, and made him his colleague in the consulship. By this means he rid himself of his presence at Capreæ. Sejanus went to Rome to fulfil the functions of the consuls. He was received with abject flattery by the Senate and people. But presently strange letters began to arrive from Capri, which kept both Sejanus and the Senate in an agony of suspense. At first he praised his colleague and hinted that the Emperor would soon succeed to the throne. Then he spoke slightingly of him, and pointedly honoured his nephew, Gaius Cæsar. Foreseeing his disgrace, Sejanus was driven to declare his hand.

He asked permission to return to Capreæ, where his betrothed bride lay ill. It was refused, the Emperor declaring that he and his family were about to visit Rome. Scenting his coming disgrace, Sejanus determined to anticipate it by striking a blow at his master. He formed a plot for murdering Tiberius on his return to Rome. But the conspiracy was betrayed. There ensued one of the most dramatic scenes in history.

The Prefect of the Prætorian Guard, with all his acquired prestige of office and power, could not be openly denounced. Cunning and caution were required. Tiberius had no lack of either. He appointed Sertorius Macro, a trusted officer, to succeed Sejanus as Prefect of the Guard. He instructed him to proceed to Rome and there cause a meeting of the Senate to be summoned in the Temple of Apollo on the Palatine Hill. The approaches to it were guarded. Sejanus, attended by an armed guard, came down to the meeting of the Senate. He was met by Macro, who informed him that the business of the Senate was to confer upon him the Tribunician power.

This was the last rung in the ladder of power, and Sejanus thought that his ambition of succeeding to the Empire was about to be achieved. No sooner had he entered the temple than Macro returned to the Prætorian Guard and informed them that the Emperor had appointed him to be their Prefect. He had first delivered to the consuls a letter from Tiberius. They proceeded to read it to the Senate. It proved to be a long and wordy epistle—so Juvenal describes it[1]—and it sealed the fate of Sejanus. Beginning with some observations on general matters, it presently introduced a slight rebuke of Sejanus. The friends who had been crowding around the fortunate minister began to move uneasily in their seats. Then the letter drifted away to other matters of little import. But just as confidence was beginning to be restored, came a passage in which Sejanus was checked. The Senators began to leave the bench on which he sat. The recital of the letter continued amidst a tension that was scarcely to be borne. Sejanus was denounced. The minister who a moment before had been fawned upon and courted by all, was now sitting alone. The Consul ordered the lictors to seize him. He was hurried off to prison, sentenced to death, and next day he was strangled and his body dragged by the executioner's hook to the Scala Gemoniæ, whilst the populace hurled down his statues.

Meanwhile, at Capreæ, perched upon the highest cliff of the island, Tiberius watched and waited for news, the prey to an agony of suspense. His fleet was ready to carry him away in safety to the East, should the signal for which he waited announce that Macro's enterprise had failed.

[1] Verbosa et grandis epistola venit A Capreis (Juv., X. 71).

CHAPTER IV

The Phlegræan Fields—Pozzuoli to Cumæ

Pozzuoli—The Macellum and Amphitheatre—The Solfatara—The birth of Monte Nuovo—"The true Falernian"—Road to Baiæ—The Lucrine Lake—The Portus Julius and Lago di Averno—The Cave of the Sibyl—Grotta del Pace—Cumæ—Baiæ—Nero and the murder of Agrippina—Miseno—The death of Tiberius—Caligula's bridge across the Bay of Baiæ—Nero at Naples—Anticaglia and the remains of the Amphitheatre.

[From the Grotta di Sejano the coast road runs to Pozzuoli by way of the little bathing station, Bagnoli. From Naples Pozzuoli can be reached direct by the *Ferrovia Cumana*, starting from the Stazione Monte Santo or Cumana. The line passes beneath St Elmo and skirts the Terme di Agnano (*Thermæ Anianæ*), a spa which derives its healing waters from the hot spring on the south of the crater of Agnano. There is an up-to-date bathing establishment close to the once famous Grotta del Cane, where visitors used to be shown how the fumes of carbide dioxide which exude from the floor to a height of two feet asphyxiate a dog. This callous show has happily ceased.

The *Direttissima* from the Stazione di Chiaia goes under the Collina di Posilipo, emerging at Fuorigrotta and terminates at Pozzuoli. Trains every half-hour. To continue the journey to Baiæ it is necessary to change stations here. The tram-line (Tram 52 from the Piazza Vittoria) follows the same route as the *Ferrovia Cumana* by Agnano and Bagnoli.]

WE have seen that Pozzuoli (Puteoli) was in Roman days a great commercial port. When the mouth of the Tiber became silted up with sand and the port of Ostia was thus rendered wellnigh useless, it was at Puteoli that the corn-ships from Egypt unloaded the cargoes by which Rome was fed. It was, indeed, the chief trading station for the East and Africa, and as such great wealth poured into its lap. The splendour of its private houses and public buildings led Cicero to describe it as *pusilla Roma*, a miniature Rome.

It was here that St Paul landed after his voyage from Cæsarea in A.D. 62, and stayed some days ere continuing his journey to Rome. Little of interest remains of all the magnificent buildings which once adorned Puteoli. But fragments of the Roman breakwater can be seen above and below the water in the harbour, which commands a fine view of the surrounding bays, from Nisida to Capo di Miseno, as Major Benton Fletcher's drawing shows. On the right rise Monte Barbaro and Monte Nuovo. Across the Bay is Baiæ, sleeping peacefully after its hectic days. The peaks of Ischia (Monte Epomeo) rise grandly beyond the turf-clad slopes of Capo di Miseno and the Island of Procida. The Roman breakwater, the *moles Puteolana*, consisted of twenty-five piers connected by arches. It was restored by Antoninus Pius in A.D. 120.

From the railway station of the *Direttissima* you make a steep descent down into the little town, the road ending in a winding stone causeway. Houses and churches, with their little domed apses, cling to the steep cliffs beneath you, so that you may almost step upon their roofs. Six Corinthian columns from a temple dedicated to Augustus by Calpurnius adorn the exterior of the present Duomo erected upon its site and dedicated to San Procolo, the companion of St Januarius, of whom more anon. Within is the tomb of G. B. Pergolesi, the musician, who died here (1736). Pozzuoli boasts a native composer in

Antonio Sacchini (1734–86). The dedication of this temple to Augustus reminds one of the scene which took place on one occasion when the Emperor landed at Puteoli. The crew of a ship from Alexandria which happened to be in port came with garlands, frankincense, and words of praise to do him honour. "To them they owed," so ran their words of homage, "their lives, their liberties, and the well-being of their trade."

Near the Cumana railway station is the so-called *Serapeum* (Tempio di Serapide). It was not really a temple of Serapis, but a rectangular forum or market-place. It is now awash with water. The general view which one can obtain from the road above will satisfy most visitors. Those who wish to examine it more closely must pay three lire for admission. Three out of six Corinthian columns which formed the portico at the entrance are still standing. Booths beneath a gallery surrounded the central courtyard of the *Macellum*, or market-place. The bases of the columns which supported a building in the centre are still visible. We mentioned in the last chapter the deductions which have been drawn from the perforations made by shell-fish upon the columns of the atrium. Just below the station of the *Direttissima*, on the right, is a fragment of the old Roman road of the Via Antiniana. It runs beneath the full circle of an amphitheatre. The fragments of this amphitheatre (entrance 3 lire) are superimposed upon the remains of an earlier one. It was completed in the reign of Vespasian. The dens in which scenery, prisoners, and wild beasts for the performances were kept will be easily recognised beneath the arena. In one of them St Januarius may have awaited his doom. In a famous passage Gibbon has described the Flavian amphitheatres. It will serve us as a guide to those which we shall see in the course of our journeys through the Bay of Naples.

"The outside of the edifice was encrusted with marble and decorated with statues. The slopes of the vast concave, which formed the inside, were filled and surrounded with sixty or eighty rows of seats, of marble likewise, covered with cushions, and capable of receiving with ease above fourscore thousand spectators. Sixty-four *vomitories* (for by that name the doors were very aptly distinguished) poured forth the immense multitude; and the entrances, passages, and staircases were contrived with such exquisite skill, that each person, whether of the senatorial, the equestrian, or the plebeian order, arrived at his destined place without trouble or confusion. Nothing was omitted which, in any respect, could be subservient to the convenience and pleasure of the spectators. They were protected from the sun and rain by an ample canopy, occasionally drawn over their heads. The air was continually refreshed by the playing of fountains, and profusely impregnated by the grateful scent of aromatics. In the centre of the edifice the arena, or stage, was strewed with the finest sand, and successively assumed the most different forms. At one moment it seemed to rise out of the earth, like the garden of the Hesperides, and was afterwards broken into the rocks and caverns of Thrace. The subterraneous pipes conveyed an inexhaustible supply of water; and what had just before appeared a level plain, might be suddenly converted into a wide lake, covered with armed vessels, and replenished with the monsters of the deep. In the decoration of these scenes the Roman Emperors displayed their wealth and liberality; and we read on various occasions that the whole furniture of the amphitheatre consisted either of silver or gold or amber."

The amphitheatre at Puteoli was the scene of two remarkable historic events. It was here that the Emperor Nero descended into the arena and fought with the wild beasts after the manner of the gladiators, intending to rouse the admiration of his guest, the Armenian king, Tiridates. The demonstration missed its effect. For Tiridates contemptuously

POZZUOLI, PROCIDA, ISCHIA

borrowed a javelin from an attendant and, without moving from his seat, transfixed two bulls with it at one cast.

It was here that San Gennaro (St Januarius) and his companions were in vain exposed to the fury of the lions before their execution. The life, miracles and cathedral of the Saint at Naples are described in the following chapter, and form as it were a commentary upon the scene now before us. Beyond the Solfatara, on the road to Agnano, the sixteenth-century convent of San Gennaro marks the spot where the Saint is believed to have been beheaded. A stone stained with the Martyr's blood is said to turn bright red when the blood of the Saint liquefies in the cathedral at Naples.

The Solfatara

From Pozzuoli, a visit to the crater of the extinct volcano known as La Solfatara forms a fitting introduction to the strange character of the Phlegræan Fields. The Solfatara—the *Forum Vulcani*, as Strabo calls it—is a Vesuvius in miniature and is in many ways quite as interesting as that more familiar volcano, although it is many hundred years since it was in eruption.

The visitor should turn to the right outside the *Direttissima* Railway Station at Pozzuoli, and then to the left, following the carriage road which bends to the right, and shortly reaches the entrance to the crater (entrance 5 lire). Once within the enclosure it is worth while to take a guide (7 lire).

As we approach the crater, fumes of sulphur dimly prepare us for the strange scenes we are about to witness. Some 20 or 30 yards below the lips of the surrounding bowl is the flat surface of a huge elliptical crater. At first sight the surface looks as if it were made of cement. But on reaching it we find that it is hot, and that, though firm, it rings hollow like an ice-covered pond. Here and there are the indentations of old *bocce*, or mouths, from which sulphurous vapour escapes; here and there are tiny holes from which jets of steam emerge at a high temperature (*fumarole*). When one mouth closes, another opens. A miniature crater forms within the crater, and whilst sulphurous clouds of steam pour forth from the bowels of the earth, within the cauldron streams of boiling mud hiss and bubble (*fangaie*). The guide adds another thrill to a sufficiently interesting spectacle by lighting a torch and laying it upon the lips of an active *bocca*. Immediately the volume of vapour issuing from it is redoubled, whilst in every direction jets of steam emerge from crevices not only in the surrounding crater, but even on the outer heights. The energy of the *fumarole* decreases when Vesuvius is active. Attempts have been made by the Armstrong Steel Works at Bagnoli to harness the energy of this volcano, but hitherto without success. The soil, which is rich in sulphur and chemicals, is largely used for manuring the surrounding vineyards and gardens and for the manufacture of stucco.

On the far side of the crater are two curious grottoes, known as the Grotta di Purgatorio and the Grotta del Inferno. These sulphurous tunnels into the bowels of the earth soon become unbearably hot and stifling, and it may well be that it was from acquaintance with them that Vergil and Dante drew their curiously intimate conception of the nether regions.

Lago Lucrino ; Lago di Averno ; Cuma ; Baia ; Capo di Miseno

[In order to make the expedition to Baiæ and the Lake of Avernus from Pozzuoli, it will be found well worth while to hire a carriage outside the station. The drivers will make a very reasonable *combinazione* for the round, which will save much time and dusty walking. Of this the pedestrian will have quite enough in exploring the shores and grottoes of the Lake of Avernus. From Naples, the *Ferrovia Cumana* (see above) takes us to the station of Lago Lucrino. Road and rail both follow the shore.

On leaving Pozzuoli we quickly reach on our left the Armstrong (Government) Ordnance Factory, and pass beneath some ruins on our right, half buried under volcanic debris, which are said to be the remains of Cicero's villa, which he called his *Academia*.]

We pass along the coast under the shadows of Monte Barbaro and Monte Nuovo. The latter is a cone-shaped hill 456 feet high, which was thrown up in a single night during a volcanic upheaval in 1538. "Pozzuoli awoke one morning," says Dumas in his lively way, " and on looking round about her, failed to recognise herself. Where the evening before she had left a lake, she now found a mountain; where she had left a forest, she found ashes; where she had left a village, she found—nothing!" (*Le Corricolo*, II. 126).

A series of earthquakes was followed on 28th September by an upheaval of the shore between Avernus and the sea. The sea fell back, and for nearly a quarter of a mile its bottom was exposed. Peasants turned fishermen, and carted away in thousands the fish that lay exposed and helpless on the dry foundations of the Bay. This phenomenon was followed by a volcanic outburst which has been recorded by more than one eye-witness. It threw up a mass of earth and red-hot stones (*lapilli*), which fell in a deluge all round the gulf, and near Pozzuoli formed this newcomer among mountains—Monte Nouvo. The neighbourhood for 70 miles around was covered with ashes. The effect of this eruption and upheaval was not only such as Dumas has pithily described. The Bay of Baiæ was also to a great extent transformed. The Roman harbour works at Portus Julius were practically obliterated, along with innumerable remains of Roman villas, and the proportions of the Lucrine Lake were reduced to those of a lakeland tarn. Monte Nuovo, though it was only born four hundred years ago, looks now as old as other hills.

From the vines which are now grown upon its terraced slopes and those of Monte Barbaro, or are trained upon canes and poles and trees at their feet, a wine is made which, if obtained in its virgin state, unblended and uncommercialised, and buoyant with the slight aeration of natural fermentation, will astonish and delight the palate of the connoisseur, and for the first time explain to the diligent œnophilist why the poet Horace grew mellow and lyric over the joys of the true Falernian. Some of the wine from this district is sold under the name of Falerno, but much of it is used to blend with that of the more potent grapes of Capri.

Before reaching Monte Nuovo we pass a turning to the right, where the old Roman road—*Via Domitiana*—strikes inland, and, skirting Monte Nuovo and the shores of Lake Avernus, leads to Cumæ through the Arco Felice, a distance of some 5 miles. Strata of lava now appear in the banks on the roadside, dotted with prickly pears.

The Lucrine Lake (Lago Lucrino) lies close to the shore, some 3 miles west of Pozzuoli. A narrow strip of land separates what is now little more than a reedy pond from the sea. The cultivation of fish and oysters, for which the Lucrine Lake was famous in Roman days, has recently been revived.

But long before the Romans used this lake for their oysters or their ships, even long before the Greeks settled at Cumæ, that narrow strip of land carried a causeway, a causeway so ancient that one cannot even guess what manner of people they were who made it. The Cumæans, being equally at a loss, attributed its construction to Hercules. On his way to Megara and Herculaneum where he rested, he passed here on his return from Gades, with the oxen of the monster Gergon, whom he slew. For their passage he made this giant causeway, nearly a mile in length, building it of large stone slabs, so large and so skilfully laid that they withstood the onslaught of the sea for ages.

A road running inland leads past the shores of the Lucrine Lake to Lake Avernus, about half a mile away.

Nobody who has any appreciation of two of the greatest poems of all time, the *Odyssey* of Homer and the *Æneid* of Vergil, can approach this spot without a thrill of what our ancestors would have described as "awful anticipation." For was it not in the forest which once surrounded the baleful lake of Avernus that Æneas, landing after his long, eventful voyage from fallen Troy, found upon a tree that Golden Bough which was to be his passport to the nether world? Was it not here, as it was said, that Dædalus, the first airman, alighted and built upon the shores of the lake a temple to Apollo, wherein he dedicated to the god the oarage of his wings, and upon the storied roof, embossed in gold, recorded the legends of Crete and the Minotaur? And here, beside the unnavigable mere,

> "Deep in a cave the Sibyl made abode,
> A spacious cave, hewed in the rough hillside,"

that Sibyl who was to conduct Æneas to the dreary shades and waste dominions of the Dead.

> "Deep was the cave, and downward as it went
> From the wide mouth, a rocky, rough descent;
> And here the access a gloomy grove descends,
> And here the unnavigable lake extends,
> O'er whose unhappy waters, void of light,
> No bird presumes to steer his airy flight;
> Such deadly stenches from the depth arise
> And steaming sulphur, that infects the skies.
> From hence the Grecian bards their legends make,
> And give the name Avernus to the lake." [1]

In obedience to the directions of the Sibyl, Æneas, before descending into Hades, made sacrifices here to Hecate and the gods of the infernal regions, as

[1] Vergil, *Æneid*, VI. 237–242. Translated by Dryden. The Greek word Aornos was incorrectly supposed to mean "birdless," and thence the legend arose which is enshrined in Vergil's poetry, that any bird which flew over the lake was suffocated by the deadly fumes which rose from the water.

Odysseus had done in similar circumstances (*Odyssey*, XI. 23–50). Such sacrifices continued to be made down to the time of Constantine. Hannibal, as Livy tells us, conformed with the local custom, and, in order to gain the favour of the natives, made sacrifice to the God of the Underworld. Truth to tell, Avernus, as we now see it, has been shorn of much of its romance. Certainly the gloom and darkness have disappeared which once led to the identification of this spot with the abode of the Cimmerians, who, according to the description of Odysseus, dwelt near the entrance to the nether regions, in a land shrouded in mist and cloud, "and never does the shining sun look down upon them with his rays, but deadly night is always outspread over miserable mortals" (*Odyssey*, XI. 14–19). The forests which once surrounded the lake have disappeared, and its marshy shores have been encircled by an edging of stone. The surrounding land has thereby been converted from a malarial swamp into a vegetable garden and vineyard. But the awesome character of the lake has been almost entirely destroyed. The stone edging lends to the near shore something of the effect of a piece of ornamental water, and to the whole rather the appearance of one of our lakeland tarns, wherein fish gaily leap and round which butterflies hover, and over which no bird could to-day find any excuse for faltering in its flight. Only the ruined baths or temples on its shores, and the cavernous mouth of the Sibyl's grotto, and the eerie cries and snatches of song of workers in the distant vineyards on the crater's slopes and crest, contribute a note of something strange and weird. The lake, which is little more than 2 miles in circumference, lies in the centre of a crater 5 miles in circumference and 112 feet in depth. It was Agrippa, as we have said in the last chapter, who cut down the

Ages. Indeed, it is said that three doctors of Salerno were roused to such a pitch of jealous fury by the cures worked by the baths at Baiæ, that they sailed across the Bay one night and destroyed the whole establishment. Divine vengeance overtook them on their way home, for they were all three drowned in a storm.

Across the Bay, on the western horn of it, we see the finely situated sixteenth-century Castello di Baia, built by Don Pedro de Toledo. "The man who knows not Naples knows not pleasure." So runs the local proverb, and certainly few towns can vie with the Siren City as purveyors of pleasure and gaiety. But with the Romans it was Baiæ, as we have seen in the foregoing chapter, which was pre-eminent as the most luxurious and demoralising of fashionable bathing stations. And indeed, when one notes its cunningly chosen site, the sandy beach of the little bay, deeply recessed and protected from the cold winds by surrounding hills, the shallow sea and the glorious views it commands, one has no difficulty in understanding why the wealthy sybarites from Rome, who had all the loveliest coast in Europe to choose from, chose Baiæ for their bathing station and *villeggiatura.* "*Nullus in orbe sinus Baiis prælucet amænis,*" says Horace. (No bay in the world outshines delightful Baiæ.) Its climate, its mineral springs, and the beauty of the scenery, attracted epicures as surely as the reputation of the wine of Falernus and the oysters of the Lucrine Lake. Nobles and emperors vied with each other in the erection of sumptuous palaces. The entrance to the modern village is through the ruins of the villa of the Cæsars, which reach down to the sea. Piso, Pompey, Marius, and a host of others had villas in the neighbourhood. When space failed, as we have seen in the foregoing chapter, the Romans built out into the sea, hewing the cliffs and finding foundations for their villas upon the submerged rocks. About their walls lapped that broad, pellucid and most lovely sea which, as it has been said,[1] along this delicious coast, seems to have renounced its prerogative of terror. So soft are the crisping winds that hover around its bosom, so glowing and so various are the hues which it takes from the rosy clouds, so fragrant are the perfumes which the breezes from the land scatter over its depths, that you might well believe it was from such a sea that Aphrodite rose to take the empire of the earth.

From Baiæ, indeed, the glory has long departed. Modern Baia is no more than a small fishing village, with a shipyard at one end of the Bay, and a pier connected with an industry in material for porcelain quarried among the cliffs on which stood the palace of Cæsar. The decadence of the Roman Empire left it open to the rapine of marauding Saracens. Devastated by malaria, shaken by earthquakes, the level of the shores sunk by volcanic upheavals in the neighbourhood, the sea completed the ruin which man and time had begun.

> "Here
> The masters of the earth, unsatisfied,
> Built in the sea; and now boatman steers
> O'er many a crypt and vault yet glimmering,
> O'er many a broad and indestructible arch,
> The deep foundations of their palaces."
>
> ROGERS, *Italy.*

During the Augustan Age Baiæ remained the Queen of Watering Places, as the advertisements would declare. But a tendency had already begun in the time of Cicero to move eastwards along the Bay.

[1] Lord Lytton, *Last Days of Pompeii.*

Two causes operated. Baiæ was becoming over-crowded. There is always a tendency amongst men of culture and refinement to withdraw from the noise and vulgarity of over-popular surroundings to spots more secluded and select. *Odi profanum vulgus et arceo* is the principle as Horace enunciated it. There was another influence at work at least as potent. These wealthy Romans came down to the sea in order to escape from the fevers and unpleasantness of the climate of Rome. But fever, bred by the malarial swamps inland, had long been creeping along the coast. Cumæ was desolated by it, was already a city of the past. Baiæ itself was beginning to be threatened. The young Marcellus died of fever caught there. It was natural, therefore, for a man like Cicero, the brilliant, hard-working advocate and man of letters, politician and connoisseur, who needed quiet and repose, but also to be in the heart of the political world, to turn his eyes along the coast, and to begin to build new villas farther east. The sites of Pompeii and of Herculaneum seemed to offer attractions equal to those of Baiæ in many ways, though they could not boast any medical properties in their waters. Cicero, then, built himself a villa, first at Puteoli, then close to the walls of Pompeii, and expressed himself as delighted with it. Calpurnius Piso selected Herculaneum. After the death of Augustus, and with the retirement of Tiberius to Capri, this tendency increased. All along the coast, as far as Stabiæ (Castellamare) and Sorrentum, the tide moved eastwards. Houses began to go a-begging at Baiæ.

It has been said that the desertion of Baiæ was hastened by that appalling Imperial tragedy which took place in its neighbourhood. For about this lovely and half-deserted coast there still lingers the memory of one of the most terrible of human crimes, terrible both on account of the deed that was enacted here, and terrible because of the fame and relationship of the protagonists. As we read Tacitus' vivid description of the murder of the imperious Queen Mother Agrippina, by her degenerate son, the Roman Emperor Nero, the shores of the beautiful Bay seem to be lit up with the lurid light of some thunder-laden sunset. The last surviving child of Germanicus, proud, implacable and ambitious, Agrippina was a type of the masculine, strong-minded women of that age, women who sinned imperially, shameless and boggling at no crime where crime could aid ambition. To her first husband, Domitius Ahenobarbus, a man infamous for his vice and crimes, she had borne a son, of whom his father declared that, with such a parentage, he must needs prove a disaster to the State. That son was Nero. It was foretold to Agrippina that if her son should become emperor he would murder her. But no such threat could curb her ambition. She married her uncle, the Emperor Claudius, and poisoned him when she had secured his adoption of her son as successor to the Empire. She could not, however, refrain from endeavouring to rule the Empire for Nero as she had ruled it for his stepfather. Nero's resentment at her domineering temper reached a climax when he became enamoured of Sabina Poppæa, the wife of his friend, Otho. Whilst Agrippina lived there was no hope that Nero would be able to divorce Octavia, a daughter of Claudius, or that Poppæa would be allowed to marry him. For Agrippina had always endeavoured to maintain the nominal union of her son and her stepdaughter. In Poppæa, however, she had met her match. That beautiful woman had every charm and every gift except that of a decent mind. She was determined to marry Nero, and ready to step over the bodies of two empresses, if need be, in order to enter the palace of the Cæsars. Nero, who had already poisoned Britannicus in the presence of his family, was easily led by Poppæa to contrive the assassination of his mother. Her support of his wife, and her attempts to form a party of her own in the State had led to an open breach. Agrippina had retired to her estates at Antium. Suddenly she received a letter from the Emperor, expressing regret for any hastiness of temper he had shown towards her, and begging her to pay him a visit at Baiæ, where he was celebrating the five days' festival of Minerva. Agrippina did not fear poison, for she was fortified by antidotes, and in any case the recent death of Britannicus barred its use in the family for the present. Her slaves were faithful, and a dagger could hardly be employed with sufficient secrecy. Nor could the daughter of Germanicus, whose name was still a talisman with the Prætorian Guard, be safely attacked in the open. Reassured by these considerations, the old lioness came to visit her son. She did not know that his former tutor and her own inveterate enemy, Anicetus, who was then in command of the fleet at Misenum, had suggested a scheme by which an accident might without suspicion happen to the Empress-mother at sea. Nero welcomed his mother on the shore, and conducted her to Bauli. "This," says Tacitus, "was the name of a villa washed by a bay of the sea, between the promontory of Misenum and the Lake of Baiæ." Agrippina was invited to a banquet in Nero's palace, the ruins of which lie now half-buried beneath the waves at the point of the Bay. A trireme prepared in her honour was ready to convey her by sea. But some hint of the plot appears to have been whispered to her. She refused to go by water, and insisted upon being conveyed to Baiæ in her litter. There the very gracious reception she met with from the Emperor calmed her fears. Nero prolonged the banquet till the evening, talking charmingly and sometimes seriously to her. When the hour at length came when she must return to Bauli, he escorted her to the shore, "clinging with kisses to her eyes and bosom, either to complete his hypocrisy, or because the last sight of the mother he was sending to her death gave a moment's pause even to that brutal heart. A night of brilliant starlight"—it is Tacitus who tells the story—"was granted by Heaven as if to reveal the crime." Agrippina entered the vessel which had been prepared for her destruction. She had with her in her cabin two intimate attendants. One of them, Crepereius Gallus, stood aft, whilst the other, Acerronia, reclining at Agrippina's feet, as she lay upon a couch, spoke joyfully of her son's repentance and of the recovery of the mother's influence. The trireme had not gone far in the direction of Bauli, when at a given signal the ceiling of the cabin, which was loaded with a quantity of lead, fell in. Crepereius was crushed and instantly killed. Agrippina and Acerronia, who chanced to be protected by the projecting sides of the couch, were uninjured. This accident was not followed by the breaking up of the vessel as had been arranged. For all were bewildered, whilst those who were in the plot were hindered by the ignorant majority. The crew then thought it best to upset the vessel by throwing their weight on one side in order to sink it. But they could not organise themselves for this manœuvre with sufficient promptitude. Others, by counteracting the attempt, gave an opportunity of a gentler fall into the sea. Acerronia, finding herself in the water, cried out that she was Agrippina, in the hope of being saved, and implored help for the Emperor's mother. She was promptly despatched by the crew with poles and oars.

Agrippina remained silent, and though she received a wound in her shoulder, she succeeded in keeping afloat until she was picked up by a fishing boat which conveyed her to the Lucrine Lake. Thence she made her way to her villa. There could now be no doubt as to the plot and its author. But the indomitable woman perceived at once that, wounded though she was, the only hope that remained to her of preventing further outrage was to ignore it. So she sent a message to her son, informing him that, by Heaven's favour and his own good fortune, she had escaped a terrible disaster. Nero knew by this time that she was wounded, and that she must be well aware whence came the peril from which she had escaped. Paralysed with terror lest she should revenge herself by arming the slaves, and stirring up the soldiery, or hasten to the Senate and the people at Rome and charge him with the attempted crime, Nero called upon Burrus and Seneca, his chief advisers, to devise some means of dealing with the situation. Now these two men—the one a soldier, the other a famous writer and philosopher—were reputed to be the two most honourable and virtuous men in the Empire. Together they had endeavoured to guide the Emperor's youth into the paths of comparative respectability. What advice, then, could they, did they give in a crisis so horrible? A long time they kept silence. Any remonstrance on their part, they probably knew, would be quite useless. Perhaps, as Tacitus suggests, they saw clearly enough that unless Agrippina were now immediately crushed, Nero must fall. Only the death of the outraged mother could save the life of the murderous son. But the son was the Roman Emperor. The embarrassed pedagogues, then, remained silent for a while. Seneca was the first to recover his presence of mind and to indicate the trend of his judgment. The philosopher cast an inquiring look at the general. Could the soldiery be relied upon to complete the bloody deed? "No," so Burrus answered the silent question. "The Prætorians are devoted to the whole family of Cæsars, and, remembering Germanicus, would not dare a savage deed upon his daughter." The pedagogues conferred. "Who," they asked, "was responsible for the plot?" "Anicetus," was the answer. "Then let him complete it." Anicetus gladly undertook the task. Nero, declaring that this day gave him empire for the first time, bade the sailor go about his business. Accompanied by a body of marines, Anicetus set out. He forced his way into Agrippina's house, and broke roughly into her chamber. A small lamp burned in the room where she lay. All her attendants had deserted her save one slave-girl. As the armed men broke into the chamber, the slave-girl fled. Agrippina turned to face her murderers. "If you come from the Emperor," she cried, "return and say that I have recovered. If you come to commit a crime, it is not my son who has ordered his mother's murder!" The assassins closed round her couch. The captain of the trireme from which she had escaped struck her a violent blow upon the head. Agrippina turned to Anicetus, and beheld him approaching with his sword drawn. Rising from her couch, with a gesture at once shameless and superb, she flung her robes from her, and cried, "Smite the womb that bore him!" She fell pierced by many wounds.

Her body was burned that night by the silent sea, a dining couch being used for a funeral pyre. Nor, so long as Nero lived, was a mound thrown up over her grave. "Subsequently," says Tacitus, "she received from the solicitude of her domestics a humble sepulchre on the road to Misenum, near the villa of

Julius Cæsar, which from a great height commands a view of the Bay beneath."

As for Nero, only when the crime was at last accomplished, did he seem to realise its portentous guilt. "The rest of the night, now silent and stupefied, now and still oftener starting up in terror, bereft of reason, he awaited the dawn as if it would bring with it his doom. He was first encouraged to hope by the flattery addressed to him, at the prompting of Burrus, by the centurions and tribunes, who again and again pressed his hand and congratulated him on his having escaped an unforeseen danger and his mother's daring crime. Then his friends went to the temples, and, an example having once been set, the neighbouring towns of Campania testified their joy with sacrifices and deputations. He himself, with an opposite phase of hypocrisy, seemed sad, and almost angry at his own deliverance, and shed tears over his mother's death. But as the aspects of places change not as do the looks of men, and as he had ever before his eyes the dreadful sight of that sea with its shores (some too believed that the notes of a funereal trumpet were heard from the surrounding heights, and wailings from the mother's grave), he retired to Neapolis and sent a letter to the Senate, the drift of which was that Agerinus, one of Agrippina's confidential freedmen, had been detected with the dagger of an assassin, and that in the consciousness of having planned the crime, she had paid its penalty" (Tacitus, *Annals*, xiv. 1–10). This story was generally believed at the time, and the Emperor was overwhelmed by sympathy and congratulations from the Senate and the people. His return to Rome resembled a triumph. He ascended to the Capitol and offered thanks to the gods for his preservation.

To-day in Baia, if you pass through some houses

on the right in the village street, and cross a vineyard, a guide will show you the remains of some Roman baths. On the roof of one of the arches some mouldering mosaic is visible, and within it a vaulted circular building, which is termed a temple of Mercury, but was more probably the cooling room of the baths (*frigidarium*). On the left of this ruin is a vaulted chamber, with traces of mural paintings and a staircase within, which is called the tomb of Agrippina.

Farther down the road on the left is a circular building of Roman brick with eight windows and the remains of a dome, which is called the temple of Venus. Opposite the railway station is a similar building attributed to the worship of Diana. In the former are placed some architectural fragments which have been recently recovered from the sea. For owing to volcanic disturbances the shore in these parts has subsided, and in the blue waters of the little bay the remains of many a stately Roman palace and villa are clearly to be seen. They may some day yield a rich harvest of ancient art.

Miseno

As the name of Baiæ was thought to be derived from Baios, the navigator of Odysseus, so the Cape of Misenum was said to take its title from Misenus, the trusty squire of Æneas, who fell overboard as the Trojans first approached this coast, and was buried with much pomp and solemnity on this headland, *Qui nunc Misenus ab illo Dicitur, æternumque tenet per sæcula nomen.* The Cape is but a fragment of a crater, the remainder of which lies buried beneath the waves. It was at Misenum that the triumvirate, Augustus, Antonius and Lepidus, signed a treaty of peace with Sextus Pompeius, who held the seas against them with a navy manned by pirates and republicans of the old order. When they had all assembled on board his ship, Menas, his second in command, whispered in Pompey's ear, "Should he cut the painter and so make him master of the world?" Pompey hesitated, and whilst he hesitated, the fate of the Roman Empire trembled in the balance. Honour triumphed. "You should have done it without consulting me," he answered, "now it is too late." The triumvirate survived to fulfil their different destinies, Augustus to unite and rule the Roman world. The scene lives in Shakespeare's *Antony and Cleopatra*:

> *Menas.* Thou art, if thou darest be, the earthly Jove:
> Whate'er the ocean pales, or sky inclips,
> Is thine, if thou wilt ha't.
> *Pompey.* Show me which way.
> *Menas.* These three world-sharers, these competitors,
> Are in thy vessel: let me cut the cable;
> And, when we are put off, fall to their throats:
> All there is thine.
> *Pompey.* Ah, this thou shouldst have done,
> And not have spoke on't! In me 'tis villany;
> In thee't had been good service. Thou must know,
> 'Tis not my profit that does lead mine honour;
> Mine honour, it.

If Baiæ recalls chiefly the luxury of Roman epicures and the matricide of a decadent emperor, this coast has memories also of the great engineering feats and naval and military grandeur which were the most permanent and important instruments in building up the wonderful system of the Roman Empire. Just as Naples is by no means merely a place of pleasure, but a busy shipping and industrial centre, so around luxurious Baiæ great works were planned and completed. We have seen how Agrippa constructed the

Portus Julius within the Lucrine Lake. Whilst these works were in course of construction, he made a temporary harbour at Misenum for the Tyrrhenian fleet. It is now represented by the *Mare Morto*, and the *Porto di Miseno*. Remains of a theatre, baths, and some other buildings, including the villa of Caius Marius, survive to remind us of the Roman occupation of this headland, which commands a magnificent view of the surrounding bays and country. The Roman colony here was destroyed by the Saracens, but remains of storehouses and reservoirs for victualling the fleet speak to the once great naval power of Rome. Notable is the so-called *Piscina Mirabilis*, a little beyond the village of Bacoli.[1] This was a huge reservoir served by an aqueduct. Its massive roof is supported by rows of columns which give something of the aspect of a basilica to a building, the dimensions of which are over 200 feet by 80 feet. It is approached by flights of forty steps, and was built for watering the Roman fleet. Like Baia, Miseno was the scene of an imperial tragedy, the memory of which still haunts the coast. For it was here that Tiberius was murdered. The powers of that clever, terrible and lonely old man were beginning to fail. He knew it, but endeavoured to conceal the fact. None the less the cry of the jackals began to be heard. There were signs that his authority was waning. Men began to ask themselves who should succeed him. Was it to be Caius Cæsar, the son of Germanicus whom the soldiers had nicknamed Caligula, or another? In search of health, though he would not allow that he was ill, Tiberius moved about from place to place. Finally he settled down on the promontory of Miseno,

[1] Bacoli has been wrongly identified with the Bauli where Agrippina stayed and was murdered. It is too far west to fit in with that story.

in a villa which had once belonged to Lucius Lucullus. At length it became obvious that he was failing. His physician, Charicles, having managed to feel his pulse by a trick, assured Macro, the Commander of the Prætorian Guard, that he could not survive forty-eight hours. There were hurried consultations with the generals and the armies. Presently the aged Emperor had a fainting fit. It was thought that he was dead. Caligula tore the ring from his finger and hurried forth to receive the congratulations of his adherents and to take possession of the Empire. Suddenly the news spread that Tiberius had recovered, and was calling for food and wine. He was demanding his ring. There was a moment of sickening and universal panic. People fled hither and thither, feigning grief or ignorance, for if the savage old man recovered, those who had welcomed his successor knew well enough that they would presently receive a hint that the moment had come for them to depart this life. It is significant of the extent and organisation of the Roman Empire that nobody ever seems to have ignored that hint, or to have endeavoured to avoid its corollary, suicide, by attempting to escape from Italy. Caligula, stunned by the turn of events, and the failure of his hopes, sat in a stupor of disappointment and terror. Only Macro, the old Emperor's trusted Captain of the Guard, kept his head. He ordered his master to be smothered beneath a heap of clothes. "And so died Tiberius in the 78th year of his age" (A.D. 37).[1]

The accession of Caligula was received by a wild outburst of popular applause. His sudden popularity and the inheritance of unlimited power turned the head of the young Emperor, whose mind had always been unsound. He soon yielded to the temptations

[1] Tacitus, *Annals*, VI. 50.

of uncontrolled debauchery, and the savage lust of cruelty. He declared himself a god, and indulged his megalomania by planning or executing engineering works of colossal magnitude. The most foolish and fantastic of these was the building of a bridge from Baiæ to Puteoli. A soothsayer had once declared that Gaius would never become Emperor any more than he would ever drive a chariot across the Gulf of

POZZUOLI

Baiæ. He determined to do so, accompanied by an army. Ships were collected from every port, in such numbers that the transport of commerce was seriously impeded and Rome half-starved for lack of corn ships. They were anchored in a double line from Puteoli to Baiæ, covered with timber and paved like a high-road. Across this bridge, before a crowd of spectators assembled on the shore, the Emperor rode at the head of his army. Clad in the armour which had once been worn by Alexander the Great, he rode into Puteoli as a conqueror. Next day he drove back in a triumphal chariot, dressed as a charioteer. On reaching the centre of the bridge a halt was called, whilst the Emperor delivered an oration. A banquet followed, and the whole coast and bridge were illuminated with torches. The banquet lasted late into the night. Many of the spectators became intoxicated, and falling off the bridge, were drowned.

ROMAN ARCHES

When we return to Naples after visiting this haunted shore, we shall find very little to remind us of the days of these lurid Roman emperors, except in the *Museo Nazionale.* That little is not well known. We have seen that the narrow, crowded Via dei Tribunali is built upon the Roman road which once bisected the city, running from the Porta Capuana to the Porta Alba. Near the Porta Capuana and north of the Via dei Tribunali is the Cathedral of S. Gennaro. It embraces, as we have explained above, the site of a temple of Apollo. At the other end the church of S. Maria Maggiore, as mentioned in Chapter I., is also on the site of a temple (*Vico del Sole*). About halfway down the Via dei Tribunali and on either side of it are the churches of San Lorenzo (south), and San Paolo Maggiore (north), facing each other. Here the rectangle formed by the Via Anticaglia, Strada di San Paolo, Vico Cinquesanti, and Via S. Biagio (Giuseppe de Blasiis) is full of old Roman brickwork and arches, now mostly covered over with stucco, here and there cut into by the Renaissance porches of old palaces, and mostly used as workshops and storehouses. The Piazza Gerolomini, near the church of S. Lorenzo, is the site of the Roman Forum. It continued to be the principal market-place until Charles I. of Anjou opened the new one. Go down the narrow Vico Cinquesanti, alongside S. Paolo Maggiore, and you will observe on the right the much damaged doorway and courtyard of a Renaissance Palace, with earlier work on the doorways and arch. It is now used as a warehouse, but is spoken of locally as the Palazzo di Nerone. Following up this narrow Vico Cinquesanti you reach the Via dell' Anticaglia, and there on the left, across the street, are two huge archways of Roman brick. Windows have been pierced in them, and they are used as houses, as was once the Colosseum at Rome. They are remains of a covered theatre adjoining the amphitheatre in which Nero gave his first public performance as a singer. That the theatre, or Odeum, was close to the amphitheatre is made certain by a line in the *Silvæ* of Statius (III. v.), where he poetically enumerates the temples and squares of the city disposed in endless porticoes, and " the twin massy theatres, this roofed, that open to the sky." The site of the Odeum is further indicated by the curve of the houses in the Via S. Paolo, near its meeting with the Via S. Pellegrino. The seats and back of the stage of the great uncovered amphitheatre faced the Temple of the Dioscuri, parallel with the Decuman streets. Parts of it were used for rebuilding S. Paolo.

The death of Agrippina removed the one influence which had restrained Nero from indulging his theatrical and artistic tastes in such a way as to lower the imperial dignity. It was his ambition to appear in public and earn the applause of his subjects by singing and playing upon the lyre, by his poetical compositions, and by his skill as a charioteer. Hitherto he had sung in private houses or gardens, but he longed for a larger stage and the plaudits of a more numerous audience. He did not dare to make a beginning at Rome, but chose for this purpose Naples, because it was a Greek city. Nero's tastes and ideals were altogether Greek. He cared little for the elaborate spectacles of the arena or the horrors of a gladiatorial show. He wished to shine as a musician, largely from vanity it is true, but also because he took a genuine artistic interest in music and art. To Naples, therefore, he came to win his spurs in the theatre, because he thought he would there find an audience which would appreciate his artistic ideals, and which would not, like the Romans, be disgusted at their Emperor's competing in musical contests (A.D. 64).

Naples, that Greek city, was moreover to be the starting-point for his theatrical tour through Greece, where he was crowned as Victor in a musical contest, and in a chariot race at Olympia. Of his appearance in the theatre of Naples Tacitus speaks with the disdain felt by every Roman :

" A rabble of the townsfolk was brought together, with those whom the excitement of such an event had attracted from the neighbouring towns and colonies, and such as followed the Emperor's train to pay him honour or for various objects. All these, with some companies of soldiers, filled the theatre at Neapolis. No sooner had the audience quitted the theatre, than the empty building fell in, but no harm was done to any one. Thereupon Nero in an elaborate ode thanked the gods, celebrating the good luck which marked so providential an escape " (*Annals*, xv. 33).

About the same time a new theatre was being

erected in the rising suburb of Herculaneum. To mark their appreciation of the imperial artist's choice of Naples as the scene of his first public appearance, or perhaps as a token of that kind of gratitude which springs from a lively sense of favours yet to come, the citizens decided to erect over the entrance of their theatre a bronze portrait of the Emperor, in his chariot (*quadriga*), driving his famous team of four Parthian horses. One of those bronze horses, full of fire and superbly modelled, may be seen pawing the air in the *Museo Nazionale* (No. 4904). It was discovered among the ruins of the theatre, some 130 feet below the ground, not far from the entrance where the tickets for the last performance were found still scattered upon the ground, some seventeen hundred years later (*see* Chap. VII.).

LAKE AVERNUS

CHAPTER V

San Gennaro

The life and martyrdom of S. Gennaro (St Januarius)—Translation of relics and sepulture—The Cathedral of S. Gennaro—Cappella Caraffa and others—The Cappella del Tesoro—The standing miracle of the liquefaction of the blood—The Saint and Championnet—S. Gennaro dethroned—The Fires of St Anthony—The Triumph of S. Gennaro—Catacombs of S. Gennaro—and Neapolitan Cemeteries.

SAINT JANUARIUS is saïd to have been a high-born youth, but whether he was a native of Naples or of Benevento is a matter of dispute. It is at any rate certain that he was Bishop of Benevento (*circa* 304) when the persecution of the Christians in the reign of Diocletian began. One record of persecution is supposed to exist in the wax mask of a headless corpse found in a tomb, which is now in the Cumæan Collection in the *Museo Nazionale* (No. 1193197). News was brought to Januarius that his intimate friend and fellow in Christ, Sosius, Deacon of Miseno, along with Proculus, Deacon of Pozzuoli, and Eutyches and Acutius, eminent laymen among the Christians of this district, had been thrown into prison by the Governor of Campania. Without a thought for his own safety, the good Bishop went straight to Pozzuoli and there visited the Christian prisoners, exhorting, comforting, and encouraging them to endure steadfastly the great ordeal through which they must surely pass. Just at this time a new Governor was appointed to the province of Campania, Timotheus by name. When he heard of the visit of the intrepid Bishop, he ordered him to be arrested. Januarius was seized, together with Festus, his deacon, and Desiderius, a lector of the Church, and haled before the judgment seat at Nola. It is said that during his examination by the cruel and malignant Timotheus, Januarius, in response to an outburst of threats, warned the Governor that he would be stricken with blindness, and that his sight would only be restored to him, at his request, in order that he might behold with what courage and devotion a Christian martyr died. Timotheus, in a fury, ordered him to be carried away from the tribunal and cast into a burning fiery furnace. This was done, but when the doors of the furnace were presently opened, St Januarius was discovered sitting in the midst of the flames unscathed, singing hymns in company of a celestial choir of angels. After inflicting the most cruel tortures upon his Christian prisoners but without breaking their constancy, Timotheus, who was about to visit Pozzuoli, compelled them to walk heavily loaded with chains before his chariot—some say to haul it—to that town. The legend narrates that, filled with superhuman strength, Januarius, Sosius, and Proculus dragged Timotheus in his chariot at a miraculous speed. They outdistanced his guards and made their first halt upon the heights of Antignano, where a little chapel was afterwards erected to commemorate the event. On their arrival at Pozzuoli, they were thrown into the same prison as the other Christians, and all seven condemned to be torn in pieces by wild beasts, in accordance with the decree of Diocletian that all who refused to sacrifice to the Roman gods and to abjure the " impious heresy " of

Christianity, should be punished with the most cruel death. St Januarius and his companions were carried to the amphitheatre, and there, as they knelt and prayed in the arena, a horde of starving and infuriated beasts of prey were let loose upon them from the dungeons. The bloodthirsty crowd of onlookers thrilled with cruel anticipation. But they were destined to be cheated of their amusement. For none of the savage animals could be goaded to touch the champions of Christ. They lay down fawning and cringing at their feet, whilst St Januarius, rising, smiled upon the people and raised his hand to bless them. At the sight of this miracle Timotheus was struck with blindness, and it was only in answer to the prayers of the saint, that his sight was presently restored. Amazed and enraged, the populace cried out that the Christians owed their impunity to magic. They were now sentenced to be put to the sword. *Homo homini lupus*. Man was more cruel to his kind than the ravening beasts. St Januarius and his companions were executed outside the city at or near the Forum of Vulcan (Solfatara), and there buried. The site is indicated by the Convent of San Gennaro, near Solfatara.

Somewhere about the year 400, when the Christian Church was triumphant, the relics of these holy martyrs were removed to more honourable places of burial. SS. Proculus, Eutyches, and Acutius were taken home to Pozzuoli, Festus and Desiderius to Benevento, Sosius to Miseno, and Januarius to Naples.

The relics of St Januarius, however, were fated to perform more than one pilgrimage ere they came to their final resting-place. During the wars with the Normans they were removed to Benevento, and later, to the Abbey of Monte Vergine. It was not till 1497 that they were brought back to Naples. There, in the Duomo, in the Chapel of San Gennaro (*del*

Tesoro), are preserved in a tabernacle behind the altar the head of the martyr and two phials of his congealed blood. It is said that during the night after his execution a devout Christian woman collected some of the blood of the martyr, which has been preserved ever since. The body of S. Gennaro is enshrined in the crypt beneath the high altar of the Duomo, in a chapel (*Cappella Caraffa*), called after its founder, the Cardinal Oliviero Caraffa, and popularly termed *Il soccorpo.*

Apart from its appeal to the devout, no lover of the beautiful should omit to visit this exquisite Renaissance chamber of white marble. The crypt is supported by two rows of five Corinthian columns each, which remind us of the adjacent temple of Apollo, on the site of which the basilica of Santa Restituta now stands. But it is the delicate carving of graceful designs, by Tommaso Malvito da Como (1504), which forms the chief attraction of this beautiful room. On either side, at the west end, are some sculptures of Venus (on horseback riding over the waves), and of Apollo, which may well have come from the original temple also. A very fine statue of the founder, Cardinal Caraffa, kneeling in an attitude of prayer, behind the altar which covers the remains of S. Gennaro, is probably by Malvito. In a casket on the north side are preserved the bones of S. Maximus.

The Cathedral of San Gennaro (*Via del Duomo*) was begun by Charles I. of Anjou in 1272, and completed by Robert the Wise in 1314. This Angevin Gothic building suffered severely from successive earthquakes. The façade was rebuilt by Antonio Baboccio in 1407 and the rest after the earthquake of 1456, by Alfonso II. of Aragon. It was restored in the nineteenth century by Raffaele Cappelli (1837–43). The striking and scholarly modern façade which includes the portal of Baboccio has only recently been completed from the designs of Enrico Alvino (1877). The interior is gorgeous with brilliant paintings by Giordano and Solimena. Beneath a magnificent roof, the nave and aisles are supported by 110 columns removed from ancient temples. Each carries the bust of a Neapolitan bishop, thus introducing us to the characteristic quality of the Cathedral which, with its many tombs and chapels, forms as it were a Valhalla of Neapolitan worthies.

SOUTH DOOR, DUOMO

One can only mention here the tombs of Charles I. of Anjou, and Charles Martel, King of Hungary, and his wife, Clementia of Habsburg, within the western portal (1599); the fourth chapel on the south side, that of Cardinal Francesco Carbone, wrought by Baboccio; and close to it, the thirteenth-century Cappella Minutolo, which was originally one of the twin towers of the *Stefania*, the basilica founded by Bishop Stefano II., and replaced by Charles I. This chapel is paved with majolica and the walls are covered with frescoes by Tommaso degli Stefani, unhappily repainted. Above the altar is the elaborately canopied tomb of Cardinal Minutolo, Archbishop of Naples, the masterpiece of Baboccio (1405). On the right is the tomb of Filippo Minutolo, Archbishop of Naples. The fourth chapel on the north side contains an Assumption attributed to Perugino, and the second chapel a beautiful Descent from the Cross by Giovanni da Nola. Of all these tombs and monuments of kings and bishops and cardinals which surround us none is more affecting than that of the unhappy Andrew of Hungary, murdered by his wife, Joanna I. (1345), with its modest epitaph; none more arresting than that of Pope Innocent IV. in the north transept. That great champion of the Church sleeps peacefully in the consciousness that he has won a victory for the Papacy over the Empire, and crushed the Emperor Frederick, "that serpent Frederick," he calls him, "the enemy of Christ"—*stravit inimicum Christi, colubrum Fredericum.* The tomb of Innocent IV., who died in 1254, was made in 1318 by Pietro degli Stefani. The features of the recumbent figure express in very lifelike manner the vigour and determination of that imperious pontiff. An epitaph in leonine verses records his benefactions to Naples, especially his reconstruction of the city walls after their destruction by Conrad. In the sacristy is a fine (? fifteenth-century) bronze bust of San Gennaro, and an Assumption of the Virgin by Pietro Perugino (1460).

When Charles I., fresh from his triumphs over Manfred and Conradin, bethought him to build a new cathedral in Naples, he chose the *somma piazza*, the noblest site in the city, where of yore stood the temples of Apollo and of Neptune. But there already, on the site of the former temple of Apollo, a basilica had been raised, which was first dedicated to the Saviour and afterwards to Sta Restituta, when the body of that saint was translated from Ischia. Tradition says that it was built in 334 by Constantine the Great, as an inscription in the baptistery, now the chapel of S. Giovanni a Fonte, the oldest part of the building, records. This pious tradition is without foundation.

But it was certainly the episcopal church of the original Neapolitan Vescovato, and is still called so in the vernacular, *ò viscuvato*. The basilica, rebuilt in the eighth century, was constructed after the pattern of S. Giovanni Laterano, in the shape of a Latin cross. It had now fallen into a ruinous condition. Charles's new church shortened and absorbed it. It is now little more than a chapel of the Duomo, the approach to which is between the third and fourth chapels on the north side. Frequent restorations have destroyed or concealed the primitive structure, and ruined the mosaics which are as old as the basilica itself and represented notable gigantic figures of the Saviour. The last unfortunate efforts in this direction were made at the end of the seventeenth century, when baroque details were added to the mixture of Gothic and Italo-Byzantine forms.

The arches of the nave are supported by eighteen columns of the Corinthian order, relics of the ancient pagan temple. The Gothic arches are worthy of attention. Another survival of pagan times is the precious vase of green Egyptian basalt, adorned with reliefs of Bacchic masks and thyrsi, which has been removed from the old baptistery of S. Giovanni a Fonte and is used in the Cathedral as a font. This vase was brought here from the temple of Mercury, on the site of which the Church of the Holy Apostles, founded in the time of Constantine, was replaced in 1626 by a new building designed by Francesco Grimaldi.

Beneath the high altar is an antique marble pillar, on which are two griffins finely carved in marble. The altarpiece, in wood, representing the Virgin enthroned, with St Michael and Sta Restituta at the sides, and, beneath, incidents in the life of the latter, is by Silvestro Buono (1500).

On the ceiling a picture by Luca Giordano portrays the body of Sta Restituta from Ischia, borne by angels above the ship, whilst S. Gennaro prays to the Virgin seated in glory above, interceding for Naples, which is represented by a siren.

A door on the right of the high altar leads into the old baptistery, S. Giovanni a Fonte, built by Bishop Vincenzo about A.D. 550. This building is square and is surmounted by a small dome, adorned by Italo-Byzantine mosaics representing incidents in the life of Christ, and the symbols of the Four Evangelists. The heads of Christ and the Virgin are of large proportions. In the centre is the Cross of Constantine.

Returning to the church, some fragments of early bas-reliefs (? eighth century), from old ambones or reading desks, will be seen in the fifth and seventh chapels on the left. They depict scenes from the lives of S. Gennaro, Samson, and S. Eustachius. The sixth chapel is the sanctuary of Sta Maria del Principio, the most ancient oratory in Naples, founded by S. Aspreno, the first bishop. Here Sta Candida and other early Christians are said to have assembled with him to practise in secret the rites of their growing sect. In the apse is a mosaic figure of the Madonna del Principio, so called, it is said, because it was the first figure portrayed in Naples. It was restored in 1322, as an inscription records, giving the name of the artist as Lellus, "*Hoc opus fecit Lellus. . . .*"

We now return to the Duomo to visit the gorgeous chapel and priceless treasury of S. Gennaro himself. The *Tesoro di S. Gennaro* is the third chapel in the south aisle. During a terrible outbreak of plague the people assembled in the church of Monte Vergine to celebrate the Festa of S. Gennaro (1527), and there vowed to erect for the Protector of the city a chapel at the expense of 110,000 ducats, if he would intercede to save them from that visitation. In 1608 the work was begun. The chapel, designed by Francesco Grimaldi, the Theatine monk, was built in the form of a Greek Cross. Magnificent in size and proportion, this chapel is adorned with a prodigal profusion of ornamentation, which is only equalled by the richness of the treasures preserved in it and the sacristy. It is impossible to enumerate them here.

The chapel is guarded by an immense and magnificent grille of gilded bronze, designed by Giovan Giacomo di Conforto, which bears two busts of the saint modelled by Cosimo Fanzaga. Within, it is decorated with many columns and brilliant marbles. It contains seven altars and the bronze statues of many saints, who form as it were the bodyguard of the Chief, S. Gennaro. Behind four of the altars are panels painted by Domenichino. A sinister memory is recalled by the frescoes which adorn the dome and lunettes. When the building of the chapel was completed, it was decided to invite some foreign artists to decorate the interior with paintings which should record the events of the life of the saint. Guido Reni, Cavaliere d'Arpino, and Domenico Zampieri, called Domenichino, were commissioned to do the work. But the group of artists who had established themselves in Naples under the Spanish regime was jealous of this invasion of foreigners. Corenzio, Stanzioni, Ribera, Lanfranco and the rest held that they were entitled to a monopoly of the home market, and determined to enforce their views by a system of picketing which even Englishmen could not call peaceful. Arpino, some say, for the story varies, was forced to retire before he had drawn a line. Guido Reni, after twice narrowly escaping assassination, thought it better to quit Naples. Only Domenichino remained. Ignoring the menaces of his brother artists, he began the series of frescoes on the lunettes and pendentives and the apotheosis of the saint in the dome (1629–44). Poor, modest, devoted to his art, serenely, persistently, he painted, absorbed in the task of depicting in his touching realistic way the martyrdom of the saint, and the miracles wrought by his relics. Guido had warned him of the fate that awaited him from the army of contractors who claimed a monopoly in covering Neapolitan churches with paintings by the acre. He would not believe him. When they saw how conscientiously he worked, in what a spirit of devotion and endeavour he strove to do his utmost for the glory of the saint and the achievement of art, surely these other artists would not interfere with him ! So he argued and entered upon his task. Soon he was forced to admit that it was advisable to work with a dagger by his side. Then he found that what he had done during the day was washed out by night. Ashes were mixed with his tempera, so that, when it dried, ugly cracks appeared in his work. There was an eruption of Vesuvius, and the people were stirred up to protest by an ugly riot that this was a sign of Heaven's displeasure at his employment. But Domenichino persisted conscientiously in his task, until at last one morning he was seized with illness as he laboured on his scaffold beneath the dome. His brother artists had poisoned him. Ribera and his friends, Stanzioni and Lanfranco, succeeded to the job and completed the series of frescoes in their rapid brilliant fashion. But the work of Domenichino remains to put them to shame by its truth and sincerity, its self-restraint and high endeavour. It was Giovanni Lanfranco, the great mannerist from Parma, who then painted the imposing composition on the dome. He refused to begin his task until the uncompleted work of the unfortunate Zampieri had first been destroyed.

The blood of S. Gennaro is preserved in the glass phials stored in a silver reliquary beneath the altar. The blood in these phials is said to have liquefied in the hands of S. Severus, when the saint's body was first translated hither from Pozzuoli. The miracle is still repeated three times a year before a vast crowd of the faithful, on the first Saturday in May at Santa Chiara (the Feast of the Translation of the relics from Pozzuoli), in the Duomo on the Saint's Day, 19th September, and on the 16th of December. The latter date commemorates the great eruption of Vesuvius in 1631, when Naples was saved by invoking the patronage of the saint. This was not the only occasion upon which the influence of St Januarius was believed to have saved the city from being destroyed by Vesuvius. The eruptions of the years 685 and 1707 are remembered as instances of his protection upon such occasions. In the latter year, we are told, "whilst the Cardinal Francis Pignatelli, with the clergy and people, devoutly followed the shrine of St Januarius in procession to a chapel at the foot of Mount Vesuvius, the fiery eruption ceased, the mist, which before was so thick that no one could see another at the distance of three yards, was scattered, and at night the stars appeared in the sky."

As to the "standing miracle" of the liquefaction of the blood of St Januarius, it is said that the blood in the old glass phials is congealed and of a dark colour, but when brought in sight of the head, though at a considerable distance, it melts, bubbles up, and upon the least motion flows on any side. It is firmly believed that the prosperity of the city for the ensuing year depends upon the successful manifestation of this miracle.

The scene in the Chapel of the Treasure on these

occasions has often been described. About the altar throngs a motley crowd composed half of well-dressed, respectable people, and half of the most ragged and disreputable rabble, the so-called *parenti di San Gennaro*—relatives of St Januarius. The priest lifts from the silver reliquary the small glass phials containing the congealed blood of the saint, and shows them to the people, at the same time proclaiming that the blood is solid (*e' duro*). The congregation, on their knees, call upon the saint with cries and tears to perform his customary beneficent miracle. "*Faccela, la grazia, San Gennaro, mio bello!*" If the liquefaction is too long delayed, adoration gives place to abuse. Terms of reproach are hurled at him in the raucous tones of a populace that lives always in crowded streets, at the top of its voice, just as natives in the East abuse and beat the idols of their rain and weather gods when the right sort of weather is not forthcoming. *Bruto muso giallo* (ugly yellow face) and other such-like things they now call S. Gennaro, who just now was *Bello! Bello! Bello!*, in order to bring him to a sense of his duty. At length the officiating priest is heard to murmur "*Muove.*" A thrill of joyful expectancy passes through the crowd. The emotion grows intense. A moment's pause of death-like stillness is followed by an outburst of sobs and cries. Then, to the accompaniment of the crash of organs and the peal of bells, and the hysterical delight of the crowd, the glad news that the blood of the saint has liquefied begins to circulate amongst the congregation in the church, and passes from the worshippers inside to the waiting crowds without. This was the signal in the old days for a salute to be fired from the forts and for the soldiers to turn out. Now the noise is contributed by the celebrations of the happy people, who dance and sing in the streets all night; the kissing is, or should be, confined to the reliquary by the faithful in the church.

Saints, like politicians, have ups and downs in popularity. St Januarius was no exception. There came a time when he was ousted from his proud position of tutelary saint of Naples. It was when the French army had occupied Naples under General Championnet and proclaimed the second Parthenopean Republic. The *lazzaroni* had fiercely opposed the entry of the French and continued to hate the victorious Republicans. Presently it began to be whispered that St Januarius did not approve of them, and that, to show his disgust, his blood would not liquefy upon the appointed day. Such failure would forebode disaster, and probably rouse the feelings of the populace to a pitch which might endanger the French. The rumour reached the ears of General Championnet. It was emphasised by the murder of several French soldiers, upon whose bodies was found the inscription, "Thus die the French heretics who are the reason why St Januarius will not perform his miracle." Championnet was not slow to perceive that it was important for his own safety and that of his army that the miracle should be performed. The May morning on which the liquefaction of the blood normally occurred in the church of Sta Chiara found the city sunk in sullen silence in ominous contrast to the usual hubbub of devotional excitement. Championnet attended the ceremony with his staff. The sacred blood remained congealed, and the cries of reproach and abuse which the *parenti di San Gennaro* were accustomed to address to the recalcitrant saint in such an event were now audibly addressed to the French Republicans. According to Dumas' account of the incident, Championnet waited until eight o'clock in the evening, whilst the saint still remained obdurate, and the crowd became more and more excited and threatening. Groans and cries mingled with abuse, and many a hand began to finger a knife beneath a cloak. The General whispered to an aide-de-camp. The aide-de-camp approached the altar rail. As the priest, who was handing the sacred phial to the faithful to kiss, came to him in his turn, he whispered a word in his ear. It was a message from the General to the effect that unless the miracle was wrought within ten minutes, the priest would be shot within a quarter of an hour. Five minutes later the phial was raised, and the priest proclaimed to the astonished congregation, "*Il miracolo e fatto.*" The blood was entirely liquefied.

The announcement was received in sullen silence. Disgusted and at first stupefied by surprise, the *parenti di San Gennaro* began presently to realise that the saint had deserted them; that he of whom it was their proud boast that he was a good saint and good patriot, and ever stood for Naples against the world, had now performed his miracle contrary to expectation in the presence of the foreigner, and thereby expressed his approval of them. S. Gennaro, the well-born bishop, hitherto thought as sound an aristocrat in feeling as any *lazzarone* amongst them, had taken sides publicly with the French Republicans. The patron saint had declared himself an enemy of his country. So the people argued. There was a terrible reaction. When, a few months later, the French were forced to retire and the Parthenopean Republic came to an end, vengeance was wreaked upon the saint along with many others who were held to have betrayed their country. His statue was torn from the Chapel of the Treasure, a cord fixed to its neck, and so dragged through the streets to the harbour and thrown into the sea. When S. Gennaro had thus suffered his second martyrdom, it became necessary to choose a new tutelary saint for Naples. The claims of many candidates were carefully considered and discussed in public conclave. At length St Anthony was chosen by secret ballot. His great merit was that he was a sure protector against fire. The danger of conflagrations was very great in ancient cities, with their narrow streets and timber houses. The worship of St Anthony was the popular form of mediæval fire insurance. He was, and still is, a much cultivated saint. On the 17th January it is the custom of Neapolitans to bring out into the streets any old furniture which they wish to get rid of and there to burn it in bonfires to St Anthony. An attempt has been made this year to stop the practice, on the grounds that it is a danger to the city. St Anthony is also the patron saint of animals, and on the same day every devout Neapolitan carter and cab-driver decorates his horse with chaplets of pastry rings (*pialli*) hung about its neck, and takes it to be blessed.

St Anthony, then, was chosen as the tutelary saint of Naples chiefly as a protector against fire. But, as Dumas observes, there are fires and fires. St Anthony was a sure bulwark against conflagrations lit by human hands, but against the fires of Heaven, against the thunderbolt and the volcano he was powerless as a child. The electors of St Anthony had reckoned without Vesuvius. After a long period of quiescence the volcano became ominously active. During the long reign of S. Gennaro, Naples itself had never suffered. Though the suburbs of Resina and Torre del Greco had been overwhelmed again and again by the rivers of lava and rebuilt only to be again destroyed, Naples itself had remained immune. But now earthquakes and tidal waves were accompanied by a terrible eruption of the mountain. There was a frightful explosion, and a stream of molten lava was seen to be pouring from the crater and descending the mountain-side, making a straight course for the walls of the city. The statue of St Anthony was brought from the Chapel of the Treasure and adjured by his presence to arrest the flood. But slowly, inexorably the boiling river flowed on, blotting out streams and dykes, burning trees and vegetation and levelling houses, on and on towards the doomed city. St Anthony was powerless against the fires of the volcano. Naples awaited the fate of Herculaneum. But lo! when the burning lava had now reached the Ponte della Maddelena and all hope seemed at an end, it came face to face with a statue of S. Gennaro which remained erect upon the bridge head. The statue was seen to raise its hand with a proud and imperious gesture. The volcano acknowledged the sovereignty of the saint. The eruption ceased, the sea grew calm, the river of fire paused and stood still. S. Gennaro had saved the city and was brought back in triumph and gratitude to his own chapel in the Duomo, the acknowledged tutelary saint of Naples, whom none may ever again challenge or supplant.

Whether it be due to S. Gennaro or another, the fact is certain that hitherto Naples itself has suffered scarcely at all from the visitations of the volcano. She is not, like the neighbouring villages, one of the martyrs of Vesuvius. The shrine of S. Gennaro still stands on the Ponte Maddelena over the river Sebeto, ready to raise a hand and say once more to the advancing streams of lava, Thus far and no farther! If faith will remove, why should it not curb mountains? And outside the south door of the Duomo rises the column of S. Gennaro by Fansaga (1660), erected in gratitude by the people for their preservation in the great eruption of 1631 (*see* Chap. VII.).

VERGIL'S TOMB

San Gennaro

S. Gennaro has given his name to the Neapolitan catacombs, which are finer than the more famous ones at Rome. The failure of the persecution of the Christians led to the toleration of the growing and stubborn sect. It was not long after the martyrdom of St Januarius that the Christians at Naples were allowed to bury their dead as they wished. For this purpose they adopted some of the old disused cemeteries which in prehistoric times had been cut in the rocks under the hill of Capodimonte. They plastered over the pagan designs, with which these catacombs had been decorated, and substituted the Christian emblems of cross and fish and so forth. Remains of old mosaics and frescoes can be seen in the *Catacombs of St Januarius*, the entrance to which is behind the little church of S. Gennaro. This eighth-century basilica replaced the chapel in which the saint was first buried. It lies to the west of the Via Santa Teresa, as the extension of the Via Toledo northwards is called.[1] The modern burying ground, the Campo Santo Nuovo, is on the hill of Poggioreale, to the north, which commands a superb view of Vesuvius and the Bay from Capri to Sorrento.[2]

Dumas in *Le Corricolo* has described in his inimitably lively fashion the old system of burial clubs, which with some modifications is not a very inaccurate description of the etiquette of to-day. The corpses are buried only a few inches deep in the ground of a subterranean crypt. Owing to the nature of the soil, the bodies are more or less mummified after lying there for a year. At the end of that period the remaining flesh is scraped from the bones, which are then placed in permanent vaults.

[1] Tram 18 from Piazza Vittoria, Entrance 3 lire.
[2] Tram 16 from Piazza Garibaldi.

CHAPTER VI

The Grotta Vecchia and the Tomb of Vergil

> " There saw we learned Maro's golden tombe,
> The way he cut an English mile in length
> Through a rock of stone, in one night's space."
>
> MARLOWE, *Doctor Faustus.*

Grotta Vecchia and Grotta Nuova—Fuorigrotta and Leopardi—Sta Maria di Piedigrotta—The Tomb of Vergil—Vergil the Christian—The Sibyl—Vergil the Magician—Vergil and St Paul—Vergil and Dante—Vergil the Protector of Naples—Neapolitan Legends—The Palladium and the Castel dell' Ovo.

IN order to shorten the length of communications between the Bay of Naples and the towns in the Gulf of Pozzuoli, the hill of Posilipo has been pierced, at different times and in different places, by several tunnels, or grottoes as they are called (*grotta*). Only one of these is now in use, having been recently constructed (1925-26) to take the place of the older ones which had collapsed, and are now blocked up. Approaching the Collina di Posilipo from the east, the Riviera di Chiaia, with its tram-service, and the Via Caracciolo converge upon the Piazza Sannazaro by way of the Via Mergellina, and the Viale Principessa Elena, a fine, new broad street. The Piazza Sannazaro lies close under the hill, the cliff of which rises sheer above a row of new houses now in course of construction. The broad mouth of the latest tunnel, which is over half a mile long, opens upon the western side of the Piazza, engulfs carts, foot-passengers and tramways, and disgorges them upon the other side of the hill. On the right of the Piazza Sannazaro, inland, and above this latest tunnel, are two others, known respectively as the Grotta Vecchia and the Grotta Nuova. The entrances to them, now blocked up, are immediately below the Stazione di Chiaia, a station on the new direct railway line to Pozzuoli. The Grotta Vecchia, the first we come to in the ascent from the Piazza Sannazaro, is traditionally ascribed to the labour of the Cumæans, but there is no historical reference to it earlier than the time of Nero. Whatever its origin, it was frequently enlarged and shortened, and ventilated and levelled, notably under the Spanish regime. This tunnel was not lit by any shaft communicating with the outer air like those near Cumæ and the Scoglio di Virgilio. It was so low that, according to Petronius, passengers were obliged to duck their heads as they walked. (*Satis constare, eos nisi inclinatos non solere transire Cryptam Neapolitanam.*)

The Grotta Nuova was pierced (845 yards long) for a tram and roadway, about halfway through which was a lift by which the top of the hill could be reached. A recent attempt to widen this grotto led to the collapse of both tunnels and the consequent piercing of the new one described above. Both these tunnels are being rapidly screened by new blocks of houses.

On emerging from the new tunnel, the exit from the old *grotta* is visible on the right, overhead. Here is the rather unattractive village of Fuorigrotta, illumined only by the memory of Giacomo Leopardi. That great poet and patriot lies buried in the vestibule of the church of San Vitale. He died bewailing the shame, the misery, the slavery of his beloved country to the hated Austrians, died in 1837, only a few years before the first movement towards the Risorgimento.

On our left, a road winds through a village street, and beneath an old wall with very picturesque bits on either side, out into country below a few large villas perched along the foot-hills, and down to the open space of the Poligono (military parade ground), the military racecourse, and the steel works at Segno. On the left foreground the shoulder of the green hill of Posilipo, dotted with umbrella-pines, stretches down to Cape Coroglio, and there the rocky mass of Nisida rises from the blue waters.

By the entrance to the Grotta Vecchia is a long inscription in Latin, dated 1668, which enumerates the medical virtues of the different kinds of baths, and concludes with the six famous lines in which Vergil is made to declare that he was born at Mantua and that Naples holds his ashes.

Between this and the sea is the church of Sta Maria di Piedigrotta, which contains a Neapolitan painting on wood of the fifteenth century, and tombs and monuments of the Filangieri family in a chapel near the choir. This spot is the scene of an annual *festa* on the evening of the 7th September, a survival perhaps of the Feast of Ceres or Harvest Festival. It is celebrated by a fearful din, for every one assembles armed with a trumpet, long or short, and blows it to the utmost of his capacity. A picture of Ferdinand driving from Naples to attend this *festa* in memory of the victory over the Austrians at Velletri (1744) will be noticed in the museum of S. Martino. Between the entrances of the newest grotto and the old, a zigzag way leads up to a Roman *columbarium*, which has for generations been reputed to be the tomb of Vergil.

The tomb, like the old grotto, being threatened with collapse, it has been taken under the care of the Italian Government. Tunnel and tomb are being propped up, and an approach by steps is to be made. The interior of the tomb is also to be renovated. At present it is in a ruinous condition and inaccessible. It will therefore suffice to say that it consists of a square chamber, 21 feet by 21 feet, surmounted by a cylindrical dome, and lit by three windows. In the thickness of the walls are two niches, in which the burial urns were lodged. The zigzag way leads up to the top of the Collina di Posilipo, a half-hour's climb up a steep, dirty and malodorous *salita*, which is barely rewarded by fine views of the Bay of Naples.

That Vergil was buried at Naples is as certain as anything can be. The wish he expressed on his deathbed (19 B.C.), that he should be buried in the city where he had chosen to live and near which his country estate lay, would naturally be complied with. It is stated in the biography by Donatus, which is thought to have been founded upon an earlier work by Suetonius, written about a hundred years after the death of the poet, that his bones were conveyed to his beloved Naples, and there placed in a tomb within the second milestone on the road leading to Puteoli. (*Qui est via Puteolana intra lapidem secundum.*) The tomb became one of the proudest possessions of Naples. Men of letters, like Statius[1] and Silvius Italicus, regarded it with such reverence that the latter made a practice of observing the poet's birthday by performing a pilgrimage to his tomb as though it were the shrine of some deity. Guilhem Augier,

[1] Born in A.D. 45, the son of a schoolmaster at Naples. Love of beauty and his native land mingle in Statius with a gentle devotion, and have endeared him to poets so different as Pope, Chaucer and Dante.

a troubadour of the twelfth century, refers to Vergil as " he who lies on the seashore, there by Naples." (*Cel que jatz en la ribeira . . . lai la Napoli.*)

These and other indications, such as the cult for his works and memory to which we shall presently refer, clearly establish the following facts: firstly, that Vergil's tomb was at Naples; second, that it was a well-known and valued shrine; thirdly, that it was within the second milestone on the road to Puteoli; finally, if we may take the troubadour literally, that it was on the seashore. M. Cocchia, in his book on *La Tomba di Virgilio*, maintains that tradition is correct in placing the tomb at the mouth of the Grotto on the road to Pozzuoli. But the Roman *columbarium* which is reputed to be Vergil's tomb is not upon the shore. It is perched upon a rock above the roadway high up on the hillside overlooking the Grotta Vecchia. Nor is it " within the second milestone on the Via Puteolana." Where, then, was Vergil buried?

The theory of the subsidence of the foreshore, as expounded by Mr Günther, offers a solution of the mystery. If it is an accepted geological fact that the shore in Vergil's time was 16 to 20 feet higher than it is now, and that by the twelfth century it had fallen to nearly 40 feet below the Roman level, and that after some five hundred years there was a rising which brought it up to the present level in the first half of the sixteenth century, then Vergil's tomb " on the shore of Naples " would have been buried deep under sand and water, and remains so buried. If, again, the evidence of the submerged buildings about Capo Posilipo be accepted, as they may well be, as proof that there once existed a coast road from Mergellina to Pozzuoli, then it remains to find the second milestone (from Naples) on that road, which, along with the villas and the tomb, has disappeared beneath the waves as the shore subsided. Mr Günther places the second milestone "down on the foreshore in what are now the broad public gardens of the *Villa Nazionale*."

Wherever it was, the tomb of Vergil disappeared, and there was need of a tomb to show. What place could be more suitable than a genuine, ancient tomb or *columbarium*, set upon a road on a way to Puteoli, and at the mouth of a *grotta* which, in his transformation as a mediæval magician, Vergil was supposed to have pierced by magic in a single night? A site having been thus chosen to suit the myth and the tourist alike, the bones of the poet *may* have been moved thither. At any rate, Villani, writing in the fourteenth century, assures us that they were placed under a marble slab on which was engraved the famous inscription:

> Mantua me genuit; Calabri rapuere; tenet nunc
> Parthenope; cecini pascua, rara, duces.

(*Mantua was my birthplace; Calabria seduced me thither; now Naples keeps me. I sang of flocks, fields, and heroes.*)

There is a story related by Gervasius of Tilbury (*circa* 1212) to the effect that the body of Vergil was disinterred by an Englishman from a grave in the mountain side, the position of which had long been forgotten. This was in the time of Roger of Sicily. Fearing that if the bones of their patron were removed from the city, as the Englishman intended, disaster would befall them, the Duke of Naples and the citizens seized them, put them in a sack, and brought them to the Castel di Mare (dell' Ovo), and there exhibited them behind iron bars. This story would seem at least to suggest that the actual site of Vergil's grave had been forgotten. If this is a fact, and there was a break in the tradition as to the actual site, it becomes easier to understand how the present "Tomb of Vergil" has come to be accepted as the traditional place of his interment.

We have mentioned the legend which attributed the construction of the tunnel to the magic art of the poet. Petrarch has recorded that King Robert once consulted him as to the truth of it. He solemnly replied that he did not remember to have read anywhere that Vergil was a stone-mason! But thanks to the changes and chances of popular superstition and mediæval theology, Vergil passed through many metamorphoses and played stranger parts than those of a mere stone-mason. For by the time that Naples had ceased to be Greek or Roman and become a mediæval town, Vergil, of all poets the supreme artist, who had sung in the *Æneid* the epic of Rome, and in his *Eclogues* and *Georgics* the country life of her people, had passed into a new incarnation and emerged as a Great Magician. He came to be regarded in popular estimation as a dread, mysterious necromancer, gifted with superhuman powers for good or evil, powers derived from his knowledge of the infernal regions he had described.

The process by which the change was achieved was a curious though natural one. As literary taste declined under a series of half-savage military emperors elected by the army, Vergil ceased to be read. But his reputation survived. His name was regarded with almost superstitious reverence. Already, under the Antonines, the habit had grown up of opening his poems at random in order to obtain a prophecy as to some future event. From the Emperor Hadrian down to Charles I. of England the custom of thus consulting the *sortes Vergilianæ* persisted, testifying to the veneration in which the author was regarded. Though the poems of Vergil ceased to be read as literature they continued to be reverenced as the great repositories of mysterious allegory. Then, when grammar and rhetoric came to be esteemed as the most important parts of culture, the author of poems whose fame was so persistent was naturally accepted as the supreme authority upon rhetoric and grammar. For Macrobius, Donatus, and Priscian, Vergil is the infallible test upon every point of learning. Thus it came about that, after the fall of the Roman Empire, the name of Vergil survived as the representative and epitome of that lost civilisation, whose art was a mystery and whose learning was as comprehensive as it was now incomprehensible. Throughout the Middle Ages he survived with the grammars in which he was quoted, and by which alone the Latin language could be taught and learned in the schools, because Latin had ceased to be a spoken language, and the European tongues which were being formed out of the old were not yet sufficiently developed and established to be used as vehicles for literature. The Christian fathers and monks inveighed against Pagan writers, but from the *Æneid* of Vergil to the *Ars Amatoria* of Ovid they began once more to read their works.

Then the reputation of Vergil passed into another phase. The high moral character of his poems, his reputation for almost superhuman wisdom, the many passages in which his words seem to foreshadow or to support the Christian faith, made a great impression upon the Christian theologians. They began to wish to purify him from what was in their eyes his only fault, the pagan spirit. It was known that the impression he made upon his contemporaries had been that of a singularly sweet and gentle personality—so much so that they had given him the characteristic nickname of *Parthenias*. It seemed sad to think that the great man whose life and works proved him, like Cicero, to have been a pure and noble soul, eminently fit to be a Christian, should have lived in the time of the false gods. Almost they persuaded themselves that he was a Christian. Into their net they swept eminent and serious pagans, who might well have been converted to Christianity, but were not; Seneca, Pliny, Cicero, Vergil, men whose writings showed them to be worthy of knowing and accepting the true faith. Not only were they struck by the many coincidences between the speculations of ancient writers and points of doctrine in the revealed religion, but in the case of Vergil there was one outstanding poem, which, alike in spirit and in detail, seemed to be undeniably a Messianic prophecy. By virtue of the fourth *Eclogue*, Vergil was hailed as one of the goodly army of prophets who had foretold the coming of Christ. "The expectation," writes Signore Comparetti in his learned work upon Vergil in the Middle Ages, "the expectation of an immediate regeneration of the world in an era of happiness, justice, love, and peace, which inspires the whole of this *Eclogue*, the connection of this expectation with the birth of a Child, and the ancient authority of the Sibyl, on which the whole prophecy is based, could not fail to induce a Christian when reading it to think of the birth of Christ and the regeneration of the world which his pure and gentle preaching promised."

The Emperor Constantine, in an address to an ecclesiastical gathering, pointed out that the Virgin who returned in this poem is Mary; that the Child sent from the sky is Jesus; the Serpent which shall cease to be is the Tempter; and that the balsam which shall grow everywhere is Christianity. Whether Vergil was a conscious or an unconscious witness to the Faith was much disputed. But in either case the evidence of one who was reputed to be the repository of all the wisdom of the ages was not to be lightly cast aside. By virtue of his prophecy that " the world's great age begins anew " (*jam nova progenies*, etc.), he was represented in art down to the time of the Renaissance, in company with Paul, Isaiah, and the other prophets, as, for instance, by Vasari at Rimini.

The Sibyl, too, was joined with Vergil in mediæval theology, as being among the prophets who had certainly foretold the coming of Christ. They both figure in the Miracle plays. Both were said to have beheld the star which guided the Magi to Bethlehem. The verses of the Sibyl were recited in Church on Christmas Day. It is natural, therefore, to find the figure of the Sibyl appearing in Christian art, and inspiring, so late as the sixteenth century, the brushes of Michelangelo and Raphael. Christian compassion for Vergil, the gentle spirit, who had foretold Christ, and yet for himself had so narrowly missed the beatitude of Paradise, inspired the author of some lines which used to be sung in the Mass of St Paul at Mantua. They relate how the Apostle, on his way to Rome, visited the Poet's tomb at Naples, and there, touched by the tragedy of it all, burst into tears, exclaiming, " What would I have made of thee, O Greatest of the Poets, had I but found thee living ! "

> " Ad Maronis Mausoleum
> Ductus fudit super eum
> Piae rorem lacrimae.
> Quem, te, inquit, reddidissem,
> Si te vivum invenissem,
> Poetarum maxime ! "

It is fancy, of course, but kindly fancy, and links up for us, as we stand about the legendary tomb of Vergil, his name with that of the Apostle who landed at Pozzuoli. Another version of the legend (*Mage du Monde*) adds that, after expressing his regret that he was too late to convert the Roman poet, St Paul discovered, after some search, the subterranean chamber in which he was buried. Access to it was rendered difficult by a furious wind accompanied by terrifying sounds. He succeeded in seeing, from without, Vergil seated between two lighted tapers, and surrounded by books lying in confusion on the floor. A lamp hung above him, and before him stood an archer with bent bow. Further entrance was prevented by two bronze men, who whirled two steel hammers about their heads. The Apostle succeeded in stopping them. But no sooner had he done so, than the arrow sped from the archer's bow and shattered the lamp. Everything straightway fell into dust, and St Paul was compelled to retire without securing the poet's books as he desired. Vergil's book of magical lore was long sought for in the Middle Ages. It was said to have been found at last by an Englishman beneath the poet's head, or, as some say, beneath the head of Chiron, in a cave on Monte Barbaro, the fabled repository of many treasures. This book is the occasion of another legend. Vergil, imprisoned at Rome, escaped by means of a magic ship in which he flew to Naples. But finding that in his haste he had left behind him his book of magic, he despatched his disciple, Merlin, to fetch it. Merlin, disobeying his injunction on no account to open the book, found himself suddenly surrounded by a crowd of devils howling for his orders. To get rid of them, he set them to work to pave the road from Rome to Naples. It is interesting to observe how these mediæval magicians anticipated modern methods of dealing with the unemployed! It was on account of Vergil's reputation for more than human wisdom, and as a prophet of Christ, but, above all, because, as a poet himself, he recognised in him both a countryman and a master-poet, that Dante chose Vergil for his guide in the infernal regions, and his poem as his supreme exemplar in art. Faithful interpreter that he is of the religious sentiment of the Middle Ages, Dante would not consign Vergil to the limbo of the damned, but places him among those whose one involuntary fault was that they were not baptised.

But Dante would have nothing to do with Vergil as a magician, or with the crude popular legends which had gathered about his name. In those popular legends, Neapolitan in their origin, Vergil had ceased to be regarded as a poet at all. As the fount and repository of all wisdom, he emerges as a magician of unbounded art and power, and appears always as the lord and benefactor of the city of Naples. It is a startling, an almost incredible transformation. The great poet of Imperial Rome becomes the leading figure in a series of grotesque mediæval fables, wherein Rome is supplanted by Naples, and poetry gives place to magic.

It was natural that these legends, which were purely popular and local in origin, should arise in Naples and be connected with the city where Vergil had chosen to live and where his tomb was preserved and honoured. It was natural that he, who had sung of these shores from Cumæ and Cape Misenum to Sorrentum, whose wanderings over the Phlegræan Fields had inspired his conceptions of the Sibyl's cave, the infernal regions, the horrors of Lake Avernus and the Acherusian swamp, should live on in local tradition. He came here, it was averred, from the north, a tall and handsome man, who wandered always with head bent, murmuring strange phrases in a language none could comprehend. He lived by the edge of the sea, where the shore curves inwards under the hill of Posilipo. But every day he would wander through the country which leads to Baiæ and Cumæ, or pass along the Neapolitan shore listening to the music of the waves which taught him his wonderful harmonies, or, at night, to the stories of the stars. To begin with, he was made Duke of Naples and Calabria by Octavian. Many were the marvels which he wrought with his magic. It was he, the chronicler assures us, who cured a plague of flies which beset Parthenope, by causing a fly of gold or bronze to be made. Into this, with magical words, he breathed life and the power to destroy all others. The bronze fly thus made by Vergil is said to have been as large as a frog. Conrad von Querfurt declares that it was placed upon one of the fortified gates. It was moved first to a window in the Castel Capuano, and then to the Castel Cicala (later called the Castel St Angelo and destroyed by the monks of Sta Chiara). There it lost its magic power. A similar creation is attributed to Albertus Magnus. Later, Vergil wrought a similar miracle when the horses of the neighbourhood were infected by some insidious disease. The magician caused a huge horse of bronze to be made, and filled it with such magic virtue, that every horse which was led round it three times was infallibly healed.[1]

So great was the efficacy of this magic beast that the farriers, finding their trade as veterinary surgeons much injured by it, at last rose up and knocked out its belly. After that, it lost its healing power. For

[1] The legends relating to Vergil in Naples were collected in the fourteenth century in the *Cronica di Partenope*, and have been popularised by Matilde Serao in her *Leggende Napoletane*.

all that, this bronze horse was still standing in the courtyard of a church as late as 1322. Then, it is said, the priests had it melted down into bells for the church. The colossal bronze head of a horse, now preserved in the *Museo Nazionale*, has been thought to be a fragment of the bronze horse made by Vergil. It is more probably Greek work of a much earlier date. Vergil made a golden leech, which cured a plague of leeches. By the exercise of his magic he banished the pestilential miasma which rose from swamps in the surrounding district, and when the fishermen complained that fish were running scarce off Porta di Massa, he caused a small fish to be engraved upon a rock there, or as some say, made a little fish of marble—the *preta de lo pesce*—uttered incantations over it, and lo! the sea swarmed with fishes. A terrible serpent devastated the district, killing many children, and always disappearing into the bowels of the earth when men went out to destroy it. Vergil was summoned to their aid. Going forth alone and unaided he slew the monster by the potency of his magician's charms. It was Vergil who set up two carven heads, the one laughing, the other in tears, at the Porta Nolana, which should be for a sign and omen. For whoever happened to pass under the laughing face might look for good fortune, whilst he who went beneath the tearful one must beware of ill. Gervasius of Tilbury, in his *Otia Imperialia*, describes an incident in his own life which illustrates the force of the belief in these magic heads. He was a professor at the University of Bologna. In the year 1190, he tells us, he was at Salerno, and happened to meet Philip, son of the Earl of Salisbury. They decided to go to Naples together and there to make arrangements for their voyage. "On arriving they betook themselves to the house of Giovanni Pinatelli,

Archdeacon of Naples, who had been a pupil of Gervasius at Bologna. He accompanied them to the harbour, and within an hour a boat was procured and all arrangements made for speedy departure. The Archdeacon was so amazed at the success and rapidity with which their business had been completed, that he asked them by what gate they had entered the city. When they told him, he exclaimed, "Now I know why you were so lucky," and asked through which part of the gate they had entered. They remembered that they had intended to come in on the left, when an ass laden with wood compelled them to cross over to the right. The Archdeacon insisted on their returning with him to the gate in question, in order that they might see what great things Vergil had done for Naples. He showed them a niche on the right-hand wall in which was a bust of Parian marble with a laughing face, while in the left-hand wall was a similar bust, only with a face of mourning. "Every one," said he, "who enters the city by the right-hand side will succeed in whatever business he has in hand, whilst every one who enters on the left will meet with nothing but disappointment." Vergil taught children the old games they love, and revealed the secret of the healing waters of Pozzuoli and the mysteries of the Cumæan cave. Other legends record the setting up of four skulls which informed the Duke of all that was happening, and the possession of a magic mirror which revealed all things to the poet.

Conrad von Querfurt, Chancellor of the Emperor Henry VI. and his Vice-Regent in Naples and Sicily, whilst carrying out his master's orders and dismantling the city of Naples, records (1194) the view held by the Neapolitans, that the walls and city he was destroying were founded by Vergil himself. The founder had deposited with them as a palladium,

CASTEL DELL'OVO, FROM POSILIPO

which should be a sure protection against all enemies, a narrow-necked bottle containing a model of the city. If the city had, none the less, fallen into the hands of the Imperialists, it was because the glass bottle was cracked. . . . The task of demolishing the walls was, however, arrested for some time when the Imperial soldiers came to the Porta Nolana. For they were afraid of setting free all the serpents which Vergil had confined there, when, in answer to the petition of the inhabitants, he had rid the country of the snakes and reptiles which used to infest the neighbourhood. For the palladium which had proved so ineffectual against the Imperialists, later legends substituted an egg, also preserved in a glass bottle. But the bottle itself was said to be enclosed in an iron vessel, and kept in the Castel dell' Ovo, which Vergil is reputed to have built.

Conrad mentions other marvellous deeds attributed to Vergil. Apart from the bronze fly and the bronze horse, there was a butcher's block upon which meat kept fresh for six weeks, and the bronze archer. In order to keep Vesuvius quiet, he set up the statue of a man with a bent bow and an arrow ready to shoot, directed towards the volcano. The threat sufficed for a long while, until one day a peasant fired off the arrow. It struck the edge of the crater, rousing Vesuvius to wrath, and straightway provoked a series of eruptions. This magical statue, which suggests faint echoes of Sicilian legends in relation to Etna and Empedocles, with his bronze statue at Girgenti, is said by Scoppa, writing in the sixteenth century, to have been set up at the Porta Reale (formerly known as the Porta Ventosa, or Windy Gate).

The renown of Vergil as a magician led to Naples sharing with Toledo the doubtful honour of having originated the Black Arts. Vergil is said to have studied at Toledo, which was as famous for necromancy as Paris for the study of the liberal arts and Salerno for medicine. It is not known exactly where Vergil died. Some think he died at Brundisium; others upon Monte Vergine, an eminence near Avellino, which is now the scene of a great pilgrimage at Whitsuntide and at the Feast of the Nativity of the Virgin (8th September). The return of the pilgrims is celebrated by a characteristic Neapolitan celebration in the streets about Sta Lucia. The people wear their gayest costumes, the horses are decorated with ribbons, and staves wound about with fruit and flowers are carried as by the Bacchanals of old. The famous Church of the Monastery on Monte Vergine was built upon the site of a temple of Cybele.

The Castel dell' Ovo, or Uovo, which took its name from Vergil's Magical Egg, or as some maintain, from the shape of the castle, stands upon a little island at the very tip of the Falcon's Beard (Pizzofalcone). The island is now connected with the heart of Naples by a narrow causeway. The luxurious villa of the Roman epicure, Lucullus, which spread over the promontory of Pizzofalcone, perhaps included it. We have seen that, according to one legend, it was first called Megaris, after the wife of Hercules. According to another, it was the wife of Sebetus. She was wrecked upon this rock and drowned there, and the River Sebeto is formed by the tears of her faithful husband, who is ever vainly seeking her in the waters of the sea. Later it was known as the *Castrum Lucullanum*, and presently, in the fourth century, when a monastery had arisen about the mausoleum founded by a rich widow of Naples for the reception of the body of St Severinus, *Monasterium Lucullanum*, or di San Salvatore. The abbot, Eugipius, set his monks to copy the ancient classics, and thus enriched Naples with many valuable manuscripts. Then came another change. It was already fortified in Norman times, for it was in the fortress of S. Salvatore that King Roger dictated his terms to the city. William I. began to build a castle there, designed by Buono, which was completed by Frederick II., and was known for some time as *Castello Marino* or *di Mare*.

At length, in 1352, we find it referred to as the Castle of the Magical Egg. For in the rules of the order of the Holy Spirit, founded by Louis of Anjou, it is then named *Castellum ovi excantati*. An inscription of about the same date, which has hitherto defied exact interpretation, refers to this name and legend :

> Ovo mira novo sic ovo non tuber ovo
> Dorica castra cluens tutor. temerare timeto.

King Ladislaus strengthened the castle and used it as a harem and a prison. It was bombarded by the French when Charles VIII. invaded Italy, and Conradin and Beatrice were imprisoned here. But its chief tragedy is that Giotto painted frescoes in the chapel of the monastery and that they have disappeared. Neapolitans believe that enormous treasure is buried in the caverns beneath the castle, which is now used for barracks. Seen from Mergellina or Posilipo, when its broader side catches the rays of the setting sun, the Castel dell' Ovo forms a striking feature in the picture of the Bay, beneath the empurpled slopes of Vesuvius, amid the crimson sea.

CHAPTER VII

Herculaneum and the Demon of Vesuvius

Early history—Pliny's description of the eruption of Vesuvius, A.D. 79—The fate of Herculaneum—The eruption of 1631—The Royal villa at Portici—Resina and the buried city—History of excavations—Bronzes, marbles, and papyri found there—Scavi di Ercolano—Torre del Greco—Torre Annunziata—Vesuvius and other eruptions.

[To visit *Herculaneum*, 6¼ miles, take a train from the terminus of the Ferrovia Circumvesuviana in the Corso Garibaldi, close to the Stazione Centrale, which will reach the station of Pugliano at Resina in about half an hour. A few minutes' walk from thence along the Strada Pugliana will take you to the *Scavi di Ercolano.* Another route is by tram No. 55, which starts from the Via Verdi nearly opposite to the garden entrance to the Palazzo Reale (1.40 lire), for Resina (Ercolano). The journey takes the better part of an hour. After passing through dusty and noisy industrial and shipbuilding suburbs, and crossing the present course of the little river Sebeto, the line traverses a region of market gardens (*paduli*) beneath the town of La Barra on the fertile slopes on the left. Beyond San Giovanni a Teduccio it emerges near Portici into a district of villas facing the sea, and stops at Resina at the entrance to the site of the excavations. (*Open*, 9–4.30 p.m. *Entrance*, 4 lire: Sundays, free.)

From Resina (Stazione Pugliano) you can ascend *Vesuvius* by Messrs Cook's Vesuvius Railway (office in Naples, Galleria Vittoria). Most people will find this by far the best method of ascending the volcano (¾ hour). There is an hotel at the Eremo Station near the Observatory, where lunch is served on the return journey. Ten minutes' walk from the terminus to the crater. Guide obligatory. A more interesting route for those who prefer to go more or less by themselves and to throw a leg astride a horse is from Pompeii to Boscotrecase by train on the Circumvesuviana and thence by a new road on horseback to the top. A day should be chosen if possible when the smoke from the crater is rising steadily into a blue sky. It should be remembered that the summit of Vesuvius is 3890 feet high, and that, therefore, the climate there is very different from that on the sea-level. Warm wraps should be taken.]

OF Herculaneum there is told a legend which has been adorned by the genius of the poet Giacomo Leopardi, that passive Protestant of Italy's servitude. Hercules, on his return from Spain, stopped here to rest after his labours. He became enamoured of the charms of the daughter of Sebetus (the *River Sebeto*) and endeavoured to seduce her. The shy nymph fled to the shore, imploring the protection of Poseidon. The god heard her prayer and changed her into a stone, and shrouded her in flowers. Hercules, baulked of his desire, kissed the stone, and declared that it should bear his name, Herakleia.

To Oscan, Etruscan, Samnite, and Greek succeeded the domination of Rome. The town fell in 89 B.C. to a lieutenant of Sulla, who founded a colony of veterans there. When the Emperor Tiberius retired to Capri, his presence there involved the development of Herculaneum and the little port of Retina (Resina). Its position on the road to Rome gave it inevitable importance. But apart from this it was already a rising town, having more of the character of a city of art and leisure than Pompeii, which was first and foremost a commercial town. The freshness of the air, the excellence of the sea-bathing, and the delicious scenery of the neighbourhood attracted the wealthy citizens of busy Neapolis. They chose the tiny promontory at the foot of Vesuvius, watered on either side by streams flowing through fertile valleys and overlooking the little port of Retina, as the site of their suburban residences in holiday or retirement.

There was no greater connoisseur in such matters than Lucius Calpurnius Piso, the retired proconsul who learned the philosophy of Epicurus from the Greek scholar Philodemus of Gadara, and whom Cicero denounced for having stripped his province of Macedonia of its treasures of art even as Verres had stripped Sicily. Here the wealthy epicure elected to build him a new and luxurious country seat, and amused himself by building a little pier from it to the sea, by which he might disembark the treasures of art and the library which he had decided to bring hither from his town house at Rome. It was a choice for which the world, as we shall see, must remain forever his debtor.

In the year A.D. 63 Herculaneum was damaged by the earthquake which shook the buildings of Pompeii to the ground. The task of reconstructing it was begun with the aid of Vespasian. We have already referred to the building of the new theatre there (*see* p. 127). Such was the state of the little town when suddenly, in the twinkling of an eye, it was engulfed by a disaster unparalleled in history.

On the afternoon of 24th August, A.D. 79, in the first year of the reign of the Emperor Titus, Caius Plinius, who was in command of the Roman fleet stationed at Misenum, had retired to his study after the midday bath and meal. He was intending to pursue his studies, for besides being a naval officer, he was the most distinguished of Roman naturalists. But he was destined to be rudely interrupted. Living with him in his villa was his nephew and adopted son, Caius Cæcilius Plinius the Younger, and his mother. About one o'clock the latter summoned the naturalist to observe a curious phenomenon. It was a cloud of very unusual size and shape, which, it was afterwards ascertained, had issued from Mount Vesuvius. The naturalist went out and climbed a neighbouring hill in order to obtain a better view of it. This cloud was afterwards described by his nephew in a letter to the historian Tacitus (*Ep.*, VI. 16). "I cannot," he says, "give a better description of its shape than by likening it to that of a pine tree, for it shot up to a great height in the form of a trunk and extended at the top as it were into branches. . . . It appeared sometimes white, and sometimes dark and spotted, as if it had carried up earth or cinders." The scientific curiosity of Pliny the Elder was aroused, and he determined to obtain a better view of it. He ordered a light skiff to be prepared. But at that moment an urgent appeal for help reached him from Retina.

"What he had begun in a scientific, he pursued in an heroic spirit. Ordering out the quadriremes, he hastened to the aid not only of Retina, but many others; for the shore is crowded with villas. He hurried to the spot whence others were fleeing, and made for the scene of danger, calmly making notes of what he saw. And now cinders, which grew thicker and hotter the nearer he approached, fell upon the ships, and pumice-stones and pieces of rock, blackened, burnt and split by the flames. Then the sea suddenly retreated, and the shore was filled with fragments from the mountain."

It was impossible to reach Herculaneum. The pilot advised putting back. But "Fortune favours the brave!" cried Pliny, and decided to make for Stabiæ. There, in order to allay the panic of his friends, he calmly bathed, supped, and lay down to sleep in the villa of a friend. He was roused when the accumulation of pumice-stones and ashes threatened to prevent escape, and the house rocked and tottered with the repeated shocks. Tying pillows over their heads with napkins, to protect them from the falling pumice-stones, the refugees made their way in the inky darkness down to the shore. All hopes of escape that way were frustrated by the exceeding roughness of the sea. Pliny threw himself down to rest. When his slaves endeavoured to rouse him to flight, alarmed at an outburst of flames and sulphurous fumes, he staggered to his feet, but only to fall down dead.

In the meantime his nephew, who had refused to accompany him in order that he might go on with his studies, had retired to rest at Misenum. For several days past, he records in another letter (*Ep.*, VI. xx.), there had been earthquakes, which had caused little alarm, because they occurred so frequently in Campania.

"But that night their violence increased, so that the whole world seemed not only to be shaken, but overturned. My mother rushed into my room, just as I was rising to call her. We sat down in a courtyard between the house and the sea. I don't know whether to call it coolness or folly—I was then only seventeen—but I called for a volume of Livy and read it. . . . It was now six o'clock in the morning; the buildings all around us were tottering, and, as there was no remaining without danger, we resolved to leave the town. The common people followed us, panicstricken and pressing in a crowd upon our rear. . . . Then we beheld the sea sucked back and driven from the shore by the convulsive motion of the earth. On the other side, a black and dreadful cloud, breaking out in gusts of igneous serpentine vapour, yawned forth long tongues of flame in fantastic shapes, like flashes of lightning but much larger. . . . Soon afterwards the cloud seemed to descend upon the earth and cover the sea: it had surrounded and hidden Capreæ and blotted out the promontory of Misenum. My mother began to pray, exhort and command me to escape as best I could. A young man could do it, she said, but she was heavy with years and flesh alike, and would die happy, if only she were not the cause of my death. I replied I would not be saved without her; then taking her by the hand, I compelled her to go on. She obeyed reluctantly, reproaching herself for delaying me. Ashes now began to fall upon us, but so far only lightly. I look back: dense darkness was pressing upon our rear, and followed spreading over the land like a torrent. 'Let us turn aside,' said I, 'whilst we can still see, lest we be trampled to death by the crowd that accompanies us.' We had scarcely sat down, when darkness came over us, not like that of a moonless or cloudy night, but of a room when it is shut up, and the lamp extinguished. Nothing then was to be heard but the shrieks of women, the screams of children, and the cries of men, some wishing to die, from the very fear of dying; some lifting their hands to the gods; but the greater part imagining that the last and eternal night was come. . . ."

At Pompeii the citizens first became aware of danger as they were keeping holiday, seated in the theatre which has never since been filled. Warned by the lurid sky and threatening darkness, they rushed to their homes. Some seized their valuables and tried to escape from the city. Some on their way felt the earth rock beneath them, and fell crushed to death by falling pillars. Some managed to reach the port at the mouth of the Sarno and were there overwhelmed. Others sought refuge in their cellars and archways. But hot, stifling dust penetrated through every crevice, noxious gases spread along the ground, and their hiding-places became their tombs. What happened to the inhabitants of Herculaneum we do not so fully know. They may have escaped or they may have been overwhelmed in thousands. They may have rushed down to the shore and there met the tidal wave and been swept to their doom. A few skeletons have been found in the piecemeal burrowings that have so far taken the place of excavations. For since the Roman admiral hauled off from the port of Retina, no mortal eye has seen more than a fragment of Herculaneum.

According to one theory, the fate of Pompeii was different in kind from that which overwhelmed Herculaneum. Whilst Pompeii was buried under three metres of cinders, ashes and pumice-stone (*lapilli*), Herculaneum, it is said, was inundated by an avalanche of hot mud. Deluges of rain, it is asserted, falling upon the mass of ash, cinders and stones flung out by the eruption onto the sides of the volcano, formed streams of liquid lava, which grew into torrents on the steep hillsides. Rushing through the streets of Herculaneum they blocked up the houses and rose over the walls, until only an indistinguishable mass was left at last, hiding what once had been so fair a city. The objections to this theory are obvious. In the first place, no ancient writer makes mention of such torrential rains during the eruption; the *outer* crust of the deposit which covered Pompeii alone bears witness to the influence of a subsequent rainfall. Herculaneum being much nearer to the crater than Pompeii, was likely to receive an even larger share of the cinders, pumice-stone, gravel and rock thrown out by the volcano. The evidence of Pliny, indeed, shows that when his uncle reached Retina, the fall of volcanic matter was so dense and asphyxiating that he was unable to land. Moreover, as might be expected, at Herculaneum, which is nearer the crater, the stones found in the tufa which covers it are often larger than those that covered Pompeii. There they are uniformly of the size of a pea or nut; at Herculaneum sometimes as large as a melon. In fact, according to the distinguished Italian geologist, Signore Giuseppe di Lorenzo, the tufa, in and under which Herculaneum now lies buried, is composed of cinders, pumice, gravel and rock thrown out during the eruption. It is of precisely the same character as that which formed Monte Nuova in 1548 without the aid of any torrents of mud, when contemporary eye-witnesses described the fall of *lapilli*. At Herculaneum subsequent eruptions of Vesuvius—from which Pompeii was exempt—added to the depth of the deposit over the buried city. This deposit was rendered compact by its own weight and hardened by the carbonate of calcium conveyed by the infiltration of water through the subsoil.

The strongest argument of all against the torrent of mud theory lies in the formation of the country as we know it to have been. The city of Herculaneum is described by ancient writers as standing upon a promontory descending abruptly to the sea. On either side of this promontory were valleys through which rivers flowed. Rivers of mud descending from Vesuvius would be bound to follow the course of these valleys and would not flow up and over the high ground of the promontory. These valleys were not obliterated until the great eruption of Vesuvius in 1631, when seven streams of red-hot lava poured down the mountain-side devouring everything on their way. Terrible in their speed as in their destructiveness, they reached the sea within an hour and converted it into a boiling cauldron. They filled with molten mud the depressions on either side of the promontory on which Herculaneum had stood, and converted them into the rising grounds which are now the sites of the Villas of Portici and Favorita. Torre del Greco, Torre Annunziata, Bosco Reale, Resina and Portici shared the fate of Herculaneum on this occasion, whilst the great waves of lava flung along the coast indicate how severely the whole neighbourhood from Portici and Greco del Torre to Torre Annunziata and Bosco Reale suffered by this visitation. Many thousands of people perished. Signs, indeed, had not been wanting of a coming eruption, and fortunately many of those who had made their homes upon the mountain slopes and seashore had removed to safety. The warnings and the course of this eruption, as described by the Abbate Braccini, were in many ways similar to those of the eruption which destroyed Herculaneum and Pompeii. The volcano had been quiescent since the year 1500. A series of earthquakes was felt all along the Bay and the water in the wells sank mysteriously. Suddenly on 16th December the expected eruption broke forth, accompanied by terrific crashes like salvoes of artillery. An ominous cloud of smoke and ashes shaped like a pine tree, exactly as Pliny had described, was seen to rise from the mountain. There was the same discharge of lightning by which many people were killed, whilst ashes ejected from the volcano were carried as far as the Ægean and even Constantinople. Huge stones were flung as far as Nola, and the streets of Naples were filled with suffocating fumes of sulphur. The darkness grew intense once more, " such as there is in some closed room where all the lights are extinguished," as Pliny had described it, and houses rocked like ships at sea. The flow of the rivers of lava—the point in which this eruption differed from that of 79, when, as we have seen, no lava was ejected—was accompanied by terrifying rumblings and growlings, which seemed to justify the Neapolitan belief that a demon dwells in the red-hot caverns of the mountain. The sea, as in Pliny's time, became excessively agitated. Suddenly it retreated half a mile from the coast, and then as suddenly returned in a huge tidal wave. Subsequent eruptions are referred to at the close of this chapter.

With undaunted courage, indefatigable industry, and a curious calm fatalism, the ruined peasants who had seen their homes destroyed, their crops scorched and burned, and the labour of years wiped out in a night, set themselves on the morrow of this, as of all succeeding disasters, to rebuild their houses and remake their farms. They have this consolation, that each eruption fertilises the already prolific soil, and will produce in the coming years redoubled crops of the beans, tomatoes, fennel-roots, melons and vines for which they toil so incessantly and pay resignedly a price so heavy. "*Napoli*," so runs the bitter aphorism, "*fa gli peccati, e Torre gli paga*." (Naples sins and Torre pays for it.) For Naples, the gay licentious city, has always remained immune from these visitations; it is the suburbs which suffer.

Nor was it only the peasants and fishermen, tied to the soil and the sea, who braved the dangers of the sleeping volcano. So long did the monster remain quiescent that Charles III., the first Bourbon king of Naples, chose Portici as a pleasure resort to which he could retire for the sake of the good air and sea-bathing. He built himself a palace and gardens there, where Murat afterwards resided, during the occupation by the French Republicans. The dilapidated remains of it border the noisy street, and are now used as an agricultural college. His example has been followed by the well-to-do Neapolitans of to-day, who delight in Portici as the scene of their summer *villeggiatura*, just as they did at Herculaneum of old.

The silence of death had fallen upon the buried city of Herculaneum. It was followed by oblivion so complete that its very existence was almost forgotten. Some seventeenth-century writers hazarded the opinion that its site was at Torre del Greco. For over sixteen hundred years it remained unheeded, inaccessible, beneath an accumulation of hardened volcanic matter, in some places 130 feet deep.

There is a little picture drawn by Macaulay in his essay upon the life and writings of Addison, which helps one to realise how rich and how recent is the heritage of interest, beauty, and knowledge of which every tourist is now the possessor. The essayist describes Addison leaving Rome and posting along the Appian Way to Naples.

"Naples was then destitute of what are now, perhaps, its chief attractions. The lovely bay and the awful mountain were indeed there. But a farm-house stood on the theatre of Herculaneum, and rows of vines grew over the streets of Pompeii. The temples of Pæstum had not indeed been hidden from the eye of man by any great convulsion of nature: but, strange to say, their existence was a secret even to artists and antiquaries. Though situated within a few hours' journey of a great capital, where Salvator had not long before painted, and where Vico was then lecturing, those noble remains were as little known to Europe as the ruined cities overgrown by the forests of Yucatan. What was to be seen at Naples Addison saw. He climbed Vesuvius, explored the tunnel of Posilipo, and wandered among the vines and almond trees of Capreæ."

That was little more than two hundred years ago. As we stand in the theatre of Herculaneum, or in the streets of Pompeii and see the life of a provincial Roman town displayed before us, as by some illusion of the *Arte muta*, the thought that all this was still hidden from the eager eyes of Addison helps us to realise, does it not, the debt the world owes to the patient labours of the archæologists and the munificence of those who help to make their work possible.

It was not, however, a particularly worthy type of archæologist who first delved among the ruins of Herculaneum. In 1706 a Frenchman, Emmanuel de Lorraine, Prince d'Elbœuf, came to Naples with the Austrian army against Philip of Spain. He was appointed commander of the Cavalry there, and presently began to build himself a villa in the select neighbourhood of Portici (1709). The story runs that in sinking a well for this villa, he happened on the forgotten site of the city. Another version of the tale states that a peasant having brought to him some stucco work to decorate his villa, he inquired where he had found it. At the bottom of the well in the field, he replied. The prince went down the well and came up with a statue of Hercules. Both stories are no doubt apocryphal. The prince probably knew very well what he wanted to do, but not quite so well how successfully he was going to do it. By an extraordinary chance, the first shaft sunk by him in the course of his excavations opened onto the back of the stage of the theatre. There he found his immediate reward in a few sculptures.

The Prince d'Elbœuf continued his excavations until the Viceroy checked his activities by requisitioning all the objects found. In 1738 the explorations were resumed by order of Charles III. of Naples, and were continued till 1776. Unfortunately the explorers pursued the same haphazard methods as the Prince d'Elbœuf. They sank shafts more or less at random, and afterwards filled them up again. Work was done again in 1828, and at intervals afterwards up till 1875, when it was abandoned on the grounds that the finds were few and poor, and that the excavations were endangering the houses above. The two great and almost insuperable difficulties which stand in the way of a thorough excavation of Herculaneum are the great depth and hardness of the volcanic tufa beneath which it is buried, and—the more difficult problem of the two—the presence of the crowded suburbs of Portici and Resina, which have been built over its site. The latter factor involves serious financial and social problems. They might possibly be overcome by some large international scheme, but that, not unnaturally, is hardly likely to prove acceptable to Italians. What the world would gain if Herculaneum were laid bare as Pompeii has been, it is, of course, idle to pretend to forecast. It is usually asserted that, because Herculaneum was a fashionable resort rather than a market town like Pompeii, more under Greek influence, and therefore with a finer taste in art, as the houses which have been uncovered and the treasures which have been found seem to show, elaborate excavations would yield greater rewards even than those at Pompeii. In support of this view, it may be argued that the best Greek bronzes known to us were found at Herculaneum; against it, that they were the collection of one millionaire, and that subsequent delving was abandoned on account of the poverty of its results. Recent experience at Pompeii tends to counter the latter argument. The *Nuovi Scavi* there have triumphantly answered those writers who recently proclaimed that Pompeii had nothing more to give us, and that the commercial quarter was sure to prove barren of art. The glorious statue of a Greek boy found there this year (1926) silences that argument. We know that the inhabitants of Pompeii were able to return after the eruption and succeeded in salving much of their wealth and treasures. It is assumed, possibly on false premisses, that the inhabitants of Herculaneum did not and could not so return, and therefore that more of the priceless works of antiquity remain buried there. This may or may not be the case. I only know that if I were a government or a millionaire I should be willing to take the risk. It might even prove more profitable than, and quite as exciting as, keeping a racing stable.

The early excavators of Herculaneum were intent only upon securing treasures and works of art. When, therefore, they had burrowed in one direction, they filled up that excavation with the debris from the next. The difficulty of the conditions I have described rendered the same procedure largely necessary

VESUVIUS, FROM ST ELMO

in subsequent operations. Streets and houses, the Forum and five temples, including that of the Dea Mater, and the Villa Suburbana, now identified as the house of Piso, were thus laid bare only to be covered up again. The result is that the actual extent of the buried city which it is possible to see to-day is very small, and bears no relation to what has really been investigated. Of the original excavations, those who now descend into the bowels of the earth can only see, and that dimly, a part of the magnificent theatre, the orchestra, which, like the temple referred to, had just been erected or restored after the earthquake of 63 A.D. An inscription records that it was built by the architect Numitius, at the expense of Lucius Annius Mammianus Rufus. It was during the excavations of 1750–65 that the *Villa Suburbana* was discovered. The outer portico had twelve columns, the *peristilium* thirty-six, and the *viridarium* sixty-five. Here was found that wonderful collection of busts and statues of Greek and Roman bronzes and marbles which is now stored in the *Museo Nazionale*, and renders it unique among the precious treasure-houses in the world. For among them were the divinely graceful Mercury Resting, the Drunken Faun, Silenus sitting on a bank, the Boys Wrestling, the busts of Sappho, an Amazon, and Polycleitus' Doriphoros, besides a score of other famous busts and statues, which not to have seen and admired is to have missed one of the greatest pleasures life has to offer.

In the library of the Villa, in presses of inlaid wood, were found no fewer than 1810 papyri. They were badly charred and much injured by damp. The task of unrolling and deciphering them was one of almost insuperable difficulty. Scholars, eagerly expecting to find amongst them perhaps the poems of Sappho, or the lost books of Livy, or a new play by Terence, tried and tried in vain. At length an ingenious method was devised by the Jesuit scholar, Antonio Piaggio. By the aid of isinglass and silken threads the charred and rotten rolls were unfolded and laid out for perusal. The manuscripts are in Greek and the letters can only be distinguished from the black carbonised ground because they have left marks that shine. Some idea of the condition of the papyri will be gathered from the mistake of the first discoverers, who thought that the library was the shop of a charcoal merchant and the charred rolls his stock-in-trade! In order to facilitate the reading and interpreting of the rolls, King Charles in 1755 founded the Accademia Ercolanese, which began to publish the result of its investigations in 1793. With infinite toil and patience about one thousand of these rolls have been unrolled and read in the course of 150 years. What was the guerdon of such toil? The works of Philodemus, practically worthless as literature! No greater disappointment ever befell a patient seeker for treasure in the realms of gold. But the papyri have not been without their use. It is from them that the identification of the owner of the villa and the collector of the gallery of Greek and Roman art found therein has been deduced. For it was remembered that Cicero in his oration against Piso had referred to his patronage of Philodemus. Philodemus was a poor Greek scholar, an inferior poet, and a worse philosopher. Who but the author himself would choose to fill a library with his works and notes? Not his own library, of course, for no needy man of letters could have afforded a villa so superb and a collection of art so priceless. The villa, the collection, the library, must have been those of his patron, who gave him a home, the epicure Lucius Calpurnius Piso.

After so much preliminary discourse it seems paradoxical and disappointing to say that the best place to study Herculaneum is in many ways not at the *Scavi di Ercolano* at Resina, but at Pompeii and the *Museo Nazionale* at Naples. For at Pompeii the town is laid out before your eyes, and the streets and temples and forum and theatres, on a grander scale and in the open air, are there for you to traverse as they were for a Roman in the age of Titus; and in the *Museo* are the unique and priceless works of art which have been recovered from Herculaneum.[1]

[1] The following is a list of the chief of these with their old Museum numbers—in many cases altered or obliterated:—
Bronze statues: Diana (4886, 4888), Claudius (5593), Augustus (5595), The "Dancers" (5604-5621), Livia (5609), Tiberius (5615), Faun (5624), Mercury Resting (5625), Boys Wrestling (5626), Satyr (5628). *Bronze busts:* Copy of head of Polycleitus' Doriphoros (4885), Amazon (4889), Sappho (4896), Demosthenes (5467), Zeno (5468), Althea (5594, 5607), Seneca (erroneously so-called) (5616), Dionysus (5618), Scipio (5634), Sulla (?), (5684). *Marble statues:* Augustus (6040), Livia (6047), Claudius (6056), Titus (6059), Pallas (6007), Apollo (6261), the Muses (6250, 6378, 6394, 6395, 6398, 6399, 6404), Æschines (or Aristides), (6618), Homer (6136), Roman Magistrates and Marcus Nonius Balbus and his family (5383, 5388, 5965-70, 6104, 6168, 6211, 6242, 6244, 6246, 6248, 6249. *Marble busts:* Euripides (6114, 6155), Lysimachus (6141), Attilus Regulus (6148), A Warrior (6151), Zeno (6152), Demosthenes (6153), Juba (6154), Archidamus II. (6156), Ptolemy Soter (6158), Anacreon (6162), Vestal Virgin (6188), Cleopatra (6189), Terentius (6245), Dionysus (6270, 6272, 6308, 6317), Doriphorus (6412). The titles given to these busts and statues are in many cases the merest guesswork. *Mural paintings:* These include, besides several portraits of mythical subjects, such as Alcestis (9026), Polyphemus (8984), Theseus and the Minotaur (9043, 9049), Bacchus and Ariadne (9271), Achilles (9565) and the Infant Bacchus (9270), and of Sappho (9084), pictures of a dressing-room (9022), and a supper party (9024).

The moisture in the ground acting upon the bronze encrusted all the bronze statues and objects found at Pompeii and Herculaneum with blue and green carbonate of copper, the colour varying according to the amount of water which percolated

But do not be discouraged from visiting Herculaneum. The descent into the buried city is a strange and unforgettable, in some ways even a fearsome and thrilling experience. The abysmal darkness of the cavernous depths wherein the greater part of the ruins lie, brings home to one more vividly the sense of the city's tragic doom than do even the open, silent streets of Pompeii. Passing through an ordinary looking doorway of a house, we dive down into the bowels of the earth by flights of nearly a hundred steps. Led and lit by the candle of an intelligent custodian, we find ourselves at once in passages and corridors ranging in and about the remains of an amphitheatre once capable of seating 4000 persons, the arches and windows of which are filled with tufa. The depth of the excavations here is over 50 feet. They are dimly lighted by the remains of the shafts sunk by the Prince d'Elbœuf. Here and there are remains of frescoes, the imprints of skeletons pressed against the walls of tufa, and of a bronze statue which has been removed. Tickets issued for the theatre were found upon the steps here and are preserved in the *Museo Nazionale*. Further on are the bases of the equestrian statues of the Chief Magistrate, Marcus Nonius Balbus and his son, now in the *Museo*.

If disappointment is felt at the comparatively small extent of the subterranean excavations, it must be remembered that much of the part explored in the

through the soil. Most of them have rightly been allowed to remain as they were found, for any attempt to clean and polish them must inevitably destroy details of modelling which can never be restored in fact or imagination. Unfortunately, some of the greatest masterpieces found in the eighteenth century were not so reverently treated. They were scraped and polished and coated with varnish, producing a smooth and brilliant patina, as, for instance, in the case of the Resting Mercury and the Wrestling Boys.

eighteenth century has been covered up and reverted to modern uses, as described above.

The more recent excavations (*Scavi Nuovi*), where work is now in progress, are about 100 yards down the street leading to the sea (*Vico di Mare*). Here we find a scene much more resembling Pompeii. Being nearer to the sea the remains here were only covered by 10 metres of volcanic matter. Part of the Baths, the foundations and part of the walls of several houses intersected by three streets have been laid bare. These houses differ in some respects from those at Pompeii, and are thought therefore to have belonged to a rather different class. The richest of these dwellings is that known as the House of Argus, frescoed and colonnaded like so many that we shall see at Pompeii. In it were found the busts of Diana and Apollo, and the mural painting of Polyphemus and Galatea. In the garden of a house adjoining, a well-preserved fish-pond has recently been uncovered. This short street of ruined, roofless houses leads down to the gentle sea. But behind, beyond, towers the giant cone of Vesuvius. Is the Demon that men still think dwells therein looking down in pride upon his handiwork? Is the trail of smoke which rises into the azure sky his warning that what he has done once he can do again?

All the way from Naples to Pompeii is a long series of orchards and vineyards, with vegetables growing beneath, broken by domed oriental-looking farm-houses built of tufa, and interrupted by the dirty crowded streets of the industrial towns of Torre del Greco and Torre Annunziata, the home of coral fishers and carvers, a centre of macaroni-making. These market-gardens (*paduli*) are cropped three or four times a year, so fruitful is the soil composed of and refreshed by volcanic dust. Torre del Greco was founded by Frederick II., and took its name from the eighth watch tower erected on the sea-shore—Torre Ottava. It received its modern appellation in the sixteenth century, being called after a Greek hermit who dwelt there and introduced the vines of Lagrima. It has been destroyed thirteen times by the eruptions of Vesuvius, and thirteen times it has been rebuilt. There are now over 50,000 inhabitants, mostly coral-workers and fishermen, whose trade has been sadly affected by the after-results of the Great War. Giacomo Leopardi, the poet, lived here in 1836, in what is now the Villa Ginestra, so called after the poem he composed there. Leopardi praised its health-giving air, and, like Shelley, enjoyed the peace and solitude it then afforded. For it was on these shores, before they were built over to the present degree, that Shelley sat "upon the sands alone," and composed his glorious tribute to the beauty of the Bay:

> "The sun is warm, the sky is clear,
> The waves are dancing fast and bright,
> Blue isles and snowy mountains wear
> The purple noon's transparent might,
> The breath of the moist earth is light,
> Around its unexpanded buds;
> Like many a voice of one delight,
> The winds, the birds, the ocean floods,
> The City's voice itself is soft like Solitude's.
>
> "I see the Deep's untrampled floor
> With green and purple seaweeds strown;
> I see the waves upon the shore,
> Like light dissolved in star-showers, thrown. . . ."

Along the coast, from Resina to Pompeii, sinister waves of black lava mark the advance of the fiery tides which again and again have descended the sides of the volcano, burning and burying all before them. An earthquake in 1861 opened a cavernous fissure in the main street of Torre del Greco. It revealed a church, buried and preserved like the theatre of Herculaneum. During the eruption of 1906 the lava flowed across the line by Torre Annunziata, as the remains of devastated houses bear witness. The lava remained hot for eight months. Its advance was believed to be checked by the Madonna del Rosario, whose picture was brought from Valle di Pompeii. The miracle is commemorated by the Campanile visible from Pompeii. The pilgrimage to this shrine is now the most popular in the district.

Vesuvius is at once the smallest, the youngest, and the most famous volcano in the world. Its circumference measures about thirty miles. It rises in isolation out of the plain of the Campagna Felice. It is separated on the west from the volcanic region of the Phlegræan Fields by the little river of Sebeto; to the south its slopes run gently down to the sea; north and east it looks across to the limestone mountain ranges of Caserta, Nola and Castellamare. The Mountain, as the Neapolitans call it, is composed not of a single cone, as one might gather from many pictures taken from the Bay, but of two peaks separated by a vast semicircular depression, the *Atrio del Cavallo*. The northern peak, *Monte Somma*, is a semicircular crest, the highest point of which (*Punta del Nasone*) is 3730 feet above sea-level. The southern peak, a truncated cone with an elliptical crater, now 3890 feet high, is Vesuvius proper. The lip of the crater of Vesuvius is not a level rim, but is broken by excrescences (*Punta del Mauro*, *Punta Sant' Angelo*, *Punta del Palo*). The interior of the crater varies from time to time, rising and falling according as the materials which form the lava accumulate or are blown off in an eruption. Thus at one time it is concave like a soup-tureen, at another a cone rises from within. The cone of Vesuvius is therefore a variable heap. Sometimes it has risen above Somma, sometimes fallen below it. Though it now measures only 3890 feet, before the terrible eruption of 1906 it was 4200 feet high. Since the mild though spectacular series of eruptions which from 1913 onwards have occurred annually from January to April, the tendency has been for a cone to form within the crater, which has thereby been reduced from 323 to 87 feet in depth. During these eruptions one can collect dust in quantities in the houses in Naples, even in rooms where the doors and windows have been tightly closed. Encouraged by the pronouncement of the savants that these ebullitions of the Demon are quite harmless, and undeterred by subterranean rumblings, thousands of visitors rush to Naples to peep into the crater. Those who are not so bold enjoy the marvellous spectacle of a pillar of smoke, rising from the volcano and outspread like Pliny's pine tree, on which the flames within the crater are reflected and cast a lurid glow over the sky. Incandescent cinders, hurled into the air, traverse the heavens like comets.

Nothing gives one so clear an impression of the terrific and overwhelming nature of the eruption of A.D. 79 as the realisation of the changes which were wrought by it in the very conformation of the volcano. Martial (iv. 44) describes Vesuvius before the eruption as clad with vines and beloved of Bacchus: "Here Satyrs danced and here was Venus' bower."

Before 79 A.D. the present eruptive cone of Vesuvius did not exist, and the quiescent crater of Monte Somma —*Mons Summanus*—was only suspected by a few men of science to be an extinct volcano. Diodorus Siculus, writing in the time of Augustus and describing the journey of Hercules through the Phlegræan Fields, compares Vesuvius to Etna, and observes that it retained signs of ancient eruptions. Vitruvius, the great Augustan architect, mentions a tradition that the mountain was an extinct volcano, and Strabo, the geographer, writing about 30 B.C., describes it as consisting of a flat table-land with one truncated cone and blackened rocks which suggested that they had once been subjected to the fire of a crater, long since extinct. Strabo's description clearly indicates that before the eruption of A.D. 79 the volcano consisted of one peak, Monte Somma, and that where we now have the cone of Vesuvius and the *piane* beyond, and the gap called the *Atrio del Cavallo*, there was then one level stretch of table-land, of which but a segment remains. Or possibly the gigantic crater of Somma embraced the site of the present eruptive cone. The eruption which overwhelmed Pompeii and Herculaneum blew off one side of the wall of the crater of Monte Somma,[1] and brought into being the truncated cone which is now called Vesuvius. This is borne out by the accounts by Florus and Plutarch (*Life of Crassus*) of an incident in the Servile War. In order to train the slaves and captives who were destined to amuse the multitude at the gladiatorial games, numerous training establishments had been set up in the neighbourhood of Capua, something after the manner of that gladiatorial school which we shall see at Pompeii. In the year 73 B.C. a number of these gladiators revolted, and under the leadership of one Spartacus, a captured brigand, sought refuge on Vesuvius. They were pursued by Clodius Glaber, the Prætor, with a force of 3000 men. Joined by other desperadoes from the surrounding country, the gladiators had ensconced themselves within the walls

[1] The effect of the broken circle is best appreciated by looking at it from the Sorrento hills.

of the crater of Monte Somma. There was only one small outlet in the steep and rocky rampart, and this was promptly blocked by the Roman forces. Spartacus and his men appeared to be caught like rats in a trap. But they were trained athletes and men of resource. The slumbering crater was overgrown with a tangle of vines and other creeping plants. These they twisted into ladders, and so letting themselves down, gave the slip to their besiegers. Evidently there was but one truncated cone then in existence, the gigantic crater of Monte Somma; it was covered with vegetation, and far from being suspected of being a volcano.

The view of the surrounding country from the summit of Vesuvius is of course extraordinarily fine: but the view into the crater baffles imagination. No amount of fine writing can convey the truly awesome grandeur of the scene which is presented by the crater in its semi-active condition. Volumes of smoke drift and coil about the surface of the gigantic cauldron, parting now and again beneath a puff of wind to reveal a lurid abyss which might be a fitting entrance to the Infernal Regions; reveal it for a moment before it is blotted out and swallowed up again by the dense fumes which rise unceasingly from the boiling depths. It is a sorry soul who brings away with him only a memory of scorched boots and mouthfuls of sulphurous fumes.

After that titanic effort of the year 79, the Demon of Vesuvius seemed to have spent his force. Only two eruptions are recorded in the next four hundred years, in 203 and 472. On the latter occasion ashes were carried as far as Libya and Constantinople. Subsequent eruptions are recorded in 512, 685, 982, 993, 1036, 1049, 1139, 1306 and 1500. The twelfth eruption was that of 1631 described above. In the long interval of quiescence the volcano had become clothed again with trees and vegetation, and had resumed something of the appearance it had in the time of Spartacus. Eruptions of varying intensity took place in 1660, 1682, 1685, 1689, 1694, 1696–98, 1701, 1704–1708, 1712, 1714, 1717, 1720, 1724, 1737, 1751, 1754, 1755, 1760, 1761, 1766, 1767, 1770, 1771, 1773, 1776, 1779, 1790, 1794, 1804, 1806, 1810, 1812, 1813, 1815, 1817, 1820, 1822, 1827–31, 1834, 1835, 1839, 1841, 1845, 1861, 1862, 1868, 1871, 1872, 1906. Not all these eruptions issued from the main vent at the summit. Occasionally the discharges issued from fissures in the lava-strewn sides of the mountains. Some of these *bocche* (mouths) break out on the lower slopes of the mountain.

The eruptions of the latter half of the eighteenth century were closely observed and recorded by the British Ambassador, Sir William Hamilton, a brilliant and versatile man, whose observations as a man of science have perhaps brought him less fame than his beautiful baggage of a wife (*see* Chap. XV.). Sir William was nearly overwhelmed by an outburst from one of the *bocche* we have mentioned, whilst he was investigating, in 1767, the flow of lava in the *Atrio del Cavallo*. He escaped by running three miles down the lava-seamed mountain-side in almost total darkness, amidst the fumes of sulphur and under volleys of stones and ashes.

Of all the eruptions enumerated above, those of 1631, which we have described, of 1779, of 1794, 1872 and 1906 appear to have been the most terrible and destructive. That of 1779 was observed with great intrepidity and minutely described by Sir William Hamilton, who actually ascended the stream of molten lava up to its source near the cone by walking over the crust of stones and earth which had formed and cooled upon its surface. This eruption was rendered memorable by a great sheet of fiery particles which was vomited forth from the volcano and hung at an immense height over the Bay. Whilst streams of lava descended upon Torre del Greco, this red-hot mass of stones and ashes was blown across to the northern slopes of Monte Somma, where it fell upon Ottaiano, a town of 12,000 inhabitants, in a deluge of suffocating dust and a hail of incandescent stones, as upon Pompeii exactly seventeen hundred years before. It covered the streets to a depth of 4 feet, and suffocated many hundreds of the terrified inhabitants. Meanwhile the people of Naples, in a frenzy of terror, clamoured for the relics of St Januarius to be taken in procession to the Ponte della Maddelena, and would not be denied. For when the Archbishop at first refused, they set fire to the gates of his palace. Needless to say, Naples was once more saved by the intercession of her Guardian Saint. This procedure was repeated in 1872 and in 1906, with the same beneficent results.

In vivid contrast to the panic and superstition of the mob stand out the courage and devotion of such scientific observers as Sir William Hamilton in 1779, of Professor Palmieri in 1872, of Professor Matteucci in 1906. Seated in the Observatory on the ridge between the two valleys down which the molten lava was descending in streams that overflowed from the *Atrio del Cavallo*, Palmieri, that devoted servant of knowledge, like his successor Matteucci, stayed for months at his post, recording the indications of his instruments, sending reassuring messages to the terror-stricken multitudes in Naples, and coolly watching the marvellous phenomena of the raging volcano, coolly, though the air was thick with sulphurous fumes and the Observatory was surrounded by torrents of fire, and the very glass of the windows grew hot and cracked.

Visitors were attracted by the reports of the marvellous beauty of the spectacle. Encouraged perhaps by the immunity of the observer whose messages were

BAKER'S SHOP, POMPEII

electrifying Europe, scores arrived in carriages at the Observatory, determined to ascend to the crater. Palmieri endeavoured to prevent them. They would not listen to him, for the streams of lava were seen to be already ceasing, and the night before they had witnessed from Naples the amazing spectacle of a vast tree of fire, whose shadow was outlined by the brilliant moonshine upon the dark surface of the mountain. They pressed on to the summit. Suddenly, once more the streams of lava broke forth and dense clouds of smoke arose on every side. Once more that ominous dense cloud in the shape of a pine-tree ascended from the crater. Fascinated by the marvellous beauty and wonder of the scene, the sightseers, instead of turning back while there was yet time, pressed on to the *Atrio del Cavallo*. There indeed they beheld a sight such as the eye of man has seldom gazed upon. But suddenly there was a crash, louder than any thunder ever heard. The great cone split asunder and belched forth floods of molten lava. The trunk of the pine-tree above them shot up even higher into the midnight sky. Craters opened around them, and a deluge of red-hot stones poured forth and fell upon the unhappy sight-seers. Over a score were engulfed or seared to death. The stream of lava which thus issued forth descended the mountain at a terrific speed and overwhelmed Massa and Sebastiano, but stopped just short of Naples and, on the other side, of Resina.

It was Ottaiano again and San Giuseppe and Bosco-Trecase which were devastated by the disastrous outburst of 1906. As by a miracle the streams of lava on that occasion stopped short of Torre Annunziata and Portici. A rain of mud and ashes fell incessantly upon the surrounding districts, whilst for many miles the country was covered with grit and yellow dust, and the vegetation of the smiling lands of the *paesi ridenti* was scorched and ruined. It is calculated that 315,000 tons of volcanic debris fell in Naples alone! An eye-witness has described the terrible onward march of the streams of burning lava which broke from the crater on 5th April and made their way relentlessly towards Bosco-Trecase, whilst hundreds of thousands of refugees fled in terror to

Naples or the seashore. "Onlookers at a distance could perceive the walls of houses bulging outward under pressure of the moving mass, until the roof collapsed in an avalanche of tiles upon the ground, whilst with a final crash the whole structure—cottage, farm, church or stately villa—succumbed to the overwhelming weight."[1]

With memories of such scenes of horror and destruction one descends the scarred sides of the volcano, gazing half-incredulously at the creeping vines and smiling gardens which are once more hiding the recent wounds inflicted by the Demon's last outburst of rage. Looking across the Bay from Naples on our return, we see, far away in the eastern twilight, the smouldering cone of Vesuvius, a crimson spot in the gathering darkness, glaring like a Cyclop's eye, bloodshot and menacing. When next? What next? *Quien sabe?* Let us at least visit Pompeii before it suffers another burial beneath the dust and ashes of another eruption.

[1] H. M. Vaughan, *The Naples Riviera.*

CHAPTER VIII

Pompeii, the City of the Dead

> "I stood within the City disinterred,
> And heard the autumnal leaves like light footfalls
> Of spirits passing through the streets; and heard
> The Mountain's slumberous voice at intervals
> Thrill through those roofless halls . . .
> Around me gleamed many a bright sepulchre
> Of whose pure beauty, Time, as if his pleasure
> Were to spare Death, had never made erasure;
> But every living lineament was clear
> As in the sculptor's thought. . . ."
>
> SHELLEY, *Ode to Naples.*

"Those disinterred remains of an ancient City, which, more perhaps than either the delicious breeze or the cloudless sun, the violet valleys and orange groves of the South, attract the traveller to Naples."

"Pompeii was the miniature of the civilisation of that age. Within the narrow compass of its walls was contained, as it were, a specimen of every gift which luxury offered to power. In its minute but glittering shops, its tiny palaces, its baths, its forum, its theatre, its circus—in the energy yet corruption, in the refinement yet the vice, of its people, you behold a model of the whole Empire. It was a toy, a plaything, a show-box, in which the gods seemed pleased to keep the representation of the great monarchy of earth, and which they afterwards hid from time, to give to the wonder of posterity; the moral of the maxim, that under the sun there is nothing new."

LYTTON, *Last Days of Pompeii*, ch. ii.

[From the Stazione Centrale at Naples the train takes us to the Porta Marina at Pompeii, which is the best starting-point for the visitor, and is nearest to the Hotels. The station on the

Mus. Naz.] *Alinari*

MERCURY RESTING

Pompeii

Ferrovia Circumvesuviana is close to the Porta di Nola. Pompeii is open to visitors from 9 to 4.30. Entrance, 8 lire. Sundays free, but the buildings are closed. Visitors are not allowed to take cameras or sandwiches, etc., into the town. Litters can be hired for viewing the ruins. A *permesso* obtainable at the *Museo Nazionale* is required for visiting the New Excavations (*Scavi Nuovi*).]

SIR WALTER SCOTT, standing amidst the ruins of Pompeii, could only murmur again and again, "A City of the Dead! A City of the Dead!" The thought was just, and the phrase has become a commonplace. But to me the marvel of Pompeii is that it yet lives, and that the life of the inhabitants, so suddenly and tragically arrested eighteen hundred odd years ago, seems to persist in the worn but silent streets laid bare by the archæologists. By their labours the whole world of Roman provincial life has been outspread before our eyes. Pompeii suffered the same fate as Herculaneum. But, unlike Herculaneum, its fascination lies not in the horror of its doom, but in the miracle of its preservation. Pompeii preserved is the whole Classical Dictionary come to life. It is Gallus illustrated, Horace explained, Petronius edited, Martial made clear, Juvenal justified!

Unquestionably one of the wonders of the world, Pompeii is in many ways the most amazing. However well one may be acquainted with the ruins of Pompeii by study of history, archæology and fiction, however familiar they may seem from paintings and photographs, the first day spent among them is certain to fill one with astonishment and delight at the size of the uncovered city, its curiosities, its romantic aspect, its lovely surroundings, and the vivid realisation of a life that is gone.

One has a notion, perhaps, of the Forum, of a

gateway, a street of ruined shops, or of a rich man's house filled with treasures and all the luxurious trappings of a bygone age. But no one, I think, can imagine, until he has seen it, the size and effect of the ruins as they now stand revealed. Ruins indeed they are, so far as roofs and porticoes are concerned—but ruins of a whole city, whereof street after street stretches from gateway to gateway, and can yet be traversed as on that fatal August day in the year A.D. 79. Temple after temple, house after house, baths, theatres, barracks, brothels, and all the public buildings of the market-place and municipal life stand in orderly array, open to the eye and the understanding of the visitor to-day, as to the citizens of over eighteen hundred years ago. And nothing else. No crowding in of mediæval streets and walls and towers, however picturesque; no superimposition of later phases of civilisation as at Rome or Nîmes; no distracting note of Renaissance buildings, however beautiful; no jarring accompaniment of modern life. Nothing but the ghosts of A.D. 79, the streets they trod, the houses in which they dwelt, the lives they lived there.

Restorations and care now lavished on the place render it perhaps a little too spick and span, and impart to it a little too much of the atmosphere of a self-conscious show place. But this, after all, though it may detract slightly from the romance of the ruins, has, like the labelling of the streets, rather added to the interest of them. The streets have been named after the heads of gods, etc., found upon the public fountains at the corners, as, for instance, Vico di Mercurio, or from adjacent buildings, Vicolo dei Teatri, etc. The names given to several of the houses are for the most part entirely fanciful and quite without authority. We would not, for all that, wish

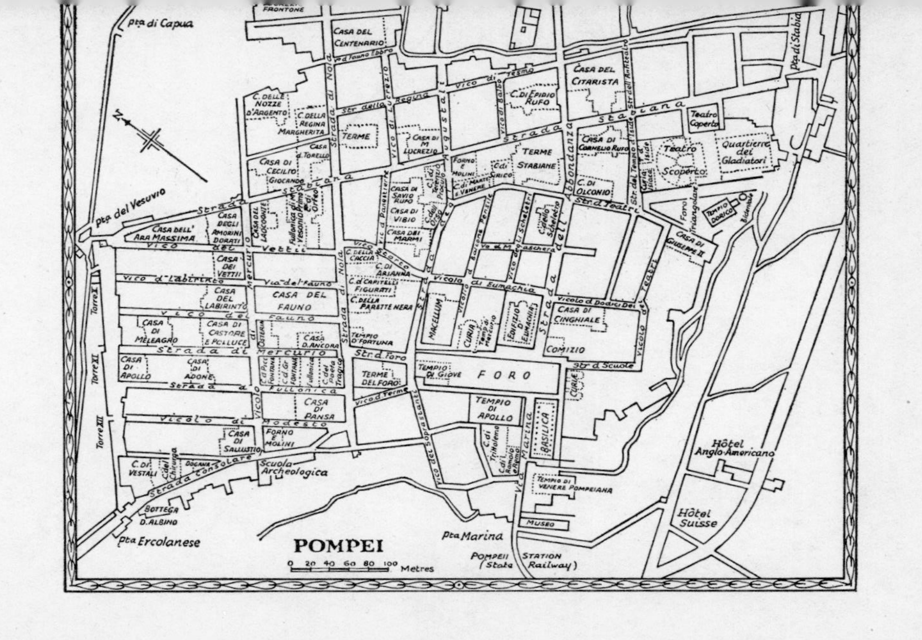
POMPEI
0 20 40 60 80 100 Metres
Pta di Capua
Pta del Vesuvio
Pta Ercolanese
Pta Marina
Pta di Stabia
Casa del Centenario
Casa del Citarista
C. di Epidio Rufo
C. delle Nozze d'Argento
C. della Regina Margherita
Terme
Casa di M Lucrezio
Casa di Cornelio Rufo
Teatro Coperto
Quartierre dei Gladiatori
Teatro Scoperto
Terme Stabiane
C. di Olconio
Casa di Cecilio Giocando
Casa del Laocoonte
Casa di Savio Rufo
Casa di Vibio
Casa dei Marmi
Casa dell' Ara Massima
Casa degli Amorini Dorati
Casa dei Vettii
C. della Caccia
C. di Arianna
C. d. Capitelli Figurati
C. della Parette Nera
Casa del Labirinto
Casa del Fauno
Casa di Meleagro
Casa di Castore e Polluce
Casa d. Ancora
Tempio d'Fortuna
Macellum
Curia
Edifizio d. Eumachia
Casa di Cinghiale
Comizio
Casa di Giuseppe II
Tempio Dorico
Foro Triangolare
Casa di Apollo
Casa di Adone
Terme del Foro
Tempio di Giove
FORO
Curie
Casa di Pansa
Tempio di Apollo
Basilica
Casa di Sallustio
Forno e Molini
C. di Vestali
Scuola Archeologica
Bottega d. Albino
Tempio di Venere Pompeiana
Museo
Hôtel Anglo-Americano
Hôtel Suisse
Pompeii Station (State Railway)
Torre X
Torre XI
Torre XII
Strada Stabiana
Strada di Nola
Strada dell' Abbondanza
Strada di Mercurio
Strada d. Fullonica
Strada Consolare
Vicolo di Eumachia
Vico dei Soprastanti
Via Marina
Str. d. Foro
Str. d. Teatri
Vicolo dei Teatri
Vico d. Labirinto
Via del Fauno
Vicolo di Modesto

to do away with them. For they introduce a touch of mingled actuality and romance singularly in keeping with the general atmosphere of the place.

Though Pompeii is now separated from the sea by nearly two miles, we must think of it during its life as a prosperous port at the mouth of the river Sarno. The course of the river was changed by the great eruption of Vesuvius, and has undergone further alteration in modern times.

The city owed part of its prosperity to sea-borne commerce, and part to the produce of a rich soil, which included wine and olives, as well as millstones and pumice which betrayed their volcanic origin. The Sarno then was navigable as far as Nola and Nuceria (Nocera). Many a ship laden with a cargo of Eastern wares or Egyptian corn passed through the Pompeian harbour to those cities, returning with the rich produce of the Campania. Some indeed derive the name of the place from the Greek word πεμπω —send—as indicating its character of seaport and emporium. Tradition, which ascribed its foundation like that of Herculaneum to Hercules, referred the meaning of the word to his herding of the oxen of Geryon. Others find its origin in the Oscan word for five, *pompe*. Though destined to be wiped out in a day the growth of the city extended over many centuries. Strabo is probably correct in saying that it was founded by the native Oscans. This primitive community was civilised, if not absorbed, by the Hellenic adventurers who, as we have seen (Chap. II.), made this shore their own some time within a thousand years before Christ. The standing monument of that civilisation is the massive Doric Temple (sixth century B.C.) in the Triangular Forum. This is the site of the original settlement. Pompeii was built upon a wave of lava which had flowed from Vesuvius in some prehistoric eruption, and this earliest part of it was set upon its southern extremity, upon a platform which projects like a promontory into the plain. It was a site admirably chosen for defence and superb as a viewpoint.

August Mau, to whom more than to any other man, our knowledge and understanding of Pompeii are owed, has classified the monuments of the city according to the material used in their composition. The Doric Temple is by far the most ancient building in Pompeii. To the first period also belong the oldest parts of the walls, of which there is a fine example outside the Stabian Gate (*Porta di Stabia*), a column, a cistern in a house (*Reg.*, IV. 14, 19), and the so-called House of the Surgeon (*Reg.*, VI. 1, 10), to which we shall refer later. These, the most ancient buildings, were constructed without mortar of huge blocks of hard limestone brought from the Sarno district and used up till the second century B.C. In the following era—the Greco-Samnite period—blocks of volcanic tufa were employed, smoothed over with a light covering of stucco. This period, to which the Temples of Apollo, the portico of the Forum, the great Theatre in the Triangular Forum, and the Stabian Baths belong, was followed by that of the Roman occupation (Little Theatre, Amphitheatre, Temple of Jupiter, Baths of the Forum, etc.), a period of comparative decadence, which was succeeded by hurried and inferior rebuilding after the earthquake of A.D. 63. Under the Romans *opus reticulatum* and travertine were used, and marble was introduced, as in the Temple of Fortune.

When the Samnites conquered Campania (*see* Chap. II.), Pompeii was occupied by them. It shared their fate when they, in turn, were subdued by the Romans. In the course of that struggle Livy mentions that the Romans landed in the vicinity (309 B.C.), attacking Pompeii as a member of the League of Nuceria. The town waxed in strength and importance. In the Social War (91–89 B.C.), when the allied nations of Central Italy rose against Rome, Pompeii was one of the last cities of Campania to be reduced. It endured a long siege by Sulla, who finally succeeded in overcoming it by delivering an assault upon the weakest point, in the direction of the Herculanean Gate. He subsequently settled one of his military colonies here (80 B.C.), with the object of holding and repeopling the countryside. He called it after the names of his family and guardian deity, Colonia Cornelia Veneria Pompeianorum.

That Pompeii was able to make so long and gallant a resistance to the army of Sulla was due to the strength of her fortifications. They were afterwards dismantled by the Romans and left in the state in which we see them to-day. But when Sulla laid siege to the city, it was defended by double walls, six metres apart, the intervening space being filled with stones covered with earth. Both walls were supported by buttresses; the outer one was crenelated, and the inner was higher than the outer. The lower parts of these walls were very old, being composed of huge blocks of Sarnian stone; the upper portions, built of tufa, were more recent. The ramparts were reached by towers, disposed at irregular intervals, of which we know that there were a dozen or more. For directions in the Oscan tongue were painted upon the walls to guide the defending troops to their stations, and one of them mentions the twelfth tower (near the Herculanean Gate). In these towers, which were three stories high and projected slightly beyond the walls, were postern gates through which sorties might be made. There were eight gates, named in Italian the Porta Marina (south-west), Porta di Stabia, Porta di Nola (north-east), Porta del Vesuvio, Porta Ercolanese, Porta di Nocera, Porta di Sarno, and Porta di Capua. The first five have been excavated. The first three are the least altered and best preserved. The Porta Marina, by which we shall presently enter the town, underwent some modifications at the hands of the Romans. But the Stabian Gate is very much as it was when the Samnites had restored the fortifications during the Social War, very much as Sulla saw it when he sat down to besiege the place.

The prosperity of Pompeii continued unchecked under the Roman occupation. For, a few years later, we find Cicero in his great speech on the Agrarian Law, referring to it as one of those rich and well-built towns of Campania which put the poor cities of Latium to shame. But a change from Oscan and Greco-Samnite to Roman forms of civilisation had already begun, and this change proceeded more rapidly after the settling of the Sullan Colony. Indications of it are to be found not only in the incised (*graffiti*) and painted inscriptions which bear witness to alterations both in language and forms of government, but also in the medium of exchange. There is a *tabula ponderaria*, of travertine, in the Forum (No. 31), which contains nine measures of capacity. The Oscan inscriptions have been erased. This shows how the Roman standard of weights and measures supplanted that of the local Oscan system. There is also a later inscription preserved, in which the *duoviri* record their work in this direction, 14 B.C. (C.I.L., X. 793). The surviving Oscan inscriptions date from the third and second centuries B.C. down to the Christian era. But the Oscan dialect gradually gave way to the Latin language. Whilst, however, the Imperial tongue became the recognised medium of official circles and polite society, the older native dialect persisted as the speech of the country folk and the market-place. Thus by the last century before Christ we find inscriptions to the same effect in both languages, showing that it was necessary to appeal in Oscan to a class of voters who had no Latin.[1]

So, too, with the forms of administration. Hitherto there had been one chief magistrate, a Quæstor, such as V. Popidius, who built the colonnades in the Forum. But the municipal administration was now placed here as elsewhere in the hands of two magistrates, *duoviri jure dicundo*, a typically Roman form of institution, and two ædiles, with a city council of aldermen (*decuriones*).

Pompeii now became a favourite resort of rich Romans. Cicero, for instance, had a villa here, a villa to which he often refers in his letters, and where he wrote his *De Officiis*. The population increased with its prosperity, and may have reached a total of 20,000 before it was overwhelmed by the eruption of Vesuvius. In the year A.D. 59 an event occurred which is of very little importance in itself, but which has acquired a curious subsequent interest. The magnificent amphitheatre, of which the imposing remains are now visible, had become the scene of frequent and famous gladiatorial shows. Sight-seers from neighbouring towns crowded into the city, just as modern enthusiasts invade the scene of a Football Cup Final. Upon one such occasion a tumult arose in which the citizens of Pompeii came to blows with a multitude of visitors from Nuceria. There was a fierce fight and many were killed or wounded. The sufferers from Nuceria, "their bodies mutilated by wounds and many lamenting the death of parents or children," as Tacitus puts it, appealed for justice to

[1] See *Italic Dialects*, R. S. Conway.

Rome. The Senate decreed that as a punishment for this violence, no theatrical exhibitions or public performances should take place at Pompeii for ten years. This incident is recorded both by Tacitus (*Annals*, XIV. 17), and by a rude mural painting in one of the houses which the excavators have revealed. Four years later (A.D. 63) Tacitus records that "an earthquake demolished a large part of Pompeii, a populous town in Campania" (*Annals*, XV. 22). Most of the public buildings were severely damaged. The citizens, however, at once set about rebuilding them, and many of those we now see were in course of reconstruction when the whole city was overwhelmed and buried in the final catastrophe.

A very striking instance of such interrupted work will be found in the Temple of Venus, on the right of the Via Marina within the Porta Marina. There the blocks of stone ready hewn, and some of them already sculptured, lie ready to be set in place upon the existing foundations just as the masons left them. The fragments chipped by their chisels are still scattered about. So living is the scene that you can hardly believe that the workmen have not just gone away for their dinner hour. You look over your shoulder, half expecting to see them returning.

The great volcano to the north had long lain quiescent. So long that none could suspect the hidden danger by which the inhabitants of the city a mile from its foot were daily and hourly threatened. So long, that the sides of the mountain were clad in verdure, and gardens and vineyards stretched up to the very rim of the ancient crater, which was itself overgrown with wild vine and eglantine. On the green slopes beneath it farms and villas of wealthy Romans were dotted about in smiling beauty. For though Pompeii was built upon an eminence of lava deposited in some former age, the period of quiescence reached back beyond the memory of man.

On 24th August, A.D. 79, the citizens were as usual immersed in their daily occupations and pursuits. It was a holiday, and for a while the busy hum of the chaffering in the market-place was still. Here and there, no doubt, a shopkeeper was busy making up his accounts,[1] a politician putting the finishing touches to an election address, or a lover inditing verses to his lady; yet for the most part the streets were empty and the shops were closed. For a great gladiatorial show was being given in the amphitheatre, and everybody had flocked to see it, perhaps to back his favourite gladiator or to see one die. Suddenly the sleeping volcano woke to life. Monte Somma broke into violent eruption, and the terrible scene began which has been depicted in such brilliant colours and with such imaginative force by the author of *The Last Days of Pompeii*. Scared by the growing gloom and oppressive atmosphere caused by the cloud of smoke which was rising from the mountain top, the sightseers began to leave the theatre. But showers of ashes began to fall fast and faster, and a hail of red-hot stones fell in torrents upon the streets. The panic-stricken inhabitants fled to their houses or the temples, to seek shelter from the terrors of the air, or to seize or to guard their treasures. Some, clutching their jewels or their money-bags, endeavoured to make their way to the Herculanean Gate and to find safety on the shore, only to meet death upon the threshold from the burning hail or falling buildings. Some

[1] In the house of a banker, M. Cæcilius Jucundus, was found a box filled with written tablets—diptychs and triptychs—containing his accounts as well as lifelike bronze busts of the owner (*Mus. Naz.*). "Posters" inviting the votes of electors were found scratched and painted around the Forum, etc.

found their way into the streets and losing their way, or trampled by the rushing mob, lay down to die. Many, reaching the shore, were overwhelmed there. For darker and darker spread the cloud above them. " It was a sudden and more ghastly Night rushing upon the realm of Noon." Others, creeping into the cellars of their houses for protection, were choked by sulphurous fumes that issued from the earth, and by the accumulation of the fine volcanic dust, hot and asphyxiating, which penetrated through every chink and buried them as they died. So some two thousand are thought to have perished, and the skeletons of many—pathetically contorted or sleeping peacefully—were found in the circumstances I have described some seventeen hundred years later.

In the house known as the Villa of Diomedes eighteen skeletons of adults and children were found in a wine cellar, all in sitting postures, and blackened places on the walls still mark their shapes and show their attitudes, like shadows. One of them, a woman, still wore upon her skeleton throat a necklace, with her name engraved upon it. Near the garden door lay the skeleton of the owner of the house, with a large key in one hand and ten gold pieces clutched in the other. Beside him lay a slave who was carrying a bag of money and valuables. They had started for the street, but the fiery tempest caught and overwhelmed them. In the *Museo* (the first building on the right within the Porta Marina) several skeletons are preserved. One, that of a woman, has her hands spread wide apart as if in mortal terror ; another, that of a young girl, shows that she was trying to protect herself with her cloak against the showers of burning ashes. Several lie with their faces on their arms and scarves drawn across their mouths, as if trying to shield themselves from the enveloping dust and cinders.

There is the agonised skeleton of a dog which had been left chained to its kennel. When the visitation was overpast, the survivors returned to find their homes buried beneath a mass of dust, ashes and stones varying from three to five metres. There was some talk of rebuilding the city, but it came to nothing. The survivors dug amongst the debris and carried off what treasures they could retrieve. Later, some of the marble and material was used for building new houses at Cività near by. Some Hebrew fugitive on the night of that dreadful catastrophe scratched upon the walls of a house (*Reg.*, IX., *Ins.*, I., No. 26) the words, " Sodom, Gomorrah." And, indeed, to any one familiar with the Hebrew scriptures, the fate of these cities must have suggested an apt parallel for the doom which had overtaken the gay and luxurious town of Pompeii.

The question whether there were any Christians at Pompeii is one which will always be asked. Probably there were. For, as we have seen, there was a congregation at Pozzuoli when St Paul landed there ten years before. It is believed that the word " Christianus " has been deciphered among the writings on the walls. But if Christians were there, we could hardly expect them to advertise their existence thus. The impious refusal of the new sect to observe the rites due to the gods of Rome, and their disgusting method of burial, compared with the cleanly Roman system of cremation, long hallowed by custom, combined with their gloomy prophecies and denunciations to render them highly obnoxious to the Roman crowd and rulers alike. Victims were always required for the games; and it seemed a good answer to their impiety to raise the cry, " *Christiani ad leones* "—the Christians to the lions—and to set a light in the arena to their tortured bodies, " butchered to make a Roman holiday." In the warning "*Tœda lucebis in illa*" there lurked the threat that the victim would be baulked of the consolation of the new form of Christian burial.

Pompeii, like Herculaneum, sank into oblivion. At length, in 1594, a new aqueduct from the Sarno to Torre Annunziata was begun. Tunnelling through the site of Pompeii the architect and engineer, Domenico Fontana, came upon some ruins and inscriptions. But it was not till 1748 that the discovery of some statues and objects of value prompted King Charles III. to give orders for excavations on a large scale. Though conducted in a haphazard fashion, they soon revealed some of the riches of the place, including the Amphitheatre, the Street of Tombs, the Triangular Forum, the Temple of Isis and the two theatres. The work was continued under the French by Joseph Bonaparte and Murat. But it was not until 1860 that it was undertaken in a scientific manner and in accordance with a well-thought-out plan. Professor Fiorelli was then appointed by the Italian Government to conduct operations which have been worthily pursued by his successors, Professors Ruggiero de Petra, Sogliano, Spinazzola, and now Mauri. The bust of Fiorelli set up in the Forum overlooks the work by which he gained the gratitude of the civilised world.

In earlier days the excavations at Pompeii were conducted upon the reverse of scientific lines. The main object was not to reveal the buried city, but to find objects of art and—too often—to trade in them. An amusing skit upon that point is to be found in Dumas' *Le Corricolo*. Even when found, statues and such-like were dealt with haphazard, and more or less according to the whim of the finder. Genuine antiques were disfigured by crude "restorations," and antiques that were not genuine were, it is to be feared, foisted upon a confiding and eager public. Of such a sort were the remains of that Roman sentry, steadfast under death, the legend of whose heroism still haunts the Herculanean Gate. Skulls were found. Helmets were found. A skull was found to fit a helmet, and thrust into it, and some lively and romantic soul breathed life once again into those dead bones in the form of a legend, which one can only wish were true. It lives on the lips of the guides as well as in the pages of *The Last Days of Pompeii*, and, fitly enough, of the *Innocents Abroad*. Only the other day I heard it described by an American visitor as the most imposing thing at Pompeii. And so in a sense it is.

The fleeing crowds, it is said, rushing through the gate of Herculaneum, passed by a Roman sentry standing livid but immovable at the post of duty. True to his duty, for no word of release had come for him, true to the proud name and stern discipline of a soldier of Rome, and " full of the stern courage which had given to that name its glory, he stood erect and unflinching, till the hell that raged around him burned out the dauntless spirit it could not conquer." This is, at least, what a Roman Legionary would have done. The story, if not true in fact, is certainly *ben trovato*.

Before entering the streets of Pompeii, it is important, in order to appreciate the significance of the rows and rows of ruined houses to be seen there, to realise the general scheme of domestic architecture which prevailed in this Greco-Roman town. Facing the street were usually two small shops (*tabernæ*), such as you may see in any Eastern bazaar, in which commodities for sale were exposed by tradesmen, or, in the case of a private house of wealthy folk, the produce of the farm. The narrow entrance (*vesti-*

bulum) which divided these two " shop windows," was sometimes paved with mosaic, displaying perhaps the image of a watch-dog and the warning *Cave Canem*, typical of the semi-Eastern privacy which the Romans maintained in their homes. This feature is emphasised by the absence of any windows opening upon the street. The shops were closed by shutters or sliding doors like the *bassi* in Naples to-day. Beyond the entrance was a corridor (*fauces*), which led into the hall or courtyard (*atrium*), where a slave was always in attendance as hall porter. On either side of this courtyard were bedchambers and storerooms. In the centre of the tessellated pavement of the *atrium* was a square reservoir (*impluvium*) for catching rain water, which was admitted by an opening in the roof (*compluvium*). This opening could if desired be closed by an awning. Close to the *impluvium* stood the images of the household gods (*penates*), and a movable brazier, or little tabernacle in the shape of a miniature temple represented the household hearth consecrated to the Lares. A huge wooden chest, bound with bronze or iron, and securely fastened to a stone pedestal, usually stood in the courtyard, and formed the family " chest," or treasury. The *atrium* was not always exactly of the same pattern. There was the *atrium tuscanicum*, as, for instance, in the House of Lucretius Fronto, the roof of which was supported by two cross beams. There was the *atrium tetrastylum*, as in the houses of the Labyrinth and Silver Wedding, in which the *compluvium* was carried by four columns at the corners of the *impluvium*. More rarely, the *atrium Corinthium*, with many columns, as in the Houses of Castor and Pollux and Epidius Rufus. Lastly, there is the *atrium testudinatum*, in which, as in the House of the Centenario, there is no opening in the roof at all.

POMPEII

At the far end of the hall, to right and left, were the *alæ* and *cellæ*, small rooms used for various purposes, and, opposite to the main entrance, the *tablinum*. This was the chief living room, parlour and dining-room in the more or less primitive type of Italic house, which ended here. But under the influence of Greek civilisation this simple design had been developed and amplified. The *tablinum*, now as a rule richly decorated with mural paintings and tessellated pavement, was converted into a sort of study or muniment room, in which were kept the family archives. The room on the right-hand side of it was used as a sort of pantry or storehouse (*apotheca*), with a passage outside it giving access to the parts of the house beyond. On the left a room was now set apart for dining, the *triclinium*, which might be closed by sliding doors or curtains of Tyrian purple. Beyond it was the kitchen (*culina*). These rooms all opened upon another contribution of Greek civilisation, a very beautiful and characteristic one. This was the *peristylium*, a square or oblong colonnade, which added a second courtyard to the dwelling, and thus converted its ground-plan into a rectangle. This Hellenic addition was by no means universal, and the old Italic design lasted on right into Imperial times. There are many examples of the latter in Pompeii, but for the most part the houses have the charming addition of the peristyle, some, as, for instance, the House of the Faun, even two. Surrounded by the colonnade of the peristyle was a garden (*viridarium*), with vases set upon pedestals for flowers, as is shown in the House of the Vettii or Loreius Tiburtinus. Within the colonnade doors led to bedrooms, a second *triclinium*, the library, the kitchen, and offices, and rooms for guests (*æci*, *exedræ*). From the peristyle a back door (*posticum*) gave access to the further street. The upper stories, of which there might be one or two, were occupied by slaves. They were reached by small flights of steps, either inside or, as is frequently the case in old farm buildings in the north of England, outside.

It strikes one at once that the houses and the rooms were small, even after making allowances for the fact that an unroofed house or room always looks smaller than it is. It must be remembered that the inhabitants lived largely out of doors, in the Forum, the theatre and the baths, and visitors were received in the hall or the peristyle, whilst partakers of their feasts, however sumptuous, seldom exceeded nine in number.

The Roman epicure knew no restraint in eating and drinking. He knew nothing of the Greek ideal of temperance and moderation. But he preferred to select his companions for their wit, their palates, their capacity, or their vices, and not to dine in a casual crowd of acquaintances. Of their habitual excess at their banquets there is one eloquent indication in a dining-room which has recently been excavated at Pompeii. It is a *vomitorium*, whither the *gourmand* might retire to relieve himself with the aid of outraged nature, or by swallowing an emetic, of the delicacies he had consumed, in order to return to feast afresh—*reculer pour mieux sauter*.

If the rooms in general seem small, the bedrooms are Lilliputian. They are mere pigeon-holes or alcoves in the wall, with a space for the bed surrounded by a dais. The inhabitants of Pompeii, to judge from the accommodation in their bedrooms and in the houses of ill-fame, must have been of much smaller stature than the average European of to-day. The couches upon which they rested were narrow and portable, so that the members of a household could easily move their beds from place to place in the house in order to find a spot suitable for the season.

It is at once obvious that the houses at Pompeii, like those of modern Italy, were built for coolness and shade. The more northern races place first the consideration of catching every ray of sunlight and the means of warmth. These objects were secured by the Pompeians in their colonnades and gardens, where they could enjoy a sun-bath at almost any time of the year, protected from the cold winds. And it must be remembered that the snow often lies low upon Vesuvius as late as March, and that the winds off the surrounding snow-clad heights can blow exceedingly cold throughout the winter and spring. But cold was endured stoically by the ancient as by the modern Romans. It was against the oppressive heat and dazzling glare of the sun in the summer solstice that they wished to guard themselves. The architecture of the round arch and the portico, the low dome and the heavy tiled roof, is therefore their natural medium. They constructed their rooms like their houses, for coolness and shade. To guard against the danger of the Evil Eye (*see* Chap. I.) they hoisted the sign of the phallus, painted, carved, or worked in mosaic, outside the threshold, or painted upon the exterior of the walls the device of two serpents (*e.g.* in the *Vico del Lupanare*).

Water was brought by an aqueduct from the mountains and stored in reservoirs (*castelli*) raised on columns, whence it was distributed to the public fountains, baths and private houses by means of leaden pipes. The fountains were adorned with heads of gods, goddesses, or wild animals. The streets were lit by the lamps hung from the shops, and the public altars dedicated to the guardian gods of the city.

The streets were paved with large blocks of lava, with high raised pavements for pedestrians on either side. Where vehicular traffic was permitted—it was forbidden in the Forum and the Street of Abundance, for instance, where chains to prevent it were drawn across the entrances—deep ruts have been worn by the passage of thousands of chariots and carts. Rings in the walls of the houses were provided for tying up the horses and mules. In the centre of the roadways large circular stepping stones were placed for foot passengers who wished to cross dry-shod. Romans who did not wish to walk were carried in litters. Those visitors to-day who are not strong on their feet will find it very advisable to avail themselves of the same method of progression.

As might be expected in an important commercial and harbour town, the number of inns (*hospitia*) and taverns (*cauponæ*) and bars (*thermopolia*) was large, and stables were provided near the main gates (VI. i. 2–4; II. vii. 6–12). One of the inns, the House of Sittius (IV. i. 45), displayed the sign of an elephant. The guests frequently scratched their names, or sentiments, or their opinions of the fare upon the walls. One complains that the innkeeper serves water to them and drinks the wine himself. Or, again, the innkeeper displays a tariff of his wines, from which we gather that Falernian was four times more expensive than the *vin ordinaire*. The best example of a tavern is in the *Via del Mercurio* (IV. x. 1). Here warm drinks kept in terra-cotta vases were sold from a marble counter, and an array of bottles and glasses on the shelves above suggests a roaring trade. In a small room at the back of the counter, where clients were regaled, is a very interesting series of wall paintings depicting a variety of scenes from the ordinary life of a drinking shop. Clients are shown drinking and calling for drinks, quarrelling and playing games, whilst the succulent viands provided by mine host are represented above in the form of hams, sausages, etc. There were many bakers' shops, in some of the ovens

THE FORUM, POMPEII

of which loaves of bread were found, stamped with the baker's name. Among the chief industries of the place were those of the tanners (I. v. 2.) and fullers. The latter were a very important guild. A series of paintings taken from the fullery in the *Via del Mercurio* (VI. viii. 20), and now in the *Museo Nazionale*, shows them in the exercise of their craft.

At Pompeii the walls in the majority of the rooms we have described were decorated with paintings. Many interesting and beautiful specimens of these mural paintings are to be studied in the *Museo Nazionale* at Naples, and have been reproduced in colour by a new process by Messrs Alinari (*Via Calabritto*). The designs are sometimes beautiful, sometimes crude; the colours very vivid, mainly yellow, black and red.

The number of well-built and decorated houses, the size and number of the baths, theatres, and gladiatorial quarters all point to the high prosperity of the little provincial town. The wealth which poured into the coffers of the Pompeian merchants from their sea-borne commerce and the handling of the wine and agricultural produce of the rich surrounding country, was spent upon the pleasures of love and feasting, of baths and shows, and upon the adornment of their houses and their city. We shall see how some wealthy citizens, like Holconius Rufus, lavished their money upon the buildings of their native town. The large place which love and feasting took in the lives of the majority of citizens is sufficiently indicated by the character of the paintings upon their walls. It is true that perhaps three-quarters of the nearly three thousand mural decorations which have been discovered, portrayed mythological subjects. They represent the gods and legends of the heroic age. That is to say, they dealt with the accepted and universal religion of the Greek and Roman world, into which the disturbing message of Christianity had scarcely begun to penetrate. But of all the myths and legends connected with the doings of their gods and heroes, which were the common religious knowledge of all the pagan world, it is noticeable that those chosen by the Pompeians for the decoration of their houses, their dining-rooms, their bedrooms, their peri-styles, were in a very high proportion those which dealt with their love-affairs. Again and again we are shown Jupiter, the King of Heaven, in pursuit of Danæ, or Leda, or Ganymede, or Europa ; again and again Apollo is portrayed in pursuit of Daphne. Venus falls perpetually into the arms of Mars or Adonis. And in most cases there is an accompanying chorus of delicious little Loves at work or play, Eros suggesting, Eros dancing, Eros fishing, or Eros at the vintage ; Eros driving a pair of swans or a team of lions, or Eros assisting his mistress at her toilette, or revealing the beautiful Endymion to Diana, or urging Paris or another to the lists of Love. These *amorini* abound on the frescoed walls of Pompeii as in the canvasses of Boucher or Watteau. Indeed, there is a strong eighteenth-century flavour in some of the Pompeian art. Look, for instance, upon that delicious little scene known as the Seller of Cupids, in which an old woman is offering for sale a little Love, which she has taken from a cage and is holding by the wings, to a young lady who, though she already has one upon her knees, is either ready to exchange it, or has not yet made up her mind which she will buy. Has it not all the charm and all the delicate suggestion of a world of gaiety and artificiality and outworn creeds which one finds in Pope's *Rape of the Lock* ?

It is fair to deduce from all this, not only how subtly the old religion accommodated itself to the tastes and pleasures of succeeding epochs, but also what those tastes and pleasures were. In the society of a small, rich and leisured provincial town, little concerned with the great business of ruling the Roman Empire, those pleasures were the Baths, the Circus, Love and Art, for Literature had little part in it. Even in the dwellings of cultivated Romans, the library—that "soul of a house" as Cicero defined it—was furnished with but a few rolls of parchment stuck on a shelf. Such a collection as that found at Herculaneum was quite a rarity, and is accounted for by the exceptional circumstance we have indicated (*see* Chap. VII.).

Love, then, was the subject which the artists chose knowingly with which to decorate their patrons' walls, love scenes drawn from the history of their gods, which might serve to excuse and idealise their pleasures, or merely to stimulate their desires.

Several periods have been traced in the decorations of the houses of Pompeii. In the pre-Roman period there was no painting. At first Greek artists encrusted the walls with stucco in imitation of marble. Figures only appear in mosaic work, as in the House of Sallust or in the House of the Faun. Under the Republic, painting begins to be applied to the stucco, and this form of decoration is developed under the Empire. The choice and treatment of subjects passes from formal architectural designs to the representation of mythological personages and scenery, and finally to fantastic landscape painting and imaginative treatment of details of daily life. In the first of these latter stages open rooms were adorned with backgrounds, columns and pediments, and corridors with landscapes, and the pictures were always copies of real objects. Under the fashion for fantastic decoration grotesque devices were introduced, when, as Vitruvius scornfully observes, reeds took the place of columns and streamered ornaments the place of pediments;

diminutive temples were supported on candelabra, and vegetable shapes sprang from tops of pediments whence issued meaningless figures and grotesque shapes of men or beasts.

With regard to the paintings of well-known mythological subjects, Helbig (*Untersuchungen über die Campanische Wandmälerei*) suggested that the pictures at Pompeii were copied from famous works of the Alexandrine school, modified and selected, no doubt, by the artist of the day. If this is the case, some of the more famous ones have an increased interest, for they may be copies, however inferior, of some of the great masterpieces of Greek art. The Perseus and Andromeda and the Io of Nicias, for instance, may have inspired similar subjects at Pompeii, and the Medea of Timomachus the Pompeian treatment of Medea about to slay her children. But whether they copied or not, the painters whose work we see to-day on the walls of Pompeii, at the House of the Vettii or in the *Museo Nazionale* at Naples, were not mere imitators. If they repeated a subject, they varied it; they could paint scenes from real life with truth and vigour; and they worked with an ease and grace and sureness of touch which give to their paintings that element of individuality and freshness and charm which remind us that Flora may be painted, but is reborn each year. They were not, of course, all of the same calibre. The difference, indeed, not only in technique but also in spirit, between some of the highly idealised and graceful scenes of domestic life, and the coarse realism of others depicting incidents in gladiatorial circles, or the lowest haunts of the town, is so marked, that some would attribute the former to Greek artists and the latter to Italian natives.

In the closing period, from the reign of Augustus

to the last days, these paintings have a further interest. For the delicious and graceful little Cupids and Psyches which adorn, for instance, the dining-room of the Vettii are portrayed as busily employed in the arts and crafts of Pompeian merchants and mechanics. They appear as makers and merchants of wine and oil, or as goldsmiths and fullers and so forth. Sharing in their airy and impish and delicate way in all the pursuits of a Roman provincial town, they seem to breathe life into the deserted city and to give back to it the inhabitants it has lost.

The other late form of decoration was the use of the painter's art for scenic effects. The garden walls were tinted, and trees and birds and temples painted upon them, in order to produce a deceptive appearance of size. According to Pliny, it was in the time of Augustus that one Ludius introduced the craze for decorating the flat wall surfaces of houses in this fashion. He describes with enthusiasm the style he brought into vogue:

> "Villas, colonnades, examples of landscape gardening, woods and sacred groves, reservoirs, straits, rivers, coasts—all according to the heart's desire; and amidst them passengers of all kinds on foot, in boats, driving in carriages or riding on asses to visit their country properties; furthermore, fishermen, bird-catchers, hunters, vintagers; or, again, he exhibits stately villas to which the approach is through a swamp, with men staggering under the weight of the frightened women whom they have bargained to carry on their shoulders; and many another excellent and entertaining device of the same kind. The same artist also set the fashion of painting views—and that wonderfully cheap—of seaside towns in broad daylight."

Artificial and scenic painting of this kind was eagerly welcomed. Vitruvius might denounce it as a decadent and meretricious form of art. But it was popular because it had the advantage of lending to the tiny rooms and miniature courts of Roman dwellings a deceptive appearance of grandeur and spaciousness. It will be noticed that, both here and at Herculaneum, the walls were divided horizontally by a bright band of colour, separating a darkly painted dado below from an upper half of lighter shade. Painted vertical stripes took the place of the pilasters of the earlier style, and divided the space into panels with red, black, yellow or white backgrounds whereon the pictures were painted.

The walls of Pompeian dwellings are eloquent in yet another way. "The moving finger writes"—inscriptions. They take two forms. The first are painted and could be washed out and replaced. They are of a more or less official character, recommendations of candidates for municipal elections, notices of public events or advertisements of forthcoming displays in theatre or amphitheatre. Secondly, there are the *graffiti*, as they are called, inscriptions scratched upon the walls as the mood seized the writer. Thus children inscribed their jokes; lovers, as they do to-day, the names of their mistresses, and messages or verses of devotion or reproach. Some of these amatory poets could turn a line as neatly as Tibullus. "*Ah! peream, sine te si deus esse velim*," writes one who had no desire to live in Paradise alone. Some are elaborate and charming in sentiment, others coarse or upbraiding, in the spirit of Catullus but without his genius.

Enthusiasts of the games scratched upon the walls the names of the gladiators of their choice; amateurs of literature the verses of their favourite poet, Vergil, Propertius, or a Greek tragedian; patriot or politician recorded the debt which the Roman world owed to Augustus—*Augusto feliciter!*—a debt which Pompeii had been the first to acknowledge by establishing there his cult as a deity. Sermons in stone, voices of the ghosts that flit by us in the silent streets, these messages from the departed fill the city with the murmurings of the dead. It is one more of those peculiarities which make this dead and ancient city seem so modern, so alive.

Whilst, then, a connoisseur like Calpurnius Piso was bringing down from Rome a shipload of Greek bronzes to adorn his villa at Herculaneum, provincial magnates at places like Capua or Pompeii followed the prevailing fashion, and adorned their dining-rooms and peristyles with works by Greek artists, or copies of works approved by the best judges as the greatest masterpieces of antiquity. Cassius the Vintner set up in the centre of his *atrium* a miniature bronze statue of a Dancing Faun, which is one of the sheerly perfect achievements of art. Balbus the Fuller, dwelling in the Street of Abundance, his coffers filled with sesterces honestly accumulated by cleaning the white togas of distinguished clients, and looking for some way to spend it and at the same time to distinguish himself from the ruck, purchased a bronze statue of a youthful Greek athlete. Or did he, possibly, accept the thing with a grimace in quittance of a bad debt, as mine host of the Crown and Thorns had frequently to do when one David Cox happened to be his guest? Who knows? Certainly he was not a man of real taste, fit to have possession of such a thing. For the tradesman in him insisted that he must turn it to some use. And the lovely lad, Pantarkes perhaps, Victor in the Boys' Games at Athens in 436 B.C., and immortalised in bronze by the hand of Phidias himself, Pantarkes offering with outstretched hand, in a gesture eloquent of all the charm and modesty of youth, a sprig of the laurel with which he had been crowned to the deity of his choice, Pantarkes must now be converted by the Roman merchant into a mere lampstand, holding a heavy bronze candelabrum in his hand, which would be forever a crime against his pose and balance. Well, Vesuvius interposed. That statue, placed in the fore-court of the merchant's house, awaiting to be converted into a candlestick (a *lichnoporos*), was suddenly, in the twinkling of an eye, covered by the ashes of the volcano as snow buries a mountain village. It was unearthed this very year (1926). Let us thank Heaven that these things were. Through Roman copies and a few rare originals, Greek art has been preserved to us in a way which defeated the vandalism of a thousand years, and in spite of Goths, Vandals and Turks, fills the rooms of the *Museo Nazionale*.

It gives one a curious sensation of contrast to pass from teeming, noisy, odoriferous Naples to the silent, empty streets of Pompeii, swept and garnished now, and fragrant with the untainted air of sea and mountain. You walk along the narrow pavements, worn by the tread of countless feet, calling at shop after shop. But the tradesmen are gone, the chafferers are silent, " home have gone and ta'en their wages." The ovens of the bake-houses are cold, and the jars that were once filled with wine and oil and fruit and vegetables are now empty or broken.

The old scheme of laying out a town was to construct an enceinte of wall and vallum, and then to draw across it two streets cutting one another at right angles. The first, running from north to south, was called *Cardo*, the second, from east to west, *Decumanus*. From these streets others might branch off, more or less at right angles. The Via di Stabia, running from the Porta del Vesuvio (north) to the Porta di Stabia (south), was the *Cardo* of Pompeii; the Via di Nola, ending in the Porta di Nola (east), the *Decumanus Major*. The Via della Marina, Via dell' Abondanza

DYER'S WORKS, POMPEII

and Via dei Diadumeni mark the line of a *Decumanus Minor*, which was slightly deflected by the construction of the Basilica and the new Forum. Smaller, subsidiary parallel streets divided the town into blocks or islands (*insulæ*) of houses in the several quarters (*regiones*), now numbered from I. to VI. The houses in the streets are numbered, and for purposes of reference are described thus: I. (*region*), ii. (*insula*), 3 (*number*).

Ascending a steep incline under the Porta Marina, partly reconstructed by the Romans, whereon a statue of Minerva guarded the seaward approach to the city, you enter the Via Marina and find the *Museo* on your right. Here, besides those skeletons we have mentioned, are preserved many relics of the domestic life at Pompeii, household utensils and articles of food. There is also a model of the Roman villa discovered at Boscoreale in 1907. Beyond it, on the same side, is what is thought to be the *Temple of Venus Pompeiana*, to which we have already referred (excavated in 1899). It will be remembered that Sulla, when he gave his own name to his new colony, added to it that of Venus, the goddess, whom he recognised as his guardian saint and protectress. Venus was not only the mother of Æneas, but also, therefore, through him the ancestress of the Roman race. *Venus physica Pompeiana* became, then, the patron deity of the city. The site of her temple was chosen near and in sight of the sea, as befitted the goddess who rose from the waves. Her image occurs frequently in the mural paintings and altars of the city, and her name in the vows and prayers of the citizens scratched upon the walls. In her was worshipped the principle of prosperity and increase, and in this local habitation of her delicious divinity was practised the cult of the universal goddess of love and fecundity.

Next to this temple are the remains of a spacious *Basilica* of the Greek type, dating from the end of the second century B.C., as one may infer from the mural paintings and the tufa employed in its construction. It was badly damaged by the earthquake. The central nave is enclosed by thirty Ionic columns of brick encased in stucco; the outer walls have engaged Corinthian columns, and are covered with stucco in imitation of marble. At the west end is a raised tribunal for the judges, for the Basilica was used both as a meeting-place and a Hall of Justice. Five portals, separated by four rectangular piers, opened into vestibules at either end, and communicated with the Colonnade of the Forum. Opposite the northern door of the Basilica, and on the other side of the Via Marina, is the *Temple of Apollo*, identified by attributes of the god in the shape of an Omphalos, painted tripod, and a sun-dial, as well as by an Oscan inscription. The temple, which dated from the best Greco-Samnite period, and was partly reconstructed after the earthquake of 63, stood in the centre of a large court surrounded by a portico. This colonnade consisted of forty-eight fluted columns with Ionic capitals and triglyphs, made of tufa covered with stucco, with a Doric entablature. After the earthquake these were converted into the Corinthian style by the application of stucco, which has now fallen off. The walls were painted with scenes of the *Iliad*, some traces of which remain. Several statues were found here, Apollo playing the lyre, probably an original Greek bronze, Venus, Hermaphroditus (son of Venus and Mercury), Diana (sister of Apollo), Minerva, and Mercury and his mother, Maia (*Museo Nazionale*, copies in site). An altar stood before the figures of Venus and Diana. The Temple, raised on a lofty *podium* surrounded by Corinthian columns, is approached by a flight of thirteen steps, before which stands a large sacrificial altar of travertine, with names of the donors inscribed. Within the *cella* the wall is covered with stucco encrusted to imitate marble—the earliest type of mural decoration—and is built of Sarnian stone. An Oscan inscription on the pavement mentions Oppius Campanius, the Quæstor. An Ionic marble column at the side carried a sun-dial given by the *duumviri*, Sepumius Sandilianus and Herennius Epidiamus.

The Basilica and the Temple of Apollo were two of the many important public buildings surrounding the *Forum*, into which we now enter. The original market-place of the old town lay between the Via della Marina and the Via delle Scuole. In the second century B.C. the city was enlarged and the Basilica built upon part of the western end of the old market-place. At the same time a more spacious Forum in the Greek style was laid out, rectangular in shape. The Samnite Quæstor, Vibius Pompidius, surrounded it with a colonnade, a fragment of which remains in the south-east corner. Fluted columns of tufa, with Doric capitals, carried an architrave adorned with triglyphs. To this colonnade the Romans added a second, of the same height, but more massive, which carried an upper story. This gallery was reached by small staircases for spectators of the gladiatorial games, which were held here before the amphitheatre was built. The space beneath was filled with shops. Alterations made by the Romans included an extension northwards for their temple for the deities of the Capitol, Jupiter, Juno and Minerva. They also began to fill the Forum, like that of Rome, with statues of people of importance. Twenty-two of the pedestals remain. One of them was of that important citizen and benefactor to the town, M. Holconius

Rufus, five times *duumvir*; others of Marcellus and Sulla. Statues of emperors, from Augustus to Vespasian, stood upon the great pedestals at the southern extremity of the Forum.

The scene, even now, is extraordinarily beautiful and impressive. For looking north, the long bare stretch of pavement and broken walls and columns terminating in the ruins of the Temple of Jupiter has for background the peaks and saddle-back of Vesuvius, whilst through the blue haze to the south are the sea, Capri and the mountains of Sorrento. How brilliant and impressive must it have been when that Temple of the Capitoline Jupiter rose in all the splendour of its Ionic and Corinthian columns complete as Sulla's veterans built it! A bas-relief in the house of the banker, L. Cæcilius Jucundus, shows us what it was like before the earthquake. The flight of fifteen steps which led up to the *pronaos* and the *cella* beyond was flanked on either side by equestrian statues. The centre of the lower part of the steps is cut into by a platform of masonry on which stood an altar. Within, the stucco of the walls is painted in imitation of marble, but not encrusted, an example of the second period of mural decoration described above. At the back of the *cella* are three rooms for the priests and the Temple treasure. On either side of the Temple was a triumphal arch. That on the west side remains. The foundations of the other are visible. Behind it was erected a later arch which carried an equestrian statue of Tiberius, and in niches statues of Nero and Drusus (*Museo Nazionale*). This arch forms an entrance to the Forum by way of the Via del Foro, which borders the Baths of the Forum (*Terme del Foro*, IV., v.), perhaps the finest building of the Roman period in Pompeii. It was built in the time of Sulla, and is very well preserved.

THE TEMPLE OF APOLLO, POMPEII

Its most remarkable feature is the *tepidarium* (warm bath), which served as an undressing room for those about to use the adjacent *caldarium* (hot bath). The low round vaulting of this *tepidarium*, with stucco designs in high relief, is carried by a row of splendid Atlases. It is massive, ponderous, efficient as the Romans themselves. Adjoining the Temple of Apollo on the western side of the Forum is (No. 31) the table of standard measures referred to above, a public lavatory, and a building that may have been a public granary. On the opposite side of the Forum, in the north-east corner of it, is the *Macellum*, or provision market, which had a very beautiful marble colonnade and was entered between a row of shops, supposed, from the many coins found there, to have been occupied by money-changers. The walls of an interior colonnade were decorated with frescoes, now sadly damaged, representing Medea helping to slay her children, Io guarded by Argus, Ulysses before Penelope recognised him, and birds, fish, fruits, etc. In the centre of the two-storied market-place, which is surrounded by shops, was a dome supported by twelve columns covering a tank where fish were cleaned. At the back of the market is a chapel dedicated to the cult of the Imperial family, Augustus, Octavia, Marcellus, etc., and on either side of it a banqueting hall and another room.

Next to the *Macellum* is a temple of the Imperial epoch, called the *Temple of the Public Lares*, with a marble colonnade in front (No. 3). Adjoining it (No. 2) is an unfinished *Temple of Vespasian*, with an altar in the courtyard adorned with bas-reliefs of a bull being sacrificed and a civic crown between two branches of laurel, a symbol of the Imperial house revived on the coins of Vespasian. Next comes the *Building of Eumachia*, as to the purpose of which there is much guess-work but no certainty. Inscriptions over the entrances state that Eumachia, public priestess, built at her own expense the vestibule (*chalcidium*), covered corridor (*cryptam*), and colonnade, and dedicated them to *Concordia Augusta and Pietas*. The building is of brick and tufa. Four niches outside the vestibule carried statues of Æneas, Romulus, Julius Cæsar and Augustus. The original inscription of the first remains. The doorway had a very fine marble frieze (*Museo Nazionale*, No. 6788). A statue of this gracious lady (*Museo Nazionale*, No. 6232) was erected by the Corporation of Fullers, with whom the building in question probably, therefore, had some connection.

Across the Via dell' Abondanza is an old building of Sarnian stone, supposed to have been the *Comitium*, where municipal elections were held. Close to it, and forming the southern end of the Forum, facing the Temple of Jupiter, are the ruins of a large building containing three large halls, the *Curia*, devoted to municipal administration. We have thus completed the circuit of the Forum, and a cursory survey of the buildings which surrounded it. For it must be understood that I am passing over an infinite mass of interesting archæological details. A study of the wall paintings in the houses of Pompeii and in the *Museo Nazionale* will enable one to form a very close idea both of the costumes and of the occupations of the busy crowds or groups of idlers who daily thronged the Forum, meeting for business, pleasure, worship or gossip, or to read the municipal notices painted up on the " albums " on the colonnade.

We now pass down the Vico delle Scuole, visiting some underground excavations where are the skeletons of some domestic animals—a horse, dog, cock, etc. —and so come to a *Palæstra* of the Roman era (II., ii.

23). This school for training athletes is elaborately equipped with baths, dining-halls, and dressing-rooms. The walls are covered with mosaics and paintings representing robust and rather brutal athletes using the strigil, boxers fighting, and so forth. Further on, following the Vico della Regina, at the corner of the *Foro Triangulare* (II., vii. 29), is a *Palæstra* of the Greco-Samnite period, for the training of youths. It has a graceful Doric colonnade, where the splendid copy of Polycleitus' Dorophorus, now in the *Museo Nazionale*, was found. It was appropriately placed here, for it represented the Greek ideal of the athletic physique. At the end of the Vico delle Scuole we find ourselves on the edge of an eminence overlooking the ruins of some houses, roofless, gaping to the skies. Beyond the plain below, the blue sea laps the promontory of Sorrento; in front of us is Mons Lactarius and the mountains behind Castellamare. On our left is the amphitheatre of Pompeii, the line of the new excavations, and, beyond them, the dome and campanile of the village of Valle di Pompei.

A graceful portico of fluted columns with Ionic capitals gives access to two gates which open upon the *Triangular Forum*. This is the most ancient part of Pompeii, and in many ways the most fascinating. A Doric colonnade extended along the sides of the triangle formed by that promontory of lava which was selected as obviously suitable for defence by the earliest founders of Pompeii. Twenty-eight out of (?) ninety-five exist. Across the base of the triangle and screening the ancient ramparts are the substructure and fragments of a Doric temple of the sixth century B.C. It had eleven columns on each side, and seven at each end, and was dedicated to Apollo and Artemis, as the remains of an adjacent sun-dial on a semicircular seat help one to conclude. The site of this temple reminds us at once of that of the Temple of Neptune at Pæstum. Both are striking examples of the skill with which the Greeks, those supreme artists, posed their buildings so as to harmonise with the beauty and formation of the surrounding scenery. As in Sicily, so here, they made their buildings a part of the landscape, and utilised Nature to enhance the loveliness of art.

As at Pæstum, the priest who stood within the *cella* looked forth upon the divinely beautiful glens among the chain of mountains which hide Sorrento and Castellamare. On the other side is Vesuvius. But there was probably more in the choice of the site than the view which the Temple commanded. It was also a site visible from afar, a beacon for mariners approaching over the sea, a sign of refuge and sure harbourage, and a call to worship the gods and goddesses who granted to adventurers fair voyages. More than that, perhaps. For I should be greatly surprised if some day an intelligent archæologist with a sufficient knowledge of astronomy were not able to demonstrate that, as in the case of the stone circles of Keswick and Stonehenge, for instance, the position was chosen with a view to observing and recording the movements of the sun and stars and so fixing the times and seasons of farming operations. One remembers that Apollo Helios was the Sun-God, and the God of Prophecy, and that sun-dials are found in his temples, for whose priests, therefore, unsuspected sources of knowledge were invaluable. In front of the steps leading up to the Temple, where the sacrificial altar usually stood, are the ruins of a curious rectangular enclosure surrounded by two walls, the outer one of which was built or reconstructed in the first century A.D. From the importance of its position before the Temple, it is thought to have been the Tomb of the Founder or Founders of the City.

Further back is a deep well, sunk through the layers of lava, which was covered with a dome carried by eight Doric columns, without bases, by the Samnite Quæstor, M. Trebius.

On the eastern side of this Forum a large uncovered theatre (*Teatro Scoperto*) of the Greek pattern was constructed some time before the second century B.C. The seats in shape of a horseshoe, which supplied accommodation for 5000 persons, were cut out of the lava rock upon which the Temple stands. The adjacent colonnade provided a delightful promenade for the theatre-goers.

The seats were covered with marble and other improvements made in the time of Augustus by the brothers Holconius Rufus and Celer, as an inscription in bronze gratefully acknowledged. The original level of the stage was that of the barracks of the gladiators beyond and below. The wall at the back of the stage (*scena*) of Roman brick, intended to be covered with marble, represented the façade of a palace. The green room is behind. Remains of the devices for spreading an awning over the spectators and sprinkling the air with cooling showers are clearly visible above the auditorium. The name of the Roman architect who restored the theatre is preserved in an inscription, M. Artorius Primus.

A little covered theatre or Odeum (*Teatro Coperto*) at the south-east corner of the great theatre was used as a concert room. It was built soon after the town fell into Sulla's hands, for inscriptions record that the design and construction were approved by M. Porcius and C. Quinctius Vulgus, the *duumviri* who presently built the amphitheatre at their own expense. Another inscription tells us that the marble pavement of the orchestra was presented by M. Oculatus Verus in celebration of his election as a *duumvir*.

Both theatres were connected with the colonnade of the Foro Triangolare, and another colonnade of seventy-four Doric columns surrounding a rectangular court. The latter was subsequently converted into barracks for the gladiators, for whom two rows of cells were constructed in the interior. Many of their weapons, fetters and sixty-three skeletons were found here.

Whilst the Little Theatre was devoted to music and the Great Theatre to the presentation of plays and mimes, it was in the arena of the amphitheatre that the gladiators fought among themselves or with wild beasts.[1] The amphitheatre was begun in A.D. 70, two years before the Colosseum at Rome. It was built outside the walls, and could hold 20,000 spectators. The present approach to it is now through the district of the New Excavations,[2] across the Via Stabiana. The vast elliptical structure of this, the most ancient of the amphitheatres known to us, is wonderfully preserved. Copies of paintings of gladiatorial fights found on the walls are preserved in the *Museo Nazionale*.

Returning to the entrance of the Foro Triangolare the Strada d'Iside on the right takes us to the *Temple of Isis* (II., vii. 28), and beyond it, to the little *Temple of Zeus Meilichios*.

In spite of the efforts of Augustus, who endeavoured to exclude foreign cults, the worship of Isis, the Egyptian goddess, had established itself alongside the old Roman religion. "We have received Isis," says

[1] On this subject, *see The Story of Rome* by N. Young in the Mediæval Town Series, pp. 41-49.

[2] In the business or industrial quarter. A special permit is necessary to view the Nuovi Scavi, obtainable at the *Museo Nazionale*. By a scheme of careful preservation and rebuilding it is being endeavoured to reconstruct a street in Pompeii as it actually was.

a poet of Nero's time, "into our Roman temples." Domitian, indeed, whilst discouraging other oriental cults, himself built a temple to Isis and Serapis. It was natural that Pompeii, which was in such close touch with Alexandria and the trade of the East, should have been among the first to welcome the mysterious deity, sister and wife of Osiris. Starting life as a corn-goddess, not unlike Demeter, her attributes had been spiritualised in the course of ages, and she was worshipped as the type of the true wife and tender mother who gave promise of Immortality to her worshippers as the mother of the infant Horus. Thus chastened and transfigured, the serene figure of Isis appealed to the more spiritually minded far beyond her native land. If her secret rites were often abused by those of the baser sort, her stately ritual, "with its shaven and tonsured priests, its matins and vespers, its tinkling music, its baptism and aspersions of holy water, its solemn processions and its jewelled images of the Mother of God," was conducted as a rule with solemnity and decorum, and gave balm to many a weary spirit, whilst in her later character as a marine deity she was worshipped as the Stella Maris by tempest-tossed sailors.[1] Something of the exquisite beauty and refinement, as well as the mystery, which attached to this cult and appealed irresistibly, in spite of persecution, to the more sensitive and spiritually minded of the Roman people from the last days of the Republic onwards, may be gathered by a study of the relics and paintings collected from the Temple before us and now preserved in the *Sala d'Iside* at the *Museo Nazionale*.

Herculaneum and Pompeii had temples dedicated to Isis before that cult was introduced to Rome in the time of Sulla. The ruins before us, however, are

[1] Sir James Frazer, *The Golden Bough*.

only those of a temple which was built after the earthquake had destroyed the previous one. It was built, as an inscription over the entrance gate informs us, by Numerius Popidius Celsinus, aged six, whose liberality was rewarded by his being inscribed by the Decuriones in their order of the Town Council. Which means that it was built by his father, a rich freedman, who thus obtained for his son the honour which could not be accorded to himself as a liberated slave. The father and mother presented the Temple with a statue of Bacchus (=Osiris), and a mosaic pavement.

The Temple was surrounded by a Doric colonnade, the columns of which were made of brick covered with stucco, fluted and painted red. On entering it, the worshipper beheld before him statues of Isis and Osiris in front of the *cella*. On the north side was the exquisitely carved statue of Isis, in a short-sleeved tunic and carrying the rattle and other symbols, which is now in the *Museo Nazionale*; and opposite to her on the south side, the lovely Venus, half draped in blue, who is coiling her hair as she emerges from her bath. The walls of the colonnade were painted with symbols of the cult. There were six altars. On the principal one, at the foot of the steps leading up to the *pronaos*, were found the remains of the last sacrifice. Close to this altar is a small rectangular building with a decorated staircase leading down into a subterranean chamber, possibly used for ablutions and purifications, and for storing the holy water of the Nile. Against the wall at the back of the Temple, where are the priests' dwellings, a staircase led up to the *cella* through a door by which, it is thought, the priest passed under the altar and made responses to the faithful, in the name of the Deity.

Other rooms served for the celebration of nocturnal mysteries and scenes of initiation in which, under the direction of the priests, the novice put off the old life and was born again to the new.

Fontana's aqueduct passed under this temple. For the harmony of its design, and the restrained grace of its artistic details, and the simple efficiency of its arrangement, this little Temple of Isis is a typical monument of the Greek genius for adapting a building to the purpose for which it was made and to the exigencies of its site.

Skeletons were found here and in the neighbouring street of many of the priests of Isis, overwhelmed as they fled with the treasures and statues of the Temple.

Beyond the Temple of Zeus Meilichios the Via di Stabia runs right and left. In the angle formed by the intersection of the Via dell' Abondanza and the Via di Stabia (left) are the Stabian Baths (*Terme Stabiane*) (III., i. 28), and beyond, on the right, where the Via di Nola crosses the Via di Stabia, the Central Baths (*Terme Centrali*, III., iv.). The part which the Public Baths played in the life of the citizens of Pompeii has been so brilliantly described and imagined by the author of *The Last Days of Pompeii* that there is no need to add anything here except that the first—the largest and best preserved—is an enlargement of a Samnite building of the second century B.C., and the second was in course of construction at the time of the catastrophe. The former, with its frescoed colonnade and bowling green, its baths for men and women, its dressing-room (*apodyterium*), its rooms for cold, tepid, and hot baths (*frigidarium*, *tepidarium*, *caldarium*), and its palæstra, dining-room, and private baths, gives one a marvellously complete idea of the luxurious bathing establishments of the Roman era.

We are now in that quarter which the day before the final disaster was, one may well imagine, the scene of such glowing and vivacious excitement as Lytton has described :—

"The gay shops, their open interiors radiant with the gaudy yet harmonious colours of frescoes, inconceivably varied in fancy and design. The sparkling fountains, that at every vista threw upwards their grateful spray in the summer air: the crowd of passengers, or rather loiterers, mostly clad in robes of the Tyrian dye; the gay groups collected round each more attractive shop; the slaves passing to and fro with buckets of bronze, cast in the most graceful shapes, and borne upon their heads; the country girls stationed at frequent intervals with baskets of blushing fruit and flowers . . .; the numerous haunts which fulfilled with that idle people the office of cafés and clubs at this day; the shops, where on shelves of marble were ranged the vases of wine and oil, and before whose thresholds, seats, protected from the sun by a purple awning, invited the weary to rest and the indolent to lounge."

Nobody but an expert will wish to look at every one of these ruined houses and to ascertain in what details one differs from the rest. Nobody but a dazed tourist in the clutches of a merciless guide will endure to be told what fancy name has been given to each and what work of art was found in each and is now at Naples. A clearer appreciation will be gained by concentrating upon the examination of a few in the light of what has been said above. The *House of the Surgeon* (*Casa del Chirurgo*, VI., i. 10, where surgical instruments were found), in the *Strada Consolare*, and the more elaborate *House of Sallust* close by, are of the earlier type. The former, by its severe simplicity and the massive blocks of Sarnian stone of which it is built, evidently dates from the earliest times of the Samnite occupation, before the influence of Greek civilisation had introduced the peristyle and all the other charming novelties to the old simple Latin life. The *House of Sallust* (VI., ii. 4) belongs to the beginning of the period when tufa had displaced limestone.

It is a stepping-stone in style to the magnificence of the *House of the Faun* (*Via del Fauno*, VI., xii. 2), with its twofold atria and Ionic peristyles. Built when Greek taste had become paramount, it formed a worthy setting for that most lovely and rhythmical bronze statuette, the Dancing Faun, which was found near the impluvium. On the pavement in front of the house is the salutation, *Have!* (Welcome!), and in the red-columned *exedra* was a magnificent mosaic depicting Alexander at the Battle of Issus (*Museo Nazionale*), marvellous for its use of material in representing a complicated battle-scene, and for the emotional expression conveyed in the faces of Darius and the other combatants.

The *House of the Tragic Poet* (*del Poeta Tragico*, VI., viii. 5), with its *Cave Canem* on the threshold, and many important pictures of a graver sort than is usual at Pompeii, is to be remembered as the dwelling of Glaucus in *The Last Days of Pompeii*.

The *Houses of the Silver Wedding and Lucretius Fronto* are instructive as showing on a larger scale of intelligent reconstruction the form and style of a Roman mansion. Here, however, as elsewhere, practically all works of art of first-rate importance, including statues, bronzes, and frescoes, have been removed to the *Museo Nazionale*. This, no doubt, is a sound policy both from the point of view of safety and also for opportunity of study. But it would be a good thing if, when the originals are removed, copies could be replaced in their approximate positions, as has been done in the case of the Dancing Faun. The *House of Fronto* (V., iv.) dates from the Empire. The magnificent *Casa delle nozze d'argento* (V., ii., the House of the Silver Wedding, so called from the visit of the King and Queen of Italy on the twenty-fifth anniversary of their wedding) is a palatial dwelling of the tufa or pre-Roman period. It is notable for rich decorations, its beautiful garden, its atrium, tetrastylum, and Corinthian dining-room. The house next to it, *Casa del cenacolo*, is notable for the loggia over the atrium. The *Casa degli amorini dorati* (VI., xvi. 7), a splendid mansion, is remarkable for the irregularity of its construction, its garden, paintings and magnificent peristyle with Doric columns (restored). Curious, too, is the little private chapel in the corner of the front colonnade devoted to the cult of Isis.

The *House of the Vettii* (*Casa dei Vettii*, VI., xv. 1), supposed to have belonged to two freedmen of that name, is the most famous of those of the later period (first century A.D.), both on account of the state of preservation and because the wall paintings are of singular charm and variety. Some, indeed, of the latter are in inferior taste, and are probably the work of inferior artists employed after the earthquake. Others are evidently the works of true artists who knew how to harmonise colours and to follow the designs of ancient masterpieces. Enchanting are the pictures of Cupids and Psyches and *amorini* playing or racing or practising the arts and crafts of the day, and forming a light and effective contrast to the more serious scenes from Greek mythology in the panel pictures. See particularly those, in black and vermilion, chiefly on the walls of the Tuscan atrium, the triclinium on the left, and the *Sala dipinta*, probably a banquet room, adjoining the north-west corner of the large peristyle.

Charming and instructive, too, is the gay peristyle, with its tinted stucco pillars. It is a trifle over-ornate, no doubt, but convincing in its atmosphere of art ministering to leisure. The shaded colonnade surrounds a charming garden, and is itself an art gallery. Statues, vases, basins of bronze or porphyry, marble chairs, and tripod tables are set amidst the flowers or beneath the portico, whilst bronze urchins holding ducks pour jets of cooling water within the garden. The garden itself has been replanted with the very flowers that grew there when Titus was Emperor, identified from the pictures on the walls. It may be compared with the garden in the House of Loreius Tiburtinus in the new excavations.

From the town one passes out through the Herculanean Gate to the Street of Tombs (*Strada dei Sepolchri*), and the " suburban " villas of those wealthy Romans who preferred to live outside the walls, and to the uniquely precious Villa of the Mysteries.[1]

The law of Rome forbade burial within the city walls. The result was that the roads leading from the city, and indeed the whole surrounding country, were lined with tombs, as we see on the Via Appia and Via Latina. So here, without the walls, we pass into a street where the ashes of the inhabitants of Pompeii were laid when they had entered upon their last sleep in the night that knows no ending. On the left are the re-covered excavations of a villa supposed to have been Cicero's, and, beyond, at the end of a series of tombs and columbaria, the famous Villa of Diomedes mentioned above. It is a serene and beautiful spot, where heaven-pointing cypresses wave above the broken monuments and the eternal mountains stand on guard.

A quarter of a mile farther on is the wonderful *Villa of the Mysteries*, in which a series of twenty-four wall-paintings has at last revealed, to some extent at least, the riddle of the Orphic Mysteries. Their celebration was forbidden by a decree of the Senate,

[1] A *permesso* to view the *Casa dei misteri* must first be obtained from the office of the Director of the Excavations at the corner of the Strada del Foro.

owing to certain scandals which had arisen in connection with the initiation of women in Campania. It is perhaps for that reason that they were held without the walls in a villa partly converted to these purposes. The theory of the ceremony—said to have been introduced by Orpheus—was that the neophyte, through sacrifice and mystical communion with the god Dionysos, should pass through the incidents of his life, should be joined to and die with him, descend into hell and rise again to a new life, purified by passion and chastisement. A series of preliminary ceremonies culminated in the final scene at the *epopheia*, in the supreme vision which has been revealed for the first time by the paintings on these walls. They show us a neophyte, a woman, passing through the final stages of her initiation. Attended by priests and priestesses and Silenus, the pedagogue of Dionysos, she is first shown donning the veil of a bride. The ritual is read to her, and she partakes of the holy supper (*agape*). A kid, representing the child Dionysos, is shown being suckled. The magical mirror—connected with the story of Dionysos as with that of Vergil—is shown as a source of divination to the neophyte, who prepares for her union with the Deity, and is chastised with rods. Finally she emerges, nude and dancing in a Bacchic frenzy, the bride and devotee of Dionysos.

Before and after seeing Pompeii, a visit to the *Museo Nazionale* is imperative. There the rooms filled with mural paintings and the room of the little bronzes, with their wealth of decorative and domestic objects, enable one to fill in the details of the picture of the daily life and surroundings of the inhabitants of the Dead City.

CHAPTER IX

Goths, Lombards, Normans and Hohenstaufen

Naples besieged by Belisarius—and by Totila—Goths defeated by Narses—Naples resists the Lombards—Held for the Empire by Dukes and Bishops—Basilicas—S. Giorgio Maggiore—Dukes and Saracens—Naples and the Normans—Robert Guiscard and King Roger—The Kingdoms of Naples and Sicily—Barbarossa, Henry VI. and Tancred—Naples and Frederick II.—Guelfs and Ghibellines—Popes bring Charles of Anjou into Italy—He is crowned King of Sicily—Defeat of Manfred—Conradin defeated at Tagliacozzo—His execution—The Mercato and Sta Maria del Carmine.

IN the year 536 Justinian, the Eastern Emperor, sent an army under Belisarius to drive the Goths out of Italy. After a triumphant advance through Magna Græcia, Belisarius anchored his fleet in the harbour of Naples and called upon the Gothic garrison to surrender. There was some parleying, from which it appears that there were two parties in the city, the aristocrats favouring the Gothic dominion and the mob the Byzantine. It was decided to defend the city. Appeal was made to the Gothic King Theodahad, for aid. No aid came. But though the aqueduct which brought water from Serino to Neapolis was cut, the city held out until Belisarius began to despair of success. He was on the point of raising the siege when an Isaurian soldier discovered that the dry aqueduct afforded a possible means of entering the city through the northern wall. A storming party penetrated through it into an empty reservoir in the heart of the city and, rushing to the ramparts, joined hands with those who were waiting with scaling ladders. The city was soon in the hands of the Byzantines. A few red arches, known as the Ponti Rossi, a little below the Palace of Capodimonte, are the remains of that aqueduct which caused the fall of the city.

The oppressive taxation of Justinian soon led to a reaction against the Byzantines. The kingdom of the Goths was re-established. Totila, their new king, a valiant soldier and able statesman, crossed the Po, captured Beneventum and Capua and laid siege to Naples. That city was held for the Empire by a garrison of 1000 Isaurian troops (542). They were soon hard pressed. A fleet laden with provisions and reinforcements from Constantinople was sent to their relief. As they rounded the Cape of Miseno they were attacked by a squadron of light vessels prepared by Totila for their reception. The unwieldy transports were easily routed or captured. In the following January a great armada was sent from Constantinople, and after some delay at Syracuse set sail for Naples. It was caught in a storm as it entered the Bay, and dashed ashore. Its crew fell a prey to the Goths who lined the coast. Amongst them was Demetrius, the Byzantine general. At Totila's bidding he was led with a halter round his neck in front of the walls of the city. There he was compelled to urge surrender upon the citizens, whilst the Gothic king promised to remember in their favour their stout defence against Belisarius. He offered to allow the Byzantine garrison to depart, and guaranteed the safety of every Neapolitan citizen. Worn as they were by hunger and pestilence, they would however

FIFTH CENTURY APSIDAL PORCH, S. GIOVANNI MAGGIORE

only offer to surrender if no succour should come within thirty days. "Three months if you will," Totila replied. Long before that time, Naples was once more subject to Gothic rule (May, 543).

It is said that Totila took such care of the people that, in order to prevent the ill consequences of sudden overfeeding after prolonged famine, he rationed them severely, gradually increasing their allowance of food. But though he treated the people and garrison with the utmost chivalry and good faith, he dismantled the walls. "For he preferred ever to fight on the open plain, rather than to be entangled in the mechanical contrivances of fortified cities."

It was nearly ten years before Justinian roused himself and despatched his chief minister, Narses, to recover Italy for the Empire. After a triumphal march through Italy, the Imperialist army reached Cumæ. There Narses hoped to capture the Gothic treasure stored in the fortress by Totila. It was at the foot of Mons Lactarius (Monte Lettere), at the spot still called Pozzo dei Goti (Well of the Goths), that the heroic Ostro-Goths, under their King Teias, met with their final defeat at the hands of Narses (January, 553).

Among the motley horde led into Italy by that aged eunuch was a contingent of savage Longobardi (Lombards). As Exarch of Ravenna, Narses filled the throne of the Gothic kings and held Italy for the Eastern Emperor. He was recalled by the Empress Sophia, who exasperated him by sending him a golden distaff. In revenge, he promised to spin her a thread not easily unravelled. Soon his messengers appeared in the banqueting hall of Alboin, the Lombard chief, bearing gifts of grapes and citrons from the promised land of Italy. The invitation was promptly accepted. Within a few years the savage Lombards were masters of Italy, except for a few isolated towns which, by virtue of their position on the sea or rivers, were able to hold out for the Empire. Among those were Naples, Pæstum, and Salerno. The rest of the land was split up into thirty-six Lombard duchies. Three years after Alboin crossed the Piave, a Lombard chief, Zotto by name, established himself as Duke of Beneventum. He extended his sway far and wide over Southern Italy. But though he laid siege to Naples (581), the citizens, led by their Bishop, Agnello, succeeded in repulsing him.

Under his successor, Arichis, the Duchy of Beneventum embraced all Samnium, Apulia, Campania, Lucania, and parts of Bruttii. But Naples still held out for the Emperor. Gregory I., the great founder of the mediæval Papacy, joined with the Imperial Exarch to save her from the grasp of Arichis (592).

Salerno, however, passed into the hands of the all-conquering Lombards about 640, and Cumæ in 717. At the instigation of the Pope the latter was re-captured by the Imperialist Duke of Naples.

For by this time Naples, too, had become a Duchy, a Republican Duchy, for the people retained their right of electing their Duke. The city militia had developed into a caste, and their commander wielded the real power in the city. As Duke, he absorbed the old offices of *Consul* and *Magister Militum*, retaining these appellations as mere honorary titles. Everywhere, in the chaos which followed the break-up of the Roman Empire, the old city institutions disappeared. But though the Lombards destroyed the Roman system of civic administration, at least the memory of old liberties persisted, magnified perhaps by tradition. At Naples, as elsewhere, it proved a strong and abiding influence, ready, under exciting circumstances, to flare up into a blaze of Republican enthusiasm. Under the dukes and bishops the old magisterial assembly—the *curiales*—sank into obscurity and was represented by the notaries who had once served it. More permanent and persistent were the *scholæ*, the old trade corporations, which were destined to develop into the mediæval gilds or trade unions.

Surrounded by the Lombard duchies of Rome, Beneventum, Capua, and Salerno, the territory of the Imperialist Duchy of Naples was rich but very small. It included little more than the strip of coast from Cumæ to Pompeii. The Duke himself nominated at first by the Exarch and afterwards by the Emperor, was subject to the Emperor's representative in Sicily.

But remoteness from the authority of the Exarch at Ravenna had already promoted a tendency to independence. Though the dukes of Naples fought for the Imperial iconoclasts against the Roman insurgents in the war of the Images, the natural tendency was for them to become less and less the nominees of the Emperor, and more and more independent hereditary princes. It is an indication of this development that Greek inscriptions cease to appear upon the ducal coins and seals about this period. Indeed, by the middle of the eighth century the office of bishop was beginning to be joined with that of duke and to become equally hereditary. But, in form at any rate, they continued to be elected by the people whose choice was confirmed by the Emperor.

It was one of these episcopal dukes, Stephen, who built the Stefania on the site of the present Duomo (*see* Chap. VI.). Other basilicas had been erected in the sixth and seventh centuries. We have mentioned Sta Maria Maggiore (Chap. I.). Within the entrance of the Church of S. Giorgio Maggiore,[1] the

[1] Via del Duomo, where it crosses the Via Biagio and Via Vicaria Vecchia. The latter was called Via S. Giorgio until the Court of Justice was removed from this spot to Castel Capuano.

remains of an early fifth century apse recall the basilica founded by Severus, saint and bishop, whose body was afterwards brought here from the church which bears his name, and placed beneath the high altar. It is recorded that this basilica was wonderfully built, and that in the apse the Saviour, seated amongst the twelve apostles and with four prophets at his feet, was portrayed in mosaic. Destroyed by fire in 1640, its reconstruction was begun from designs by Cosimo Fansaga, but not completed until the eighteenth century. All the frescoes are early works by Solimena. Robert of Anjou, Prince of Taranto and Emperor of Constantinople, was buried here in 1364. His tomb, erected in 1471, has disappeared.

For four centuries Naples remained a duchy of this sort. The ducal bishops sometimes allied themselves with the Pope, sometimes even with the Saracens in their desperate endeavour to keep the Lombard foe at bay. At other times they joined with Salerno and Amalfi, or the Papacy, in resistance to the piratical raids of the infidels who held Sicily, established themselves at Misenum and plundered all the cities of the coast. The treaty of 803, by which Rome was abandoned to the Franks, left Sicily, Naples and Calabria to the Eastern Empire. But the sovereign authority of the *Basileus* grew more and more shadowy as Byzantium proved itself less and less able to protect the provinces it claimed. Naples, however, though besieged by successive princes of Beneventum during the ninth century, remained to some extent a centre of Greek culture, both ecclesiastical and literary. Its connection with the Empire had important results. For we owe many of the surviving manuscripts of the Greek authors to Duke Giovanni III. His ambassadors at Constantinople had copies made of the originals which the Saracens subsequently destroyed. Giovanni encouraged letters and collected books. It was in his time (*circa* 950) that Giovanni the Deacon compiled his *Lives of the Bishops*, a work invaluable for Neapolitan chronology.

In the administration of the city the dukes were aided by a body of councillors, who acted as municipal assessors. These *boni homines*, as they were called, or Notables, were not nobles, but chiefly merchants, shippers, and landowners. When the duke was in difficulties they seized the opportunity to filch or extort from their sovereign some of his functions and prerogatives. Thus we find Duke Sergius IV. in 1030 agreeing not to make peace or war or to change established customs without their consent. At the same time the nobles obtained the concession that no noble should stand trial without the consent of his peers.

Surrounded by the Saracens, who held Sicily, by the Papal State to the north, and the Lombards at Capua and Benevento, Sergius had trouble enough within and without. Most imminent was the aggressiveness of his Lombard neighbour, Pandulf, Prince of Capua, the "Wolf of the Abruzzi." Now a little before this time (1016), a party of Northmen returning from the Holy Land put into Salerno. They were received as pilgrims, but when, shortly afterwards, siege was laid to the city by a strong force of Saracens, they demanded arms, and, attacking the infidels, routed them by the force and ferocity of their onslaught. The repute of the military prowess of these fair-haired, blue-eyed giants from the north quickly spread abroad. They were invited to return as auxiliaries to Lombard princes warring against the Byzantines, or fighting amongst themselves. Tempted by the riches of the south, bands of Normans came to fight, and stayed to plunder.

The Greek armies, we are told, disappeared before these fierce Northmen "as meat before devouring lions." The services of such a band were secured by Duke Sergius to help him in resisting Pandulf, who had occupied the city of Naples. He rewarded their leader, Rainulf, by granting him the county of Aversa (1029). Like the *condottieri* of later times, the idea of gratitude entertained by the leaders of these Norman bands was to sell themselves to the highest bidder, their idea of loyalty to rat to the stronger side. Reinforced by others of their countrymen, fierce and fearless and ruthless in robbery, these Norman adventurers began to devour the country. Among them came several sons of Tancred of Hauteville, who established themselves at Salerno. Crafty, courageous, ambitious, unscrupulous, Robert Guiscard left Normandy, it is said, with less than fifty followers to join his brothers, and died Lord of Southern Italy.

After a vain attempt to expel the Normans, the Papacy came to terms with them. Leo IX., after being defeated and taken prisoner by them, recognised their conquest, though it is very doubtful if, as was afterwards claimed, he granted them Calabria and Sicily as an hereditary fief of the Holy See (1053). Nicholas II. conferred upon Robert Guiscard, in return for an oath of fealty and yearly tribute, the investiture of the Duchy of Apulia, Calabria, and Sicily (1059); and that of Capua upon Richard, Count of Aversa. Henceforth, until the time of Ferdinand II., the Regno (Puglia) and Sicily were to be held in fief of the Holy See. Duke Robert had now to fight his fellow Normans in Apulia (for they were by no means willing to accept his supremacy), and to expel from Italy the Byzantine power which supported them. He accomplished these ends by the capture of Bari (1071), after a long struggle. He then joined his brother, Count Roger, in Sicily, with whom he achieved their cherished ambition of turning the Saracens out of that fertile island.

Alarmed at the progress of the Norman chiefs, and disappointed at the results of their alliance with them, it now became the policy of the Popes to paralyse their activities by encouraging them to fight amongst themselves. In pursuance of that policy and of his design to help the Greek Empire against the Moslems, Gregory VII. came to an open breach with Duke Robert. Promptly composing his differences with Richard of Capua, the indomitable Norman laid siege to Naples, Salerno and Benevento. Revolts stirred up by the Pope in Apulia and Calabria were triumphantly suppressed, and Gregory was at length compelled to come to terms. At Ceprano (1080) Robert took an oath of fealty to the Pope, but at the price of what amounted to practical recognition of himself as master of Southern Italy. For he received the investiture of Apulia, Calabria and Sicily, and permission to hold Salerno, Amalfi and part of the March of Ancona. Of his great expedition against the Eastern Empire, of his long siege of Salerno and subsequent residence there, marked by his patronage of its famous School of Medicine and the building of its great cathedral, this is hardly the place to write, nor of his deliverance of Gregory when besieged by Henry IV., the Emperor of the West, in the Castle of Sant' Angelo.

When death at last removed the strong hand of Robert (1085), anarchy reigned in Apulia until the death of Robert's grandson provided Count Roger II. of Sicily with the opportunity of proclaiming himself Duke of Puglia and Calabria. His right was challenged by the Pope, Honorius II., who claimed these duchies for the Church, refused to grant him the investiture he sought, and finally excommunicated him. Roger replied by transporting a formidable army from Sicily, in the presence of which the rebellious barons in the Papal camp melted away. Honorius thought that the time had come to turn the other cheek, and granted him the investiture of Puglia and Calabria in 1128. After consolidating his position in Southern Italy, he prepared to change the title of Duke for that of King. In return for his support of the Anti-Pope, Anacletus II., against Innocent II., he received, on Christmas Day, 1130, the crown of Sicily, Puglia and Calabria, the principality of Capua, and the protectorate of Benevento and the honour of Naples, though that Dukedom was still dependent on the Eastern Empire. Duke Sergius VII., after bewailing the last day of that illustrious Republic, helped to place the crown upon his head.

Neither the Eastern nor the German Empire recognised the Norman right. Nor would the Papacy long accept the establishment of a powerful rival state in Southern Italy. The Popes did their utmost to destroy, when they were not obliged to use or to humour the Norman kingdom. Supported now by the Emperor, now by the Pope, Roger's rivals were encouraged to revolt, and amongst them, Duke Sergius. Roger laid siege to Naples (1135), but it was relieved by a fleet from Pisa. After several years of struggle for the possession of Puglia and the coast towns, the death of the Emperor Lothair and the capture of Innocent II. turned the scale in favour of the Norman. Innocent II. was forced to grant him the investiture of the kingdom of Sicily, the duchy of Puglia, and the principality of Capua, in return for his allegiance and tribute to the Holy See.[1] The

[1] It is a disputed point whether the Italian provinces were at this time regarded as dependent on the kingdom of Sicily, or

Neapolitans were now obliged to submit (1137). Roger rode in triumph through the Porta Capuana, and crossing next day to the Castle of S. Salvatore (Castel dell' Ovo), dictated his terms. He appointed his eldest son Duke, and the last remnants of Republican liberty disappeared. Among his measures was the grant of five *moggie* of land and five serfs to each noble, in return for feudal service. For whilst in the north the rise of the Communes was about to develop each little city state into an independent republic, the Normans imposed upon the cities of the south their characteristic feudal system and administrative organisation, by which the country and the towns were held for the king by a hierarchy of officials.

Roger's son, William I., continued his policy (1154). The descent of Frederick Barbarossa into Italy led to an alliance between the Pope and the Byzantine Emperor, which encouraged William's vassals to revolt. They were ruthlessly suppressed. Taking the field, William defeated the Byzantine troops, and by the Treaty of Benevento forced the Pope to grant him the investiture of the kingdom of Sicily, the duchy of Puglia, and the principality of Capua, as well as Naples, Salerno and Amalfi, subject to the payment of tribute (1156). It was he who began to build the Castel Capuano and the Castel dell' Ovo.

The Papacy was now obliged to ally itself with the Normans in the endeavour to prevent the Emperor Frederick from invading Southern Italy. But in 1177 peace was made, and some years later William consented to the marriage of Constantia, a posthumous daughter of Roger II., with Barbarossa's son Henry. As William had no issue, Constantia was his legal

formed a distinct kingdom. Giannone (*Hist. di Napoli*, II.) gives good reasons for maintaining that they were independent of Sicily.

heiress. Thus began the fatal connection of Sicily with the Empire.

On William's death, besides Constantia's husband, two other candidates appeared in the field, Roger, Count of Andria, and Tancred, Count of Lecce, an illegitimate son of Duke Roger. Hatred of the Germans led the Barons to choose Tancred for their Duke (1190). The partisans of Roger of Andria thereupon revolted and espoused the cause of Henry, who sent an army of Germans against Tancred. They were, however, compelled to retire, and Tancred made himself master of Puglia, securing the support of the towns by granting many privileges to the burghers. Soon, however, Henry, having now succeeded his father as the Emperor Henry VI., entered Italy with a powerful army. He was joined by many exiled Normans and discontented nobles, and laid siege to Naples (1191). But the walls were strong, the sea was open, and his repeated assaults failed. The hot weather came, and with it a new ally for Tancred. For an epidemic broke out and compelled Henry to retire. Salerno, which had submitted to him, thereupon made amends by surrendering Constantia, who had taken up her abode there, to Tancred. The death of Tancred in 1193 left the field open to Henry, who was crowned King of Sicily on Christmas Day, 1194. He treated the supporters of Tancred with the most abominable cruelty. Naples had submitted to him at once, but Salerno resisted, was taken by storm and sacked, and its walls destroyed. Following upon the sack by the Pisans in 1135, this proved a deathblow to the old rival of Naples, which had once been the chief port for the Levantine trade.

Henry was succeeded by Frederick II., for whom Constantia at first acted as Regent and the Pope as his guardian. Frederick was a man born out of due time, a prototype of the despots of the Italian Renaissance. Poet, epicure, freethinker, he loved art, letters, wars and women, all with a passionate intensity. After a period of unrest during his minority, his kingdom, under his enlightened rule, emerges as a rare instance of an almost ideal monarchy, where the people enjoyed liberty and justice, the licence of the barons was kept in check, and a sovereign such as Bolingbroke imagined, inspired by the highest ideals and assisted by ministers chosen for their merits, ruled, and ruled benignly, promoting at once the welfare of his subjects and the culture of the arts.

Valorous, learned, courteous, but with a touch of the barbarian in his cruelty, as instanced by his massacre of the Sanseverini, he was himself a troubadour, and gathered round his court at Palermo poets who formed the first school of Italian poetry. He was the one Western Emperor who chose to live upon these lovely shores. Soon after he received the Imperial Crown at Rome, he decided to reside at Naples, attracted by the beauty and accessibility of its position. Here he established his high court; here he completed the Castel Capuano, bringing Niccolò Pisano to work for him there, and the Castel dell' Ovo; and here he erected the private schools into a *Studium Generale*, or university, inviting to it professors in all faculties from abroad (1224). Under such patronage Naples became a centre of learning and the city of most importance in the kingdom.

The Normans had imposed an alien civilisation upon an alien land. They had gradually given to it unity and comparative order, though indeed the record of their wars, if I should set it out here, would hardly give the impression of peace and security. They offered a united front to the emperors of the East and West alike. But their right was the right of conquest from the Eastern Empire. They had sought to regularise it, and, by acknowledging the overlordship of the Pope, gave grounds for the claim that it was a Papal fief, carrying the right of the Pope to direct the succession. The union of the kingdom of Naples and Sicily with the Empire in one so strong and self-reliant as Frederick, involved inevitably a clash with the Papal claims. For Frederick was as determined not to abate one jot or tittle of the temporal overlordship of the Empire as was his relentless foe, Innocent IV., not to forego his feudal rights or spiritual dominion. The whole of Italy was divided into the warring factions of Guelfs and Ghibellines, supporters of the Pope and supporters of the Empire, and Frederick wore out his life in the unceasing struggle.

Upon the succession of Frederick's son Conrad, in 1250, Naples declared for the Pope, refusing to acknowledge any king who had not the Papal benediction and investiture. Conrad, with an army of Germans and Saracens, laid siege to the city, and, after a ten months' siege, forced it to capitulate (September, 1252). He allowed his soldiers to pillage the place, razed the fortifications, and punished the rebellious citizens with great severity. Meanwhile the Pope had offered the investiture of the kingdom of the two Sicilies first to Richard, Earl of Cornwall, brother of the King of England, and upon his refusing it, to the Count of Anjou, brother of St Louis of France. On Conrad's death, Manfred, an illegitimate son of Frederick II., acted as Regent for his infant son Conradin, and presently himself assumed the crown (1258). Innocent IV., still intent upon asserting the claims of the Church, came to Naples to oppose him, and there died. Manfred maintained his position for a while and gained acquiescence in his rule by the clemency, generosity and justice which proved him a true son of Frederick II. He married his daughter to the son of the King of Aragon. But Urban IV. and Clement IV. now succeeded where Innocent had failed, and "by a master stroke of policy," as an admirer called it, brought the French into Italy. Charles, Count of Anjou, on undertaking to pay homage and tribute to the Papacy, was crowned at Rome King of Sicily *citra et ultra pharum*, and, marching rapidly on Benevento, there defeated and slew Manfred. Beloved by his people for his liberality, charm and good rule, *Biondo e bello*, as Dante describes him, and a lover of learning, Manfred was deserted by the Puglian barons in the middle of the battle. Being excommunicated, his body was dug up and flung beyond the borders of the kingdom (26th February, 1266).

There remained Conradin. Charles proved himself a ruthless tyrant, oppressing his new subjects and overburdening them with taxes, parcelling out their lands to his French followers and mercilessly destroying the supporters of the Suabian line.

The discontent of his subjects and the call of the Empire roused the youthful Conradin to brave the excommunication of the Pope and march into Italy. Many Ghibelline cities joined his standard, and he advanced upon Naples in great hopes of recovering his kingdom. But he was outgeneralled, defeated and taken prisoner by Charles in the plains of Tagliacozzo (23rd August, 1268). Charles punished his rebellious subjects with savage reprisals. His cruel oppression of the Sicilians resulted a few years later in the terrible massacre of Frenchmen, known as the Sicilian Vespers. Helena, the widow of Manfred, and her children, he kept prisoners until death released them. The Guelfs had triumphed, and were taking their revenge. But there remained Conradin. Charles thought it wiser to get rid of the kingly lad—he was but seventeen—by a judicial murder. For the hopes of the Ghibellines still centred upon him.

On 26th October, 1268, a scaffold and a throne were raised in the Piazza del Mercato, then an open space without the walls, intersected by a stream and overlooking the sea. Side by side stood Corradino, as the Italians call him, the last of the Hohenstaufen, and his boy friend, Frederick of Baden. Villani records that when the Grand Protonotary read the sentence, Count Robert of Flanders drew his sword and ran him through the body, and the bloodthirsty Angevin monarch, seated on his throne, dared not punish him. But he was to have his fill of blood that day. For besides these two gallant boys, two Neapolitan nobles were beheaded, and nine hung that day, and in the days to come many were tortured, blinded, killed.

Ere the axe fell, Conradin turned to the people and justified his actions. "Before God," he cried, "I deserve death as a sinner, but not for this." So saying, he threw his glove among the throng. There were many sympathisers in the crowd, one of whom, the story goes, secured the glove and carried it to Don Pedro, son of the King of Aragon, seeing in it the lad's last proud call for vengeance and the gift of succession to his kingdom.

Just before he received the fatal stroke, Conradin cried out in sorrow to his mother, "What grief I am inflicting on you!" His mother, indeed, had endeavoured to dissuade him from this adventure, and when she heard of the danger which threatened him, had set forth with great sums to ransom him. She arrived too late. The money she had brought she handed over to the Carmelite monks to pray for her son's soul in the little church of the Carmine, which then stood near the scene of his death. Here, too, the body of her son was presently interred. For at first it was buried in the sand near the scaffold, in unconsecrated ground, since he was excommunicate.

In 1631, when the pavement of Sta Maria del Carmine was being lowered, a leaden coffin was found beneath the high altar, on which the letters R.C.C. were roughly cut. Within lay the skeleton of a youth, the head severed from the body, and a sword unsheathed. This confirmed the belief that the initials stood for Regis Corradini Corpus—the body of King Conradin. In the Church of S. Croce, too easily distinguished by its glittering dome of green and yellow glazed tiles, on the north side of the Piazza, are preserved a column of porphyry which once marked the place of Conradin's execution, the block on which he was beheaded, and a cross with an inscription in which Charles savagely records his triumph over the last of the Hohenstaufen kings of Sicily.

The busy fishmarket and the streets surrounding the Piazza del Mercato still retain some of the characteristics of old Naples. But it is only a faint echo of the crowded and noisy scene of former years. At the southern end of it are two fountains with obelisks of the fifteenth century, and at the eastern end is a fountain of the time of Philip IV. (1663), restored and converted into a shrine in 1788. Round about it are some more old shops, or *bassi*, under arches with huge double folding doors, such as we have noticed in the neighbourhood of S. Eligio. Crossing the Piazza Pepe (formerly Garibaldi), we are confronted by the façade and campanile of the Church of Sta Maria del Carmine, with a striking memorial in bronze to those from the Mercato quarter who fell in the Great War. On our right are the remains of the Porta and Castel del Carmine. The Carmine Church of Conradin's day had been founded by some hermits from Mount Carmel, who fled hither from the Saracens in the seventh century. They brought with them a picture of the Madonna, painted, it is said, like so many others, by St Luke, and placed it in a grotto beneath the church. This Madonna della Grotticella, or La Bruna, as it is called, became one of the most famous of the miracle-working Madonnas in Italy. She wrought her first miracle here in 1500, when her healing gaze fell upon a wretched beggar who had lain before the church door paralysed for thirty years, and he thereupon arose and danced before the Lord. Whereat the bells of the church pealed aloud in joy and thanksgiving, so loud, indeed, as to deafen the monkish chronicler who tells the tale, and no wonder, seeing that they were "rung by all the hosts of Heaven." Another prized relic in the church is a figure of Christ on the Cross. When Alfonso of Aragon was besieging the city in 1439 a cannon ball fell into the church, and would have decapitated the image of the Saviour, had it not suddenly bowed its head and allowed the shot to pass.

Sta Maria del Carmine was rebuilt in 1769. It is a wonderful example of the way in which at that period architecture was subordinated to painting. The whole aim of the builders seems to have been to provide light and space for acres of paint and gilt. The gilded roof is flat and heavy, the arches between the square marble piers are surmounted by heavy scrolls containing angel-heads. Above them, the heavy, harp-shaped windows of the clerestory show to what depths of ugliness baroque and rococo could descend (*v.* Chap. XIV.).

The fall of the House of Suabia put an end to any movement towards a fusion of the south of Italy into one homogeneous nation developing its own national life and culture.

The development of architecture, sculpture and the beginnings of poetry, which had begun, was suddenly checked. Art disappeared with the Suabians, together with the commerce and silk industry they had developed, fled into Tuscany and Venice, and there broke into the dawn of Italian Renaissance.

It disappeared because it had never been anything but an alien inspiration, fostered by a cultured and intelligent court, and was not the indigenous product of the genius of a prosperous, free and united people. If the father of Niccolò Pisano came from Apulia, it was from Rome that he drew his inspiration, and in Tuscany that he worked.

The Apulian barons, a term which then included the Neapolitans, had no share in the military ardour of the Normans, or in the civilising greatness of Frederick. They preferred the profits of brigandage, varied by the occasional effort of civil war, to the discipline and hardships of Roger's campaigns. The foundation of the evil reputation for pusillanimity and double dealing was already laid, which was to pursue them throughout the Middle Ages and beyond. The State which had shone both as the model of good government and the pioneer of civilisation in the twelfth and thirteenth centuries was destined, when the strong hand of the leonine rulers from the north was withdrawn, to become throughout the succeeding centuries a byword for disorganisation and brigandage, of political degeneration and rotten administration.

CHAPTER X

Naples and the Angevins

Naples the Angevin capital—Castel Nuovo and S. Lorenzo—Charles II.—Sta Maria la Nuova—S. Pietro Martire—S. Domenico Maggiore—Sta Maria Donna Regina—Robert the Wise—Boccaccio and Petrarch—Belforte and S. Martino—Giotto's frescoes—Sta Maria l'Incoronata——Guglia and Church of Gesù Nuovo—Sta Chiara—The Angevin tombs—Giovanna I.—Murder of Andreasso—Disputed succession—Charles III. and Ladislaus—Struggle with Louis II.—S. Giovanni a Carbonara—S. Angelo a Nilo—Monte Oliveto—Tasso—S. Giovanni dei Pappacoda—Giovanna II.—Sergianni Caracciolo—Réné of Anjou—Stma. Annunziata.

CHARLES I. never recovered from the loss of Sicily and his exhausting efforts to regain it. Outwardly Naples benefited. For it now took the place of Palermo as the capital of the Angevin kingdom in the south. Charles's policy was to secure the devotion of his French followers, high officials and supporters among the Puglian barons, by rewarding them with fiefs, honours and privileges. The rest of his conquered subjects he taxed without mercy and ruthlessly oppressed. In Naples he confirmed the privileges of the nobles and their *seggi*, open-air tribunals of separate wards, derived from the old Greek *phratriæ*, in which the nobles met, taxed and governed themselves, without regard to the rest of the people. Charles inaugurated the policy pursued by his successors of rendering the city worthy in strength and magnificence of being the capital of the Angevins. To this end, he invited the barons and nobles to reside in the city, and enlarged the university and granted it new privileges. To this end, he paved the streets with great flagstones taken from the Appian Way, and repaired and enlarged the fortifications, extending them so as to include the scene of Conradin's execution, which he converted into a fine new market-place, the Piazza del Mercato. To this end, he began to build himself a palace and castle more suitable for his royal residence and a place of strength to hold Naples than the old Castle of S. Salvatore. The Castel Nuovo, with its high walls and moat and great round Angevin towers, designed by French architects, was completed by his son. So, too, was the Church of S. Lorenzo, which he began as a thank-offering for the victory of Benevento. Sanfelice rebuilt most of it after it had been damaged by the earthquake in 1732. But the graceful door, chapel and ambulatory survive as instances of that charming French Gothic style which was now introduced by the Angevins into Neapolitan ecclesiastical architecture. Elsewhere for the most part it has been gutted, destroyed, or overlaid by their successors. In the chapels are a picture of Robert the Wise being crowned by St Louis, by (?) Simone Martini, and a tomb of Aldomoresco by Baboccio, and in the Choir the tomb of Catherine of Austria (*see* p. 272), and a charming sarcophagus of the little Maria of Durazzo, daughter of Charles III.

The design of S. Lorenzo, like that of the Castel Nuovo, is wholly French. If style goes for anything, it is difficult to see what share Giovanni da Pisa or his father Niccolo can have had in them. It is said, however, that Frederick II. brought Niccolo to Naples in 1220 to complete the Castel Capuano, and that he stayed there for ten years and returned in the time of

Charles I. to work on the Duomo. Giovanni, his son, is said to have been invited by Charles to help in building his new castle and this Church of San Lorenzo.

Whoever the architect, there is more than one reason for visiting this church. For not only is its primitive architecture more intact than that of any other church in Naples, but it was in this church that Petrarch prayed, and that Boccaccio in 1346 first beheld and loved the lovely Fiammetta, a daughter, it was rumoured, of King Robert himself. The result of that meeting was to make literature which all the world still reads, literature in which the gay scenes of Neapolitan Court life are for ever enshrined, literature by which the very streets of Naples and the neighbouring coast are haunted to this day.

The sceptre of Sicily had passed to Don Pedro of Aragon, husband of Constantia, daughter of Frederick II. There was talk for a time of a duel between the two kings to settle their claims to Sicily. It was during the absence of Charles in Provence on this business that Roger di Loria, a Calabrian refugee in command of the Aragonese fleet, sailed into the harbour of Naples. His taunts provoked Prince Charles to put to sea, though his father had strictly charged him not to be drawn into battle. Deceived by Loria's Parthian flight, he was completely defeated and taken captive. Two days later, Charles I. arrived with a fleet from Provence. On learning that the mob had shown sympathy with the Sicilians by shouting for Roger di Loria, he at first determined to burn the city, but was presently induced to content himself with hanging 150 of the chief rioters. Upon his death (1285), Prince Charles being still a prisoner, the Pope appointed a Cardinal Legate as Governor of Naples, under whom many laws were passed for the immunity and benefit of the ecclesiastical state and entrenching upon the royal prerogative. Loria gained another brilliant victory over the Neapolitan fleet, which induced the Cardinal Legate to sign a truce with the Sicilians for two years. In the following year (1288) Charles came to an understanding with King Alfonso of Aragon, through the mediation of Edward I., King of England. As soon as he was set at liberty, Pope Nicholas IV. absolved Charles from his agreement, crowned him King of the two Sicilies, and joined him in an attempt to recover Sicily. Roused by this act of rascally bad faith, Edward I. threatened to intervene, denouncing the Pope as the incendiary of Christendom, and so put an end to that adventure.

Charles II. returned to Naples, and there busied himself in building churches and palaces for his family in the precincts of the new castle, and also in developing the resources of the city. In order to attract citizens and increase their numbers, he established a cloth industry, and exempted the town from taxes. He also built the Molo Angioino forming the Porto Nuovo close to the castle. Like his father he encouraged the University, granting it new privileges and paying illustrious professors large salaries to reside and teach in it. He was a patron of art too, as well as of letters. For he brought Montano d'Arezzo from Tuscany to paint the chapel of the Castel Nuovo. The close connection of the Angevin kings with the bankers of Florence, who financed their wars and handled the corn and produce of the Regno, helps to explain how it was that from this time onwards one Tuscan artist after another was brought by them to the joyous task of beautifying Naples. Art follows trade as trade follows the flag. One is forced to conclude, too, that there was a curious absence of native talent. Patriotic Neapolitan writers have discovered or invented the names of certain aboriginal artists, and attributed to them works of which the authors are otherwise unknown. But other evidence of their existence is lacking (*see* Chap. XIV.).

The seductive air of the Siren City was already beginning to influence the Angevin princes. Life was gay in the time of Charles II., affording a sharp contrast to the gloomy atmosphere of his father's court. Charles II., however, was by no means wholly frivolous. When his father cleared the ground for the Castel Nuovo, he removed a Franciscan monastery from that site and built Sta Maria la Nuova [1] for the monks in its stead. His son favoured the Dominicans. He built for them S. Pietro Martire, which is opposite to the University building and contains a Coronation of the Virgin by the sixteenth-century Neapolitan painter, Silvestro Buono. Nor did he forget a vow which he had made in the time of his captivity. On the site of a church which had passed from Basilian monks in the fourth century to Benedictines, and from Benedictines to Dominicans, he began to build the great French Gothic Church of S. Domenico, wherein his heart is preserved. It was designed, the Neapolitans say, by their imaginary "Masuccio I.," who incorporated in it the previous Dominican church. San Domenico Maggiore stands on rising ground at

[1] The first street on the right as you ascend the Via Diaz leads into a piazza surrounded by old Renaissance palaces and conventual buildings. The church, said to have been designed by Giovanni Pisano, was rebuilt by Agnolo Franco in 1525. The fine Renaissance façade has engaged Corinthian columns reduced to mere decoration. The flat roof of the aisleless nave, richly painted with pictures and portraits in gilt frames, gives the impression of an inverted picture gallery. The frescoes of the cupola are by Corenzio. In the south transept, against the west wall, is a fine early Renaissance monument. In the chapel opposite is a wooden Crucifixion by Giovanni da Nola, by whom also is the Ecce Homo on the south wall.

the end of the Largo San Domenico, on the western side of the old Greek wall or ditch, the Via Mezzocannone. It is surrounded by remains of the splendid palaces of the noble families which dwelt here in the days when this was the fashionable quarter. The main entrance to the church is reached through a courtyard opening upon the street which leaves the Strada dei Tribunali, near S. Pietro a Maiella. A baroque porch and remains of baroque alterations of a Gothic façade increase the general air of decadence and neglect upon this side. The more popular entrance seems to be from the Largo San Domenico, in which is the baroque obelisk—the Guglia di San Domenico—designed by Cosimo Fansaga. Heavy and ornate with meaningless decoration, it is at least beautiful in comparison with the Guglia del Gesù. There is another obelisk by Fansaga, set up in honour of S. Gennaro after deliverance from the plague, outside the Duomo. These distressing monuments are a peculiarity of Naples, though there is a similar one at Ostuni in Apulia.

The entrance from this piazza into the east end of San Domenico is through a chapel in the apse, whence a winding staircase leads into the south transept. The colour scheme of the fresco work of the interior is French grey and light blue, relieved by light brown and darker brown. This note is echoed by the painting of the ceiling and by the grey-blue tint of the engaged pillars which carry lofty pointed arches. The church has been much mutilated in the course of several alterations at the hands of Renaissance and Baroque artists.

In the *Sacristy* a dashing and brightly coloured fresco of the Last Judgment, by Solimena, that brilliant tradesman, covers the ceiling and draws the eye upwards to the gallery wherein, above the presses, are ranged the coffins of some five and forty "people of importance," including ten Princes of Aragon and the Marquis of Pescara, the great sixteenth-century soldier, and his wife, Vittoria Colonna.

Facing the Sacristy, in the last chapel of the north aisle, is an exceedingly charming and graceful group by Giovanni da Nola, representing the Virgin and Child, with St John the Baptist and (?) Joseph on either side, and angels in relief above. The whole is set in a Renaissance frame of pilasters and pediment. The fine tomb of Galeazzo Pandono (1514) in the south transept is possibly by the same artist. The Chapel of the Crucifixion, the seventh chapel on the south side, contains a relic which reminds us of the connection of St Thomas Aquinas with the Dominican monastery. For this was the original seat of the University, and it was here that the angelic doctor studied and taught philosophy. One day, as he prayed before the Crucifix by Tommaso de Stefani, now preserved in the chapel referred to, he heard the Saviour speaking to him and commending his doctrine—"*Bene scripsisti de me, Thoma.*"

Charles had married Maria of Hungary. On the death of her brother, Ladislaus, King of Hungary, without issue, he obtained the crown of that kingdom for his eldest son, Charles Martel, by right of his mother. Maria has other interest for us. For not only did she found the Dominican Nunnery of S. Pietro a Castello, but also the church and monastery of Sta Maria Donna Regina.

Ascending the Via del Duomo, the first street on the right after passing the Cathedral—the Via Donna Regina—leads us into the piazza of that name. Here, on the left, opposite the Archbishop's palace (1638, restored 1886), a flight of steps forms the approach to the church built by G. B. Guarini in 1620. The interior is terribly over-decorated in the seventeenth century manner. There are frescoes by Solimena and Giordano. But in a chapel in the north-west corner is the early fourteenth-century tomb of Queen Mary of Hungary. This is the work of the Sienese master, Tino di Camaino, assisted by Gallardo Primario. Within an ornamented Gothic canopy two angels hold aside a curtain screening the recumbent effigy of the Queen, which is raised upon a pedestal adorned by bas-reliefs (*see* p. 272).

Leaving the church, turn to the left up a narrow, dirty street bordering the south side of it, the Vico Donna Regina. At No. 25, on the left-hand side of it, knock loudly at a rusty old gateway over which hangs the sign, *Museo Civico Pitture.* A custodian will lead you through a dilapidated courtyard up some flights of stairs into a strange, bare room. So it seems at first, for it is hard to recognise at once that this is the remnant of the monastic chapel founded by Queen Mary. The very handsome sixteenth-century ceiling has just been renovated. At the east end it cuts across the Gothic arch of the apse. But the chief feature of this chapel is that the walls are covered with frescoes, which, though much damaged, form a magnificent and spirited series, dating from the first or second quarter of the fourteenth century, and telling the story of the Passion of Christ, the Last Judgment, and the Legends of St Elizabeth of Hungary, St Catherine, and St Agnes. The vigour and breadth of design, and the masterly arrangement of colour proclaim the inspiration of some great artist. The large figures on the north-east wall recall the frescoes in Sta Maria Incoronata, and, it may be hazarded, are by the same hand. Those over the south and south-west door are very fine. They date from the first quarter of the fourteenth century, and owe at least their inspiration to Pietro Cavallini, if not by that master himself, or to Giotto. More than one hand is clearly traceable. Probably these frescoes were painted by pupils of Cavallini, and perhaps in part by the artist himself. Some of the pictures of that pioneer in the new art of religious paintings, of which the banner was raised in Rome at the end of the thirteenth century, may be studied in the picture gallery of the *Museo Nazionale*.

Apart from these activities, Charles II. spent most of his reign in vain attempts to recover Sicily. He died in 1309, having gained the affection of his subjects, it is said, by his clemency, courtesy and liberality.

The accession of his third son Robert, Duke of Calabria, was challenged by his grandson, Carobert, King of Hungary, but decided in favour of the former by the College of Cardinals. Robert took the oath of fealty and homage to the Pope at Avignon, and received the investiture of both Puglia and Sicily. Robert, like his predecessors, spent his force in continual attempts to recover Sicily, attempts in which he was opposed by the Emperor and supported more or less ardently by the Papacy. It would be wearisome to enumerate the many invasions and counter-invasions of Sicily and Calabria which took place in the course of this long struggle betwixt Angevin and Aragonese. Nor can we stay to recount Robert's activities in the wider world. Villani tells us that he was the wisest and most learned prince that had reigned in Christendom for five hundred years, and that he was as just as he was liberal. As a statesman he was clever enough to steer his course successfully between Pope and Emperor, to manage Genoa, Milan and Florence, and to leave his kingdom stronger than he found it. That was no mean achievement, and we need not grudge him the title of The Wise, which his contemporaries awarded him. For as leader of the Guelfs and vicar of the Papal States whilst the Pope was his guest at Avignon—for he was Robert of Anjou and Provence as well as of Naples—he became, indeed, little short of dictator in the affairs of Italy. At the height of his power he was shattered by the untimely death of his only son, Charles the Illustrious, Duke of Calabria (1328). "The crown is fallen from my head," he cried, and arranged for the succession by betrothing Giovanna, Charles's eldest daughter, to Andrew, the second son of the King of Hungary who, as the son of his eldest brother, had an hereditary claim (1333). Andreasso, as the Italians called him, was at that time seven years of age, and Giovanna five. For himself Robert now desired to lay down the sceptre and to don the habit of a Franciscan, but he was dissuaded by his nobles.

The Court of Robert the Wise reflected the increasing importance of the Regno. The Piazza delle Corregge was the scene of many gay and splendid festivities, among them a tournament described by Boccaccio. For Boccaccio came to Robert's Court when he visited Naples on his father's business, and in *Filocolo* and *Fiammetta* he has enshrined for ever the gay life of Neapolitan society in those days—the shows, the jousts, the hunting, the picnics and bathing parties along the shores of Baiæ, and the eternal love-making. Robert himself was by no means averse from the latter pastime, though he was also a student of divinity and philosophy, and, under the influence of Petrarch, dabbled in poetry in his old age. As a patron of letters, he gained the eloquent gratitude of Petrarch. For after adroitly flattering the greatest and most learned monarch of the day, Petrarch came to Naples to obtain the approval and support of Robert before receiving the laurel crown at Rome.

To the Castel Nuovo Robert added the Torre dell'

Oro to serve as a treasury, and he extended the gardens. A more important step was the fortification of the heights of St Erasmo (St Elmo) by a castle then called Belforte, and the completion of the adjacent Carthusian monastery of S. Martino, begun by his son (*see* Chap. XII.). He completed the Duomo also, as we have seen, and he built Sta Chiara.

Robert was a patron of art as well as of letters, and certainly a wise one. Like his father, he was in close touch with Florence, whose bankers financed his ruinous wars and the lavish expenditure to which his Spanish wife, Sancia of Majorca, contributed not a little by her religious foundations at Sta Chiara and elsewhere. It was from Tuscany, therefore, and especially from Florence and Siena, that he brought artists to adorn his castles and churches. Chief among these was Giotto and Tino di Camaino. It is one of the great tragedies of Naples that whilst the frescoes of 79 A.D. have been preserved, of the frescoes of Giotto little or nothing remains. Vesuvius was not so destructive as Spanish viceregency. The frescoes which Giotto painted in the chapel of the Castel dell' Ovo have long since disappeared. The Tuscan artist painted the walls of the chapels of Sta Chiara. But a Spanish officer in 1732 held that they made the church too dark, and thought that a coat of whitewash would be an improvement. Frescoes, not by Giotto, but certainly of his school, survive above the Tomb of Robert the Wise, and in the four chapels on the right is one faded work possibly by him (Madonna della Pietà). Some fourteenth century repainted frescoes in the Duomo are said to be by him, but without reason. We have mentioned those in the Church of Donna Regina, thought by some to be by Giotto. There remain the paintings in the Church of Sta Maria l'Incoronata. This church (Via

Emanuele Filiberto di Savoia, leading from the Piazza del Municipio) was rebuilt and renamed in 1352 in honour of her coronation by Giovanna I., of whom presently. It retains much of its original Gothic character. Above the organ is a series of fourteenth-century frescoes representing the Seven Sacraments and the Triumph of the Church. Now the fresco representing the marriage sacrament is said to depict the wedding of Giovanna I. and Louis of Taranto in 1345. As Giotto died in 1337, that fact might seem to dispose of the possibility of his authorship. But it has been suggested that what he did was, by command of Robert, to adorn an apartment of an adjoining palace in which his children dwelt, and that this apartment was afterwards incorporated in Giovanna's church, and that the features of the fresco were altered after her wedding to likenesses of herself and her husband. *Credat Judæus Apella.*

Whilst Giotto was engaged upon his work King Robert would often come and chat with him, for he appreciated his shrewd speeches as much as his art. " If I were you, Giotto," he remarked one summer day, " I would stop painting now it is so hot." " And so would I, Sire," replied the painter, " if I were you."

Tram No. 2 from the Villa Nazionale takes one to the Largo del Gesù, or Piazza Oberdan. It halts beneath the extreme example of baroque frightfulness in Naples, the *Guglia del Gesù*, or *della Concezione*, by Giuseppe Gennino (1747), an obelisk whereon involution rolls up on involution in meaningless contortion.

It is a relief to turn from this noisy and restless multiplication of waving cornices and fatuous contortions to the Renaissance porch of the adjoining Church of Gesù Nuovo, which was applied in 1580 to the *diamanté* façade of what was once the palace of Roberto Sanseverino—a Renaissance palace built by Novello da San Lucano in 1470. The interior is a blaze of baroque decoration, with seventeenth-century frescoes by Francesco Solimena and Giovanni Lanfranco. The famous *Expulsion of Heliodorus from the Temple* by the former, over the doorway, is a picture of great force and no little depth of meaning.

A narrow street leads from the piazza to a very different scene. Surrounded by a quiet courtyard on one side and by houses on the other, rises the dignified Gothic façade of Sta Chiara, the Royal Chapel and mausoleum of Robert the Wise. The ornate portal, partly composed of marble of different hues, is more perfect than its predecessors at St Eligio, the earliest Angevin building in Naples, the Duomo, S. Lorenzo and S. Domenico.

The building of the great foundation of the Corpus Sanctum Christi, known as Sta Chiara, was begun in 1310. The architects were Lionardo di Vito and Gallardo Primaro, Tuscan and Neapolitan trained in the Angevin school. Queen Sancia chose for it a site amongst the gardens which then filled the space between the Roman and the mediæval walls, north of the Convent of Sta Maria di Donn' Albina. Church and monastery and nunnery alike were richly endowed by Robert to please his pious wife. Sancia, indeed, would have preferred for herself the chaste life of a nun to that of a royal spouse. She did finally take the veil and the name of Sister Chiara, dying in the adjacent nunnery of Sta Croce, one of her own foundations close to the Franciscan monastery of the Trinity. Robert himself, sobered by the death of his son, had leanings towards the religious life, and donned the Franciscan garb three weeks before his death.

The campanile, like those of San Lorenzo and San

Domenico, is not attached to the church. Only the lower story, of marble and travertine, dates back to Angevin times. Inscriptions on it record the history of the foundation. The tower was intended to consist of five stories, in the five orders of architecture, but was not completed until the seventeenth century. The austere Gothic of the aisleless nave was converted about 1751 by the architects Domenico Antonio Vaccaro, Gaetano Buonocore and Giovanni del Gaizo into what can only be described as a baroque ballroom, the ceiling of which was painted by Giuseppe Bonito, Francesco de Mura, Sebastiano Conca, Paolo di Majo and others.

The chapels contain several fourteenth-century tombs, and by the north door that of Antonia Gandino, who died on her wedding day (1530), by Giovanni da Nola.

There are several fragments of fourteenth-century frescoes, so faint and so repainted as to be of little interest. But in the third chapel (north) is a Madonna and Child, and in the fourth chapel (south), a Madonna della Pietà, which are attributed to Giotto. The former is probably by a Sienese painter under the influence of Giotto. The latter, which has been taken from the wall and placed upon the altar, is the merest ghost of a picture, but the tender grief of the mourning mother and the realistic rigidity of the dead Christ might well have been suggested by the Master's hand. The head of the Madonna, however, and other details seem rather to indicate a later date.

There are other remains of late fourteenth-century frescoes in the adjacent monastery of the Minors. Whilst the church was a-building the barren aspect of the nave and its side chapels is said to have suggested to Charles the Illustrious, Duke of Calabria, the idea of a stable with rows of stalls. So he told his father, when he asked him what he thought of the work. "God grant," replied Robert, "that you be not the first to eat in it." But a few years later he was laid to rest here (1328). His tomb and that of his second wife, Marie de Valois (1331), by the side of the magnificent tomb of his father, were wrought by Tino da Camaino, the Sienese master, who came to Naples before 1323 and stayed here till he died (? 1338).

The most obvious characteristic of the tombs of the Angevin kings of Naples is their unanimity of design. All have Gothic canopies covering a Virgin enthroned above an effigy recumbent upon a sarcophagus, and other details described below. Just as the churches and castles of the Angevins were built by French or Tuscan architects, so their tombs were sculptured and their chapels painted by Tuscan artists, followers of Giovanni Pisano, in harmony with the Gothic traditions of the north. The earliest of these tombs is probably that of Catherine of Austria, the first wife of Duke Charles, who died in 1323 and is buried in S. Lorenzo, and is by an unknown artist, though some attribute it to Tino and others to later hands. Here the Gothic canopy is supported by two Cosmatesque twisted columns with female heads appearing through rich foliage of Puglian capitals.

Probably Tino's first sepulchral work in Naples was the tomb of Mary of Hungary in the Donna Regina, and his next the lighter, more graceful and harmonious tomb of Duke Charles, completed in 1332, now before us. In all his work he shows himself an apt pupil of Giovanni Pisano, and he probably owed his conception of these tombs to a study of the work of Arnolfo di Cambio at Rome. Within a graceful Gothic canopy supported by pilasters, the body of the duke, wearing a ducal cap, is stretched upon a sarcophagus, which is revealed by two winged angels

Mus. Naz.] [*Alinari*

DANCING FAUN

(From the House of the Faun, Pompeii)

drawing aside the curtains. In the background very finely carved groups of priests give absolution or mourn over the corpse—a detail which, like that of the angels, is an echo of Arnolfo. On the front of the sarcophagus groups of knights and courtiers do homage to the duke, above whom, and beneath a Gothic arcade, the Madonna and Child sit enthroned. On either side of her are rather poor statues of St Francis and Sta Chiara. Graceful winged figures of the Seven Virtues adorn the supports of the sarcophagus. Their drapery is reminiscent of Giovanni Pisano.

The tomb of Marie de Valois (sometimes wrongly called that of Giovanna I.) is on the same lines as that of the duke, but in several parts the workmanship is inferior, and is probably that of a pupil. The duchess, in a blue mantle sprinkled with lilies of gold, lies on a sarcophagus supported by figures of Temperance and Charity. Sta Chiara, faced by St Louis of Toulouse, presents her to the Madonna. Five niches between the pilasters carry statues of Mary and her four children.

A month after the death of Robert the Wise, in 1343, Giovanna I. commissioned the Florentine brothers, Giovanni and Pacio da Firenze, to make the tomb recognised as the finest Italian monument of the Trecento. The artists derived directly from Giovanni Pisano and Tino, but improved in detail upon the latter's work in Naples, and produced a more perfect balance of architectural and sculptural elements than he achieved.[1] Unfortunately the Angevin tombs were moved and mauled when the Gothic church was converted into baroque gilt and gaudiness. The tomb of Robert in particular has been so blocked by

[1] Many writers—M. Maurel amongst them—think that Robert's tomb was the first of these Angevin monuments and the prototype of all the rest.

the high altar, that it is exceedingly difficult to see many of the details or to appreciate it as a whole. The upper portion repeats the scheme of Charles's tomb, but the Madonna above is noticeably good. Remains of the colour scheme show how magnificent it once was.

In niches on the pilasters, beneath rich canopies with a blue background, stand statues of saints, apostles and prophets. Beneath the Madonna the King sits enthroned, with a line in Gothic letters, said to have been written for his epitaph by Petrarch: *Cernite Robertum regem virtute refertum.* But the effigy on the sarcophagus below wears the Franciscan robes in which he died. The place of the mourning priests on Charles's monument is taken by figures representing the Liberal Arts, beautiful, humanised female forms which are the best work of the artists here. On the face of the tomb are Robert and his family. Beautiful, heavily-draped figures representing the Six Virtues (omitting Hope) are applied to the front columns supporting the tomb.

Other Angevin tombs at the side of this splendid monument are those of Agnes and Clementia, daughters of Maria (posthumous daughter of Charles the Illustrious), and Charles of Durazzo, and also of their little son Ludovico, possibly by Giovanni and Pacio (1344), and of little Maria of Calabria. The tomb of Maria di Durazzo (*see* p. 259), in which the heavy twisted columns spoil the grace and harmony of the Gothic canopy, is by some unknown follower of those Florentine masters, who was also the author of the tomb of Drago de Merloto in the second chapel on the north side of the church. Opposite Robert's tomb, and forming a frieze along the organ gallery, are eleven cameos on a black ground representing incidents from the life of St Catherine. They are among the loveliest things in Naples. These, too, are the work of Giovanni and Pacio (1345). Delicately wrought, but full of vigour, every detail of these graceful figures is inspired by that directness of outlook and that sincerity and freshness of spirit and workmanship which constitute the peculiar charm of early Tuscan artists.

Parallel to the High Altar, and in the south-east wall of the church, is the entrance to the cloisters and chapel and other remains of the Franciscan monastery, and the extensive conventual buildings founded by Queen Sancia, where once three hundred nuns of noble blood followed the religious life.

The Chapel of the Monks, adjoining the southern wall of the church, is a large rectangular building divided into a nave and aisle by piers with engaged columns. The aisle contains two hundred eighteenth-century stalls. The whole interior is a blaze of colour, every inch of the walls, the piers and the lofty Gothic vaulting is covered with seventeenth-century fresco work by Massimo Stanzioni and by Paolo di Majo (1763), and majolica work. The beatification of Sta Chiara is the central figure. Along the walls are seven altars representing the seven stations. The cloister outside repeats the extraordinary scene of colour within. The centre is draped in vines. But the alleys of the cloister and the garden walks are lined and coated with majolica work, representing scenes of eighteenth-century life in Naples. Fourteenth-century statues gaze in innocent bewilderment at fountains raised on majolica, whereon fishes are depicted sporting in azure waves, and the whole wilderness of spirals and semi-cylindrical cornices, gigantic snails and brilliantly coloured octagonal piers and seats. This wonderful invention is the work of Domenico Antonio Vacaro (1740). It will be observed that, like the church and chapel, the south alley of the cloister has Gothic windows, whilst elsewhere in the conventual buildings the rounded arch is retained.

At the south end of the cloister is the old Refectory, and a passage through some ruined arches leads to the Little Cloister with fourteenth-century Gothic vaulting. On the walls of the present Refectory hang two magnificent pieces of tapestry, one of the fourteenth century, and one, of silk, of the sixteenth century, worked by the nuns.

The first Angevin line was drawing to its end. It was destined to expire in a crescendo of iniquity. Robert, after the death of his son, had proclaimed his granddaughter, Giovanna, his heiress, with much pomp and circumstance in the Castel Nuovo. Clever, fond of gaiety, unbridled in temper, and passionate in temperament, the young Queen found herself yoked to a dull and boorish youth, incompetent as a husband. Moreover during her minority the Hungarian party, led by the monk, Fra Roberto, Andrew's tutor, took charge of the kingdom, and began to intrigue with Louis, King of Hungary. In order to forestall Hungarian claims, Charles, Duke of Durazzo, nephew of the late king, married his cousin Maria, Robert's other granddaughter, posthumous child of Charles the Illustrious by Marie de Valois. The surviving daughter of this marriage, Margherita, married her cousin, Charles III. of Durazzo, the successor of Giovanna I., and was mother of King Ladislaus I. and Giovanna II.

Meanwhile Petrarch was sent to Naples to assert the right of the Pope to the regency. He met with no success. Louis, on the contrary, by a well-placed bribe and a heavy one, obtained from the Pope a bull for the coronation of Andrew. The Neapolitan barons, led by Charles of Durazzo, were indignant.

In such times, in such circumstances, the issue was almost inevitable.

With or without the privity of the Queen, Andrew was called out of his bed one night at Aversa, on pretence of urgent news from Naples. He was strangled by a silken cord (woven, as the story goes, by the Queen herself), and hanged from a balcony. Civil war at once broke out, one party fighting for the Queen, the other for Durazzo. Some of the murderers were hung; others shut themselves up in their castles, and the whole land fell a prey to disorder and brigandage. King Louis of Hungary seized the opportunity to march into Italy to avenge his brother and claim the kingdom for himself by right of his grandfather, Charles Martel. He met with little opposition. For Giovanna had disgusted her supporters by marrying her paramour and cousin, Louis of Taranto. She fled to Florence, and there, making over Avignon to the Pope, received his proclamation of her innocence and of her husband as King of Sicily. Meanwhile, Louis of Hungary put the Duke of Durazzo to death and had him thrown over the balcony at Aversa, where Andrew had been hanged. Then he entered Naples, displaying a black standard with a picture of the strangled prince as a sign of the vengeance he was about to take (1348). He did not stay long in Naples, however, and presently came to terms with Giovanna, who was crowned with great pomp in 1351, after explaining to the Pope that any failure as a wife on her part had been due to witchcraft.

A period of brigandage and confusion followed, interspersed with endeavours to reduce Sicily, and tumults at Naples, where the taxes levied to pay the Grand Company of Count di Lando—a body of freebooters retained by Louis — were found too burdensome.

Whilst the Hungarians still held Naples, the Admiral Ugo del Balzo had sailed from Provence to recover it for Giovanna. He forced an entrance into the Castel dell' Ovo, where he found Maria, widow of Charles. He proposed that she should marry his son Robert, and when she refused, Robert violated her in his father's presence. The two ruffians then carried her off to Giovanna's Court and demanded assent to the marriage. Louis, however, slew the Admiral with his own hand, and sent Robert to prison in the Castel Nuovo. Maria now took her revenge. Entering his prison with four assassins, she had her violator murdered before her eyes, and his body flung out upon the seashore (1352).

On the death of Louis in 1362, Giovanna married James, the Infante of Majorca. When he died, eleven years later, Giovanna adopted Charles III. of Durazzo as her heir. But as she still had hopes of an heir, in 1376 she married Otto of Brunswick. Charles, then, in order to secure the succession, entered into negotiations with Urban VI., promising in return for the investiture to surrender portions of the Regno, which the Pope coveted for his nephew. Unhappily for herself, Giovanna supported the Anti-Pope, Clement VII., whom she entertained in the Castel dell' Ovo, till a furious riot by Urban's supporters obliged him to flee to France.

The state of the Regno was more than usually pitiful. Plagued by two popes and at least one epidemic; ravaged by warring barons and great troops of wandering banditti; taxed, bullied, plundered and perplexed, the majority decided to throw in their lot with Urban VI., when he excommunicated Giovanna and induced Louis of Hungary to support Charles in an effort to depose her. Giovanna retorted by adopting Louis, Duke of Anjou, by the second creation, her distant cousin, and brother of the King of France, as her heir, an appointment which was confirmed by the French Anti-Pope. This Francophil policy ruined her. Charles, at the head of a Hungarian army, advanced upon Naples almost unchecked, in spite of Otto's endeavour to raise a force to prevent him (July, 1381). His cavalry surprised the city by wading through the sea, and laid siege to Giovanna in the Castel Nuovo. Otto was taken prisoner in an attempt to relieve her. She was forced to surrender, and Margherita was crowned in her stead. To secure his position, Charles caused Giovanna to be smothered with a bolster (July, 1382). Although she is credited with having murdered at least two of her husbands and lived a life of the most abandoned profligacy, she was undoubtedly a woman of great ability and force of character.

Louis of Anjou, her appointed heir, was soon invading Naples to establish his claim, but died without making any headway against Charles. The latter, having refused to fulfil his bargain with the Pope, was involved in hostilities with him which kept the Regno in a perpetual state of civil war. At one time he held Urban prisoner in the Castel Nuovo, at another laid siege to him at Nocera, whilst Butillo Prignano, the Pope's nephew, whose claim to the Duchy of Capua he was supporting, ravished a nun in Naples, and was excused by Urban on the plea of his youth. He was only forty.

Charles died in Hungary, whither he had gone to be crowned king, and was succeeded by his son, Ladislaus, aged ten (1386). The Neapolitans at first accepted him. But, rejecting the regency of his mother, the *Seggi* set up a magistracy of eight Lords of good Government—*Otto del buono stato*—to administer the city. Tommaso Sanseverino, however, took up arms on behalf of Louis II. of Anjou, who had received the investiture from Clement at Avignon. Margherita retired to Gæta. Sanseverino, supported by Otto of Brunswick, gained possession of the city, and was declared Viceroy. When Margherita appeared with a fleet before Naples in the following year, they appealed for help to Louis and Clement. Clement sent them ships and money, but also, to their disgust, a Viceroy in the person of his nephew Montjoy. In the summer of 1390 Louis himself arrived with a strong force of men and ships, and took possession of the city. For several years the claimants struggled for the mastery, alternately supported and betrayed by the Sanseverini and other barons. At length Naples opened her gates to Ladislaus, and Louis resigned his pretensions to the Crown (1400), leaving the barons who had supported him to the vengeance of his rival.

Strong, ambitious and perfidious, devoted to the tourney, and keeping a sort of harem in the Castel dell' Ovo, Ladislaus spent most of his reign in warfare outside his kingdom, for which the great schism of the Church gave him ample opportunities. More than once he invaded and plundered Tuscany and Rome itself. He died from the effects of his debaucheries, and was buried in S. Giovanni a Carbonara (near the Porta S. Gennaro), a fourteenth-century church he had himself enlarged, and where his sister, Giovanna II., who succeeded him, erected his monument. Curious winding steps at the end of the Via Carbonara lead up to the Church of Sta Monica, which has a poor Gothic doorway, attributed to Baboccio, and contains a tomb by Andreasso da Firenze. Through a doorway on the left is the entrance to S. Giovanni a Carbonara. It is an ugly box-like church, with a blank north wall. The French Gothic has been converted into Renaissance. The fine Gothic chancel arch encloses a narrow apse with pointed vaulting, which is half-filled by Ladislaus' tomb. This monument, as well as the unfinished tomb of Giovanni's lover, Sergianni Caracciolo in the Cappella del Sole, is by Andreasso da Firenze (*see* p. 285). Other tombs of the Caracciolo family are in the Cappella di Caracciolo di Vico, by Giovanni da Nola. The monuments of Ladislaus and Sergianni are both adaptations of the Angevin type of tomb, still Gothic after the order of King Robert, but more heavily ornate with trefoils and pinnacles. Ladislaus on horseback surmounts his monument, and below it he is shown with Giovanna at his side. Yet the Renaissance had already appeared in Naples, and placed there one of her most exquisite possessions.

The Church of S. Angelo a Nilo (Via Nilo) was founded by Cardinal Brancaccio in 1385. Its fine Renaissance doorway, and the happy blend of the Gothic and Renaissance styles prepare us for the lovely tomb of the founder (d. 1427), in which Donatello collaborated with Michelozzo. The relief of the Assumption, the realistic figure of the Cardinal in the sleep of death, and the two angels raising the curtain that shrouds the sarcophagus, are all of singular beauty and power. Nor can the three figures that support it be easily surpassed for vigour, grace and charm.

The church and monastery of Monte Oliveto (or Sta Anna dei Lombardi) belongs also to the closing years of Ladislaus's reign (1411). It is approached through a little piazza with a fountain facing the Post Office in the Via Diaz, a fountain formed, according to the pretty legend, by the tears of a monk who wept unceasingly over the passion of Our Lord. The Post Office itself was once a magnificent Tuscan Renaissance palace, the Palazzo Gravina. Its grand façade with splendid Corinthian pilasters was half ruined in the nineteenth century by the addition of an upper story. Another very fine Renaissance palace of rather later date is the Palazzo Cuomo (*see* Appendix I.).

In the monastery of the Olivetani, which was of vast dimensions and included seven cloisters, Tasso the poet took refuge from the persecution of Alfonso d'Este, Duke of Ferrara, and wrote part of his *Jerusalem Delivered* (1588). He was a native of Sorrento, and had been educated by the Jesuits at Naples.

The porch of the basilica contains monuments to Domenico Fontana, the architect (1607), and Giuseppe Trivulzio (1757). Within the entrance—a beautiful wooden door—are altars by Giovanni da Nola and Girolamo Santacroce. There are several other works by these artists, but they are overshadowed by the beautiful Renaissance altar (bas-relief of the Adoration of the Shepherds), and tomb of Maria of Aragon (d. 1470), daughter of Ferdinand I., by Antonio Rossellino, works so beautiful in design and masterly in workmanship that they were for a long time attributed to Donatello. A curious contrast to these masterpieces is offered by the terra-cotta Pietà by Guido Mazzoni, the Modenese sculptor (1492), in the chapel of the Holy Sepulchre (south). They have the same sort of interest as Madame Tussaud's realistic waxworks, of which Michelangelo might equally have said, as he did of these, " If this could become marble, woe to the statues of antiquity ! " For these statues are all likenesses of contemporaries. Sannazaro is Joseph of Arimathea ; Alfonso II., St John ; Nicodemus is Pontano, and so on. Much more delectable are the medallions of the Four Evangelists by Luca della Robbia. In the choir the *in-*

tarsia work of the stalls (Giovanni da Verona) and frescoes by (?) Simone Papa are notable; in the apse the tombs of Alfonso II. and Guerrello Origlia, Ladislaus's favourite, who founded the church, by Giovanni da Nola; in the third chapel (south), an altar relief of St Anthony preaching to the fishes; and in the first chapel (south) an Annunziata, with an exquisite effect of perspective by Benedetto da Maiano (1489). Another building of this period, founded by Ladislaus's Grand Senechal, Antonio Pappacoda, is the Church of S. Giovanni dei Pappacoda, close to S. Giovanni Maggiore, opposite to the Pappacoda Palace. Here, too, is a mixture of the Gothic and Renaissance styles. The most notable features are the campanile and the exceedingly graceful and charming Gothic portal (1415), highly ornate, but deriving obviously from the doorway of the Duomo.

When Giovanna II. came to the throne in 1414, she was in her forty-fourth year. She had had already a long and lurid career, distinguished by an endless succession of lovers. Her unsavoury reputation survives to this day. "Siccome la Regina Giovanna" is a very odious comparison in popular speech. She was proclaimed Queen without seeking investiture from the Pope, and immediately appointed her low-born favourite, Pandolphello Alopo, chief minister. But when she married Jacques, Comte de la Marche, that Bourbon prince quickly had him put to death, placed Frenchmen in command of all the fortresses, assumed the administration of the kingdom, and shut up Giovanna in the Castel Nuovo. The Neapolitan nobles who had at first supported Jacques against Alopo, were disgusted by his Francophil policy, and presently carried off the Queen to the Castel Capuano and laid siege to Jacques in the Castel Nuovo. At the instigation of the Pope, with whom Giovanna formed a defensive alliance, Jacques was finally released, and retired in disgust to France, where he relapsed upon religion.

There ensued a struggle for predominance in the State between favourites old and new, and between French and Neapolitans. The Pope and the nobles sided first with one party, then with the other, whilst the soldiers of fortune, Braccio, Orsini and Sforza, alternately fought for and betrayed them. The Queen resigned herself entirely to the direction of her new favourite, Sergianni Caracciolo, a famous knight, and head of a family famous in Neapolitan story. She had ensnared him as a lover, against his will, so the story runs, by the following device. As he ignored her advances, she engaged her courtiers one evening in a discussion as to what each feared most. Sergianni confessed to a horror of rats. Next day a cageful of rats was let loose in the passage as he passed along a corridor. The gallant knight fled in terror, and tried first one door, then the next, hoping to escape. Each was locked. At length he came to one which yielded. It was the Queen's.

When the Pope, Martin V., invited Louis III. of Anjou and Sforza to invade Naples (1420), Giovanna replied by adopting Alfonso, King of Aragon and Sicily, as her son and heir. The latter sent ships to Naples, which compelled Sforza to raise the siege. Alfonso himself arrived presently with a large force, and turned the scales against Louis, Sforza and the Pope. His presence provoked the jealousy of the domineering Caracciolo. Suspecting a plot on his part, Alfonso seized the favourite and kept him prisoner in the Castel Nuovo. Giovanna shut herself up in the Castel Capuano, and summoned Sforza to her aid. He succeeded in confining the Spaniards to the Castel Nuovo until the arrival of a fleet from

Aragon put them once more in possession of the city, part of which they burnt, plundering Giovanna's supporters (1423). As it was obvious that Alfonso designed to make himself master of Naples before her death, Giovanna now declared Louis of Anjou her heir. With the aid of Louis, the Pope, Filippo Maria Visconti of Milan, Sforza, and later of his son, Francesco, Giovanna regained possession of Naples (12th April, 1424). Alfonso had retired to Spain, but his brother Don Pedro and the remains of the Spanish garrison maintained themselves in the Castel Nuovo.

Caracciolo now again resumed the direction of affairs, and made many enemies by his ruthless treatment of offending nobles and his overweening ambition. Louis of Anjou he kept in Calabria subduing rebellious barons. At length his ambition overreached itself. He demanded that the Queen should grant him the principality of Salerno. His enemies persuaded her to refuse. Caracciolo was so furious that, after abusing her violently, he ended by boxing her ears. The Duchess of Sessa, the Queen's cousin, seized the opportunity to put an end to his arrogant career.

Giovanna ordered his arrest. In the evening, after the celebration of his son's wedding in the Castel Capuano, Caracciolo was summoned from his bed to attend the Queen, who, he was told, had been seized with apoplexy. He opened the door, and a body of assassins rushed in and hacked him to pieces. Next day all his relations were summoned to the Castle and forthwith imprisoned (1432). He is buried in S. Giovanni a Carbonara (*see* p. 281). Louis of Anjou died two years after Caracciolo, and, a few months later, Giovanna (1435).

By her will she appointed Louis' brother, Réné of

Anjou, her heir, and a Council of Barons to act as regents. For Réné was at that time held prisoner by the Duke of Burgundy. Giovanna rests after her highly ornate career in the Church of Santissima Annunziata. Her grave is marked, as she wished, by a simple flat stone. This fourteenth-century church was rebuilt by Luigi Vanvitelli (*circa* 1780). The graceful cupola and Corinthian columns form a fine interior. There are sculptures by Giovanni da Nola, and frescoes of the seventeenth century Neapolitan artist, Belisario Corenzio, in the sacristy and treasury (*cf.* Chap. I.).

CHAPTER XI

Naples and the Aragonese

Réné and Alfonso—Triumph of Alfonso I.—His Court—Giovanni Pontano—Ferrante and John of Anjou—Lorenzo dei Medici—Revolt and murder of the Barons—Charles VIII. and Alfonso II.—Ferrantino and Federigo—The Regno divided between France and Spain—Ferdinand triumphs—Jacopo Sannazaro—SS. Severino and Sosio.

WITH Giovanna II. the first line of Anjou had died out. By birth Réné could only claim as a Valois, Marie de Valois having been Giovanna's mother, and not as a Count of Anjou. His brother Louis, however, had been popular in the country, and a strong party in Naples supported him. But there was another candidate in the field. Alfonso, King of Aragon and Sicily, was the descendant, through Constantia, of Frederick II. and Roger of the Two Sicilies. He promptly sailed for Ischia and laid siege to Gæta. There he gained the title of Magnanimous by displaying some small consideration for the inhabitants. But Filippo Maria Visconti, Duke of Milan, sent a Genoese fleet to its aid. Alfonso was made prisoner and carried to Milan. There he gave proof of that diplomatic ability which won the admiration of Machiavelli himself. For he converted his captor to his cause, and Visconti entered into an alliance with him to prevent the French becoming masters of Southern Italy. The Pope and

Francesco Sforza supported Réné, for whom his wife, Isabella of Loraine, acted as Queen Regent, until he ransomed himself and came south to face Alfonso (1438). The chivalrous Frenchman challenged his rival to settle the succession in single combat. But Alfonso was sure of his prize and saw no reason for risking his life. Caldora, the condottiere noble who had at first sided with Réné, came to the same conclusion, and deserted Réné. The Pope followed his example, and Alfonso, advancing upon Naples, laid siege to the city. Réné made a gallant defence, but on 2nd June 1442 Alfonso, like Belisarius, effected an entrance through an aqueduct, but not the same one. This was the "della Bolla," which brought the water from Monte Somma, and entered through the eastern wall. Another incident of the siege was the death of Alfonso's brother, Don Pedro, who was shot by some Genoese troops from the campanile of the Carmine Church. Guns were trained on the tower, and occasioned the miracle of the Crucifix related above (p. 256).

After the Spaniards had sacked the city for four hours, Alfonso rode through the streets and put an end to violence. Summoning a parliament at Benevento, he caused the barons to swear homage to his bastard son Ferdinand, whom he created Duke of Calabria. In the following year he ordered forty yards of the city wall to be levelled, and entered through the breach in a triumphal chariot drawn by four white horses, and followed by all the nobles of the kingdom on foot. The memory of this triumphal entry is preserved in the magnificent Renaissance Arch of Triumph which Alfonso set up in the Castel Nuovo (*see* Chap. XII.). The day was concluded with tournaments and feasting. Pardon was granted to all the Anjou faction, and honours were showered

[*Alinari*

CASTEL NUOVO

[The Angevin Towers were built by Charles I of Anjou; the Renaissance Triumphal Arch by Alfonso I, to commemorate his entry into the City]

with so liberal a hand that the number of titled folk was doubled. A few months later the Pope Eugenius granted bulls of investiture to him and Ferdinand (1443) as *Rex utriusque Siciliæ*—King of both Sicilies. Alfonso agreed to attack Sforza, whose increasing power they both dreaded, and also to grant to the barons the same privileges as they had enjoyed under William II. A swarm of Catalan adventurers now descended upon Naples, and took the place of their Angevin predecessors. For Alfonso made Naples his royal seat, and so far established order and good government that in after years his was regarded as the Golden Age. He simplified taxation, instituted a militia, personally administered justice, and became so popular that he was able to walk in the streets unattended. "A father," he explained to his protesting courtiers, "has nothing to fear from his children." A kindly prince, proud, clever and accomplished, he was a typical product of the Renaissance. His Court was brilliant and cultured. An enthusiastic scholar himself, he never travelled without his volumes of Livy and Cæsar. His coat of arms bore an open book. When Greek scholars fled to Italy after the fall of Constantinople, they found a warm welcome at the Neapolitan Court, and posts in the University, where the King himself would go on foot to hear their lectures. His patronage of Valla and Filelfo and other famous scholars brought him rich rewards in eulogy. But the chief ornament of the Court of this early Humanist was Giovanni Pontano, Alfonso's secretary, whose little Renaissance chapel we have seen near Sta Maria Maggiore, and whose Latin verse enshrines very charming descriptions of Naples. For he had a genuine lyrical gift, and was as lively and animated as if he had been a Neapolitan born. As a writer of satirical dialogues he has been deservedly described as the Lucian of his age. It is only to be regretted that he did not write in the vernacular. After Alfonso's death these scholars formed with him the famous *Accademia Pontana*, devoting themselves mainly to the cultivation of style and discussions of questions of literary and dramatic forms.

Alfonso engaged for some years in a war waged by the Pope and Venice against Florence under Cosimo dei Medici and the condottiere, Francesco Sforza, who presently succeeded to the Duchy of Milan, to which Alfonso himself had been named heir by Filippo. The war was concluded in 1455, when all parties joined in a defensive alliance against the Turks. But before that happened, the Florentines, hard pressed, had asked for help from Charles VII. of France, who sent Réné to their aid, and afterwards John of Anjou, Réné's son, took possession of Genoa in the name of Charles VII. Alfonso sent a powerful fleet to besiege that city (1457), but died suddenly on 27th June 1458. Long separated from his queen, Margaret of Castile, whom he refused to see after she had caused his mistress, the mother of Ferrante, to be strangled, he had found consolation in his later years in a romantic attachment to Lucrezia d'Anagno. Daughter of a Neapolitan noble, Lucrezia was as good (or as ambitious) as she was beautiful, and as clever as she was charming. She refused to be the King's mistress, and could not be his queen, for the Pope refused to grant him a divorce. So she remained, it is said, virtuous, whilst still retaining the devotion of her passionate lover. On his death the kingdom of Sicily remained attached to Aragon; that of Naples was devised to Ferdinand.

Pope Calixtus tried to blackmail Ferdinand, or Ferrante as he was called, into sharing the kingdom with his nephew, Borgia; but his successor, Pius II., granted him the investiture. A large party of Neapolitan barons, however, espoused the cause of John of Anjou, who inflicted a crushing defeat upon Ferdinand. He would probably have captured the kingdom if he had advanced against Naples, but he was dissuaded from doing so by the Prince of Taranto. For Queen Isabella, leaving the city disguised as a Franciscan monk, had flung herself at his feet and besought him, as he had made her a queen, so he would let her die a queen. Taking advantage of this respite, Ferdinand in the following year defeated John at Troja (1461), who finally retired to Provence. This victory is commemorated in the bronze gates of the Castel Nuovo (*see* Chap. XII.). On the death of Queen Isabella in 1467, Ferdinand married his cousin Giovanna, daughter of John, King of Aragon. Shortly afterwards he made an alliance with Sixtus IV., and sent troops into Tuscany to support him in his attempt upon Florence (1478). Florence was hard pressed. To save the State, Lorenzo dei Medici, taking his life in his hands, voluntarily went to Naples and placed himself in the power of Ferdinand. It was a noble and courageous action, for Ferdinand was a monster of cruelty, avarice, lust and treachery. He was perfectly capable of murdering his guest if he thought fit. But if he had the defects, he also had some of the qualities of the typical Italian tyrant of the Renaissance. He was sensitive to art and literature, and his mind was open to argument and appreciative of eloquence. His father, Alfonso, according to a well-known story, was once so enthralled by the eloquence of a Florentine ambassador that, rather than interrupt, he heard him to the end, before raising his hand to brush a fly from his nose. Ferrante, too, was fascinated by the eloquence, and convinced by the arguments of Lorenzo the Magnificent, who returned to Florence with an honourable peace. The occasion lives in art. For Botticelli's great allegorical picture in the Pitti Gallery at Florence, in which Pallas, the beautiful Goddess, is seen subduing the Centaur, the beast of war and disorder, with a background of a ship at anchor in the Bay, commemorates Lorenzo's triumphant return.

In the following August the Turks landed in Italy, and stormed Otranto. They had been invited into Italy, it was said, by the Florentines and Venetians, in order to compel Alfonso to withdraw his troops from Tuscany. The warring states of Italy united for a moment in the presence of the common enemy. The Neapolitan fleet, in conjunction with its allies, recovered Otranto (1481). Before long, however, Ferdinand was at war with the Pope and Venice in defence of his son-in-law, the Duke of Ferrara. Peace was concluded in 1484. Ferdinand presently assisted Florence against Genoa. By so doing he provoked the resentment of the Genoese Pope, Innocent VII., who was already sore at the non-payment of his tribute. He took his revenge by espousing the cause of the Puglian barons, and offering the investiture to Réné. This was the occasion of one of the most horrible crimes in the bloodstained annals of the Renaissance, a crime of which the ghoulish traces remain to this day.

The barons had been provoked by the conduct of Alfonso, Duke of Calabria, Ferdinand's son, who respected neither their property nor the honour of their womenkind. Alfonso, cruel and arbitrary, was determined to curtail their privileges, and was imprudent enough not to disguise his intentions. They rose in revolt. But neither party was able to crush the other, and in the following year, 1486, a peace was concluded. The barons, not without reason, distrusted Ferdinand's good faith. But when the Kings of Aragon and Sicily, the Duke of Milan and the Florentines stood sponsors for the Treaty, they came to terms. Ferdinand agreed to pardon all concerned and to pay tribute to the Pope when convenient. The Duke of Salerno, head of the House of Sanseverini —whose palace is now the Church of Gesù Nuovo— chose the better part. He fled, disguised as a muleteer, to France, after inscribing on his palace gate the adage, *Passero vecchio non entra in caggiola*—an old sparrow does not enter the cage. Among the leaders who remained were Antonio Petrucci, who had won credit by his upright administration as royal secretary, and the Conte di Sarno. Ferdinand and Alfonso, with cunning dissimulation, prepared for these less wise sparrows a trap, which places them on a pinnacle by the side of Cesare Borgia as exponents of Italian statecraft in the fifteenth century. A marriage was arranged between Sarno's son and the daughter of the Duke of Amalfi, Ferdinand's nephew. A splendid banquet was given in the Castel Nuovo to celebrate the occasion, in the room now known as the Sala dei Baroni (*see* Chap. XII.). Ferdinand and Alfonso (who had for some time been practically master of the kingdom) entertained them royally. Suddenly, in the middle of the feast, when all was gaiety and goodwill, the signal was given. Soldiers entered. The bridegroom and all the barons were seized and hurried into the dungeons of the Castle. The sponsors of the Treaty protested against this signal stroke of cunning and bad faith, but without avail. After the show of a trial, princes, dukes, and barons by the dozen, with their wives and children, were butchered. Their property was seized to swell the coffers of the King. The Conte di Sarno and Antonio Petrucci were executed in front of the Castle, some time after the two sons of the latter had been beheaded in the Piazza del Mercato. The fate of the rest was less public. Food, indeed, was daily sent to their dungeons. But when one day the executioner was seen wearing a gold chain which had belonged to the Prince of Bisignano, the truth was recognised. The grisly skeletons of four of them—one a strangled cardinal, distorted in his last agony, two barons and a princess, beheaded—are to be seen in the Castel Nuovo (*see* Chap. XII.). Their presence is explained by the ghoulish habit recorded of this king and prince, of keeping the salted bodies of their victims in chambers beneath their palaces, so that they might, when the mood seized them, go down and gloat over the agonised features of their dead enemies.

Among the few who escaped was the Princess of Bisignano, who with her children sought refuge in the Church of San Lionardo, which then stood in Chiaia, outside the walls. As the virtue of that saint as a protector of fugitives was strong and deeply respected, she was able to persuade a boatman to carry them to Terracina. But there were other fugitives in the same church, barons and their ladies and children, who, it is believed, were less fortunate. For Alfonso, returning one day from Pozzuoli, is said to have butchered them all with nameless cruelty. Certain it is that some atrocious crime of the sort in connection with that church haunted even his soiled conscience, and the horror of it is said to have caused him to flee from Naples at the approach of Charles VIII. For he had not been a year upon the throne when the French King marched into Italy.

Of Alfonso there is nothing good to be said. But Ferdinand, treacherous and greedy as he was able, was much admired for the successful duplicity of his statecraft. He raised a revenue of some 700,000 ducats from his kingdom, partly by confiscating the estates of the Francophil nobles and largely by a system of commercial monopolies. Whilst remaining a feudatory of the Holy See, he succeeded in avoiding payment of tribute. Though delighting in cruelty for its own sake, oppressive, and taking his subject's wives and daughters as freely as he took their money, he yet did not a little for Naples. Not only did he enlarge the city and build new walls, but he also gave the Regno a lasting source of prosperity by introducing the manufacture of silks and woollens. He was a great patron of learning, encouraged the University, and introduced the new art of printing. According to Guicciardini, he would have been accounted a good prince had he continued as he began, for he gave the kingdom many wise laws, and raised it to a greater pitch of grandeur than any of his predecessors. The arrogance, oppression and treachery of his later years are to be attributed, at least in part, to the predominating influence of his son. The dread of a French invasion is said to have hastened his end. For Charles VIII. was preparing to enforce his claim to the Regno, and the Sanseverini and other Neapolitan exiles were eager to return in his train. For the claim of Réné, through the adoption of Louis of Anjou by Giovanna, had passed through his nephew, the Comte de Maine, by will and succession to Louis XI., and thus to Charles VIII. Ferdinand, King of Spain, also had his claim, and, but for trouble nearer home, would have made war upon the violators of the treaty he had guaranteed.

Gian Galeazzo, the weakling Duke of Milan, had married in 1489 Isabella of Aragon, daughter of Alfonso. Lodovico il Moro, his uncle and guardian, the real ruler of Milan, had married her cousin, Beatrice d'Este. Stung to the quick by the usurpation which threatened her, Isabella urged her father to come to the aid of the rightful duke. The answer was prompt. Ambassadors arriving from the Court of Naples suggested that it was time for the guardian to retire in favour of his ward. Lodovico replied by entering into a defensive league with Venice and the Papacy and inviting the French King to seize Naples.

So he opened the gates of Italy to the foreigner, and from that moment the end of the independence of the Italian states was in sight, an end, too, of the petty wars and leagues and intrigues by which they had been endeavouring to maintain the balance of power between them. The Alps became once more the highways of European armies, and Italy a mere counter in the game of European politics. For, once the great Powers of Europe had set foot on the Italian stage, it was absurd to suppose that they would be content to serve the petty despots. Italy, henceforth, divided and rotten with unscrupulous intriguing of small states against each other, became but the arena where Austria, France and Spain might fight their battles and glut their appetite for spoliation.

To stay the advance of the French, Alfonso sent his son Ferrantino, with an army strengthened by a Papal contingent, into the Romagna, whilst his brother, Federigo, protected the coast with a powerful fleet. But Charles VIII. conquered Naples almost without a blow. The great condottieri, with their bands of mercenary soldiers, had by this time reduced warfare in Italy to a mixture of chess and cheating. They marched and counter-marched for position, and surrendered as soon as they were out-manœuvred or outbribed. To their horror and amazement, they found in the French army soldiers who fought and slew. Charles entered Rome on 31st December. A large part of the Regno declared for the French. Three weeks later Alfonso abdicated in favour of his son, and fled to Sicily (22nd January 1495). He had long been haunted, it was said, by the ghosts of the barons he had murdered, and his nerve was shattered by nightly visions in which his father appeared and warned him that their line was doomed as a punishment for their murderous deeds. Apparently, too, he hoped that Ferrantino, who was young and popular, might be able to stem the tide. Ferrantino retreated before Charles to Capua. Then Trivulzio, the renowned soldier of fortune, showed that if the condottieri had forgotten how to fight, they still remembered how to betray.

At Poggio Reale, where Alfonso II. had built himself a beautiful villa, an embassy from Naples saluted Charles, who entered the city almost unopposed. "It only lacks Adam and Eve to make it a Paradise," he wrote enthusiastically, after his triumphal entry on 22nd February. Ferrantino, after destroying the greater part of his fleet, endeavoured to hold out, first in the Castel Nuovo and then at Ischia. But within a month the whole kingdom had submitted to the French. Charles granted an amnesty to those who had served the Aragons and restored the property of the Angevin exiles. But six weeks later he was obliged to beat a precipitate retreat. For the Emperor Maximilian joined a league of all the Italian states to drive the French out of the country. Before he left (21st May), Ferrantino had landed in Calabria. With the aid of the "Great Captain," Gonsalvo de Cordova, and some Spanish troops lent him by Ferdinand, King of Spain, and the Venetian fleet, he quickly recovered his kingdom, and was received with tumultuous joy by the Neapolitans, who had welcomed Charles with similar enthusiasm. After marrying his aunt, niece of the King of Spain, he died prematurely, on 7th October 1496, to the great grief of the whole kingdom. He was succeeded by his uncle, Federigo, "a prudent prince," we are told, "of mild disposition and a great encourager of learning." He soon became aware that his Spanish and Venetian allies were, under one pretext or another, clinging to the places they had taken from the French. And his general was Gonsalvo, Ferdinand's man.

Ferdinand the Catholic had, indeed, already entered into negotiations with Charles VIII. for a partition of the kingdom of Naples. Louis XII., on succeeding the latter, immediately took the title of King of France, Jerusalem, the Two Sicilies, and the Duchy of Milan. The Pope, Alexander VI., after vainly endeavouring to get hold of the Regno for his son by marrying Cesare Borgia to Federigo's daughter, entered into an alliance with Louis. After making himself master of the Milanese, Louis concluded a treaty with Ferdinand of Spain for the partition of Naples (November 1501). Ferdinand's claim was based on the right of conquest by his uncle, Alfonso I. This treaty—shamefully sanctioned by the Pope—provided that Spain should have Apulia and Calabria, and France the rest of the kingdom, with the title of King of Naples and Jerusalem. Before such a combination of forces, betrayed by the Spaniards who held his fortresses, and weakened by the usual division of warring parties at home, Federigo could do nothing. The French army advanced unopposed. After storming and barbarously sacking Capua (25th July 1501), they entered Naples. Federigo retired to France, where Louis created him Duke of Anjou. The French and Spaniards fell out over the division of the territory, which had not been sufficiently explicit. The French Viceroy began hostilities against Gonsalvo, and succeeded in shutting him up in Barletta. But next year

(1503) having received reinforcements from Spain, he severely defeated the French in Apulia, and on 14th May entered Naples in triumph. Ferdinand thereupon repudiated a settlement which had been made in the meantime by his son-in-law Philip, Archduke of Austria, with Louis. Louis sent a fleet and army to assert his rights. They were heavily defeated by Gonsalvo on 21st December 1504. The French were driven out of the Regno. Louis resigned his claims, and Naples became a mere province of Spain (1505).

Federigo was accompanied into his exile by Jacopo Sannazaro, a loyal and high-minded man of letters, to whom his patron gave a beautiful Renaissance villa at Mergellina (destroyed in the French war of 1528), and whose church there we have visited (Chap. III.). Though not a writer of the first rank, Sannazaro's position in literature is of importance. Apart from his Latin poetry, he was the first to prove that excellent Italian prose could be written out of Tuscany. His immensely popular pastoral romance, *Arcadia*, published in 1504, fixed the form of that type of pseudo-classical composition and directly inspired both the spirit and many of the details of Sir Philip Sidney's equally famous romance of that name. In spite of its artificiality of style and subject, it reveals the genuine grace and poetical character of the writer's mind.

The Church of SS. Severino e Sosio, rebuilt and enlarged at the close of this period, contains some tombs by Giovanni da Nola, in his best manner, with inscriptions by Sannazaro. That of Giovanni Battista Cicara is notable for its lovely frieze. By the same artist are the realistic figures of the three Sanseverini brothers, who were poisoned, whilst out hunting, by their uncle in 1516. There is also a fine polyptych by Andrea da Salerno, perhaps the best of the early Neapolitan painters (*circa* 1520). The sixteenth-century choir stalls are noteworthy. The ceiling was painted by Corenzio, who fell from a platform whilst at work here and is buried in the church. The four cloisters of the old Benedictine monastery are decorated with sixteenth-century frescoes, illustrating the life of St Benedict. They are generally ascribed in part to Antonio Solario (Lo Zingaro). (*See* Ch. XIV.) One must be content to say that they are by some Venetian or Florentine artists. Restoration has not entirely destroyed the vigour and variety of the figures and the charm of the Tuscan background. The third cloister is called Il chiostro del Platano, after a plane tree said to have been planted by St Benedict. The monastery itself is now the repository of the great collection of Neapolitan archives.

CHAPTER XII

The Castles and the Walls

Roman Naples—The walls—Porta S. Gennaro—Porta Capuana—Castel Capuano—S. Pietro ad Aram—Porta Nolana—Castel Carmine—Castel Nuovo—Castel St Elmo—San Martino.

THE Neapolis of the Roman Empire was roughly about the same size as Pompeii. It formed an oblong of about 1000 by 800 yards, occupying little more than the space of one of the modern *quartieri*, S. Lorenzo. The three *Decuman* streets—Anticaglia, Tribunali, Biagio—were intersected by over a score of *Cardines*, which still lend to this part of Naples an air of rectangularity very different from the winding streets of mediæval growth. The western boundary, as we have seen (Chap. I.), is indicated by the Via Mezzocannone, at the southern end of which was the Porta Ventosa, leading down to the seashore and harbour-suburb (*proasteion*). The south wall, two or three hundred yards from the coast, ran along a little ridge of higher ground, from the Sma. Annunziata to the New University buildings. The line from the Annunziata to the Castel Capuano is roughly that of the western boundary. The Piazza Cavour and Strada Carbonara lie a little outside the northern limit. The western gates of the *Decuman* streets were the Porta Romana (Anticaglia), Porta Alba (Tribunali), and Porta Puteolana (Biagio). The Porta Capuana and Porta Nolana were the eastern exits of the

Via dei Tribunali and Via di Biagio. Outside the walls and Porta Nolana, and a little to the north of the Via Annunziata, were the Baths, which were rebuilt under Titus. South of the Via Annunziata, and stretching down to the Via S. Giovanni a Mare, lay the Hippodrome. And at the northern end of the Via del Duomo, the great Stadium. Here, every

CASTEL NUOVO

five years the great Games were held, which rivalled those of Olympia and Rome. Practically nothing of all this remains.

Under the dukes and bishops the walls were strengthened, and forts (*castelli*) built outside the walls to serve as places of refuge from Saracens and other marauders. We have seen how the walls were dismantled and destroyed by Totila and Conrad (1194). They were rebuilt, and the circumference of the city extended first by Narses and Innocent IV., and afterwards by Charles I. (1270), Charles II.

(1300), Charles III. (1382), and by Alfonso I. and his successors. Charles V. and the Viceroy, Don Pedro de Toledo (1537), rebuilt and extended the fortifications from Carbonara to the height of St Elmo and, leaving the scarp of that mountain to serve as a wall, continued them to the Gate of Chiaia. Giulio Capaccio, writing in 1607, describes the circumference of the walls as extending for five miles. There were then, he tells us, no fewer than thirty-one land, and five sea towers, the names of which he gives, and the following gates :—Porta Capuana, San Gennaro, Sta Maria di Constantinopoli, Reale or Toledo (the old Porta Ventosa), and Nolana. These gates marked the lines of Toledo's walls, which also included both St Elmo and Sta Lucia, the arsenal and Castel Nuovo.

Apart from the Porta Alba and the Castel dell' Ovo, which we have already dealt with (Chap. V.), and the Castel St Elmo and Castel Nuovo which we shall presently describe, the only remaining section of the fortifications of any importance is that which stretches from the Porta San Gennaro to the Castel and Porta del Carmine.

A considerable section of the old city walls runs along the Piazza Cavour to the Porta San Gennaro, near the intersection of the Via del Duomo. The two huge round towers here are now used as barracks. Another tower is passed on turning down the Via Cirillo and the Strada Carbonara in the direction of the Stazione Centrale. This brings us to the Porta Capuana, within which is the Castel Capuano. The Porta Capuana, always the principal entrance to the city, received its present form under the Angevins (1485), and was enriched with trophies to commemorate the victorious return of Charles V. from Africa. The handsome gateway is by Giuliano da Maiano (1485); and the statues are by Giovanni da Nola

(1535). On the right rises the lofty dome of Sta Caterina a Formello. Within and without the large round towers of the Gate is a crowded fish and vegetable market, where, as of old, *cittadino* meets *contadino*, and chaffers over the produce brought in from the countryside.

Within the Gate, and formerly surrounded by a beautiful garden, but now flanked by the Piazza dei Tribunali, is a square barrack-like building, consisting of one story raised upon porticoes and entirely without ornamentation. This is the Castel Capuano, which King William began, and which Frederick II. is said to have brought Niccolo Pisano to Naples to complete (1220-31). It remains much as it was when it ceased to be used as a royal residence and was converted into a central Court of Justice by Don Pedro de Toledo. Since then it has been known as La Vicaria (*circa* 1537). Toledo made its dungeons healthy and up-to-date as prisons went in those days, but under the last Bourbon kings it gained a hideous notoriety for the barbarity with which political prisoners were treated in its noisome dens. In the Museum of S. Martino a stone column—*La Colonna della Vicaria*—is preserved, which used to stand outside the castle gate, and where debtors were exposed stark naked in proof of their insolvency.

Working southwards and towards the sea, we come to the Church of S. Pietro ad Aram, at the end of Corso Umberto I., and close to the Stazione Centrale. This church was restored in 1914. The remains of an old doorway are embedded in the surrounding shops and houses. The principal entrance is in the street to the left of it. The altar from which the church takes its name is preserved on the north side of this entrance, and was once dedicated to Apollo. But it is sanctified for the faithful by the tradition

BRONZE DOORS (CASTEL NUOVO)
(A cannon-ball is shown embedded)

that St Peter used it for the baptism and communion of the first Neapolitan Christians, St Candida and St Asprenus, after healing the latter at St Candida's request.

Close at hand, in the Corso Garibaldi, between the Stazione Centrale and Stazione Circumvesuviana, are the low round towers and archway of the Porta Nolana. It is built over and about with houses. It was here that the magic marble faces were set up, which tradition attributed to Vergil (*see* Chap. V.). Scoppa, a sixteenth-century writer, says that he saw them there as a boy, before Alfonso II. of Aragon destroyed the Gate and removed them to his villa at Poggio Reale.

Of the Castel del Carmine, only part of two huge round towers and the gateway—Porta del Carmine—remain to remind us, amidst a scene of much clearing and reconstruction, of the undistinguished building begun by Charles III., and completed by Ferdinand I. (1382). It was called Sperone from its shape, and was rebuilt after the failure of the Duc de Guise, who made it his headquarters (*see* Chap. XII.) at the time of Masaniello's rebellion.

Landwards, the three huge, round, machicolated Angevin towers of the Castel Nuovo frown over the east end of the Piazza del Municipio. Seawards, two similar towers guard the Porto Beverello. This harbour, whence the steamers for Ischia and Capri sail, is enclosed by the prolonged Molo San Vincenzo on the west, shorewards by the Molo Beverello, and on the east by the Molo Angioino, built by Charles II. (1300), and enlarged by his successors. The lighthouse upon it was built originally in the following century. Beyond are the Molo San Gennaro and the Commercial Harbour and docks for ocean liners.

Castel Nuovo—New Castle—was the name given to this famous castle and palace, isolated, outside the city walls and close to the sea, to distinguish it from those older fortresses, the Castel dell' Ovo and Castel Capuano. So Charles I. dubbed the stronghold which Pierre de Chaul and Pierre d'Agincourt built for him in 1277; so did all the Spanish Bourbons.

LIGHTHOUSE, NAPLES

But to the man in the street it is *Maschio Angioino*, the Angevin Keep.

As a fortress it was soon out of date. Military history does not stand still any more than any other. Between weapons of offence and the reply to them there is a perpetual see-saw. Not long after it was completed, the vaunted Angevin stronghold, built on the French mediæval plan, was out of date. The development of artillery, in weight and range, made it necessary for the defence to push the assailants further back from what had been intended to be an impregnable fastness. With this object, the Spaniards constructed an outer range of fortifications consisting of low bastions, which are still traceable here and there, but have for the most part disappeared. They are clearly indicated on the seventeenth-century map reproduced on p. xvi. Rebuilt by Alfonso the Magnanimous, and enlarged again by Charles III. (1735), the castle and palace were used as the royal and vice-regal residence. The five gloomy and threatening towers have been known by different names from time to time. The two facing the sea, now called St Louis or Beverello (east), and S. Ferdinando (west), were named Bibirella and Telasia, or Torre dell' Oro, in the sixteenth century. Of the two towers on either side of the Triumphal Arch, that on the right is called S. Francesco, and that on the left S. Carlo. The fifth, formerly named the Governor's Tower or Sta Barbara, is now termed S. Alfonso.

The outer wall, which used to block the view of the approach to the castle, has recently been removed, and other work is now in progress upon the approach to the main entrance. The surrounding moat is also being excavated at the present time (1926). The massive towers are impressive rather than beautiful. But beyond the drawbridge, and squeezed in between the two huge gateways which glower over the town, there has been inserted—somewhat inharmoniously—a rich and graceful archway. This beautiful piece of Renaissance work is the Triumphal Arch which was raised to commemorate the entry of Alfonso I. into Naples (1442). It was erected between 1455 and 1470, and has been attributed to Giuliano da Maiano, who worked on the Capuan Gate, and to Leon Battista Alberti. But it lacks several of the chief characteristics of the work of the great Florentine architect, and is more probably the work of the Milanese, Pietro di Martino.

Four Corinthian columns rest upon bases richly ornamented with fruits and rosettes. In the tympanum of the archway, between these columns, two winged dolphins, rampant, hold horns of abundance on either side of the arms of Aragon. The cornice is adorned with *putti* holding garlands and musical instruments, and carries the inscription:

ALPHONSVS REX HISPANVS SICVLVS ITALICVS
PIVS CLEMENS INVICTVS

The second story displays the triumphal entry of Alfonso into Naples. Above this compartment is another arch similar to Roman triumphal arches, over which are four statues in niches representing the virtues of the King. The whole is crowned by statues of St Michael, St Anthony and St Sebastian, added by Giovanni da Nola. The interior of the archway is covered with bas-reliefs in which barons and people are shown doing homage to the king.

Niches for the gates will be noticed in the main archway. We enter into a large square courtyard. Before us is the famous building which again and again since the time of Manfred has been the scene of fierce and terrible conflicts, of royal splendour and triumphant pomp, of treacherous cruelty and grim tragedies, some traces of which yet remain. In the right-hand corner is the chapel of Sta Barbara, the patron saint of gunners. The portal is a lovely work by Giuliano da Maiano, who also designed the Madonna and angels in the lunette. The Madonna above is by Francesco Laurana. The ceiling paintings are by Luca Giordano. A chapel reached by a staircase is shown as the chamber wherein S. Francesco da Paola rested on his visit to Naples. It is in a subterranean chamber beneath this chapel that the skeletons of the victims of Alfonso and Ferrante are to be seen (*see* Chap. XI.).

A stone staircase in the left-hand corner of the courtyard leads up to the *Sala dei Baroni*, so called

STEPS TO HALL, CASTEL NUOVO

from that scene of triumphant treachery described in the last chapter. The room shows traces of the fire by which it was gutted in 1919. But it is well worth while to ascend the stairs and pass into the vast empty room. Remains of a musicians' gallery confront us as we enter, on the left of which is a passage leading down to the ramparts and bastion of Beverello's tower, which command a fine view of the harbour and the eastern end of the Bay. On the right are winding staircases and secret passages, believed, erroneously, to communicate with the strongholds of St Elmo above and the Castel dell' Ovo below. A bas-relief on the door leading to the King's apartments repeats the representation of Alfonso's triumphal entry (? by Luciano di Lauria). Inside the hall at present are the double bronze gates by Guglielmo da Monaco, which formerly closed the entrance to the castle. They are signed *Guilelmus Monacus fecit*. The panels contain spirited bas-reliefs of exquisite workmanship, depicting scenes from the battles fought by King Ferrante against the barons in Puglia, and his victory at Troia, etc. (1461). The incidents are described in Latin verses at the foot of each panel. The doors have been dented in several places by cannon balls. The bottom panel of the left-hand wing still holds a cannon-ball embedded in the folds of the half-pierced bronze. It is usually said that these were shots fired in the commotion of 1799. But the type of cannon ball is an early one. The incident occurred in Gonsalvo's days, possibly in 1495 (*see* Chap. XI.). The thin, evil features of Ferrante are portrayed in life-like fashion. Both these gates and the triumphal arch are of interest for their portraiture of that cruel and treacherous dynasty and its contemporaries.

Upon the heights of the ridge above the city, directly above the Castel Nuovo, towers that other castle, the Castel St Elmo. It takes its name from the hill of St Elmo, or St Ermo, as old writers called it, deriving it from a chapel dedicated to St Erasmus, an early Neapolitan martyr. It is said that a Norman tower was erected here in 1170 and called Belforte. But, so far as we know, Robert the Wise was the first to fortify this hill and build a fort of that name, of which Francesco di Vito was the architect (1329).

Don Pedro de Toledo replaced it in 1537 by the Castel Sant' Elmo. It was strongly fortified, and held by a Spanish garrison which dominated the city.

San Martino

[The Castle of St Elmo and the old Carthusian monastery of S. Martino may be reached

(i) From the Piazza Dante by the funicular railway (*Funicolare di Montesanto*), or Tram 7 to the Piazza Vanvitelli, or

(ii) From the west end of the Villa Nazionale (Via Piedigrotta) by Tram 4 or 6, which winds round and up the Corso Vittorio Emmanuele to the Piazza Salvator Rosa. Thence by Tram 7 to Piazza Vanvitelli. This goes by the Strada della Cerra and Gennaro ad Antignano, turning left-handed to the village of Antignano and past the villas of the Vómero quarter, and along the Corso Alessandro Scarlatti.

Alighting at the Piazza Vanvitelli, the Scarlatti road leads you on to a flight of steps, at the top of which is the station of the funicular railway mentioned above. From this point the road winds to the right of the station, round the battlemented walls of St Elmo Castle.]

As we walk under the frowning walls of the castle, whose crumbling battlements now guard a military prison, we see through loopholes in the arches of the walls on our left hints of the marvellous view soon to be obtained from the ramparts. The Apennine range and the high hills of Caserta frame the Campanian plain, from which the separate peaks of Vesuvius rise in the foreground to the right. At our feet lies a huddled mass of houses, broken here and there by a cypress or umbrella pine, and here and there by domes, towers, or fragmentary arches. The centre of the picture, at the end of a ridge in the middle distance, is the imposing L-shaped front of the Royal Palace of Capodimonte. This palace was built as a shooting box for Charles III. of Bourbon in 1738 by Giovanni Medrano, the architect of the Teatro S. Carlo. There Charles established the famous factory of porcelain, many interesting specimens of which are preserved in the *Museo* there and in S. Martino. The fine park is a favourite resort on Sunday afternoons.

From distant Campanili the sound of bells is borne upwards upon the breeze, in a greeting, as it were, from the crowded city to the silent monastery on the promontory.

A more extensive view seawards—a view of unsurpassable beauty—is obtained from *Belvedere*, balconies projecting from a room in the *Museo* within.

The Certosa of S. Martino was begun by Charles the Illustrious, Duke of Calabria, and completed by his father, Robert the Wise. Francesco di Vito was associated with Tino da Camaino in designing it (1325-29). But the Carthusian monastery we see to-day is not their work. It is the masterpiece of Cosimo Fansaga, the Bergamese architect (1591-1678). The design of the whole demonstrates his greatness as an architect, and the details his superiority as an artist to most of his Neapolitan contemporaries. His orderly mind was able to control the use of acres of marble and stucco, and his artistic sense to exercise a certain restraint in the application of the florid embellishments beloved by the degenerate taste of his time. The Certosa is now a National Museum, and, with the Duomo and *Museo Nazionale*, is the *locus classicus* for the study of Neapolitan painting and the virtues and vices of seventeenth-century baroque (*see* Chap. XIV.). The monastery was dissolved in 1866. The monks, who had long been a byword for their wealth and luxury, particularly distinguished themselves in the Revolution of 1799, when they welcomed the French by making the new Republican flag of red, yellow and blue out of ecclesiastical hangings, and entertaining the leaders of the Parthenopean Republic to a sumptuous supper and dance in the Prior's rooms.

The church is approached through a passage in the left-hand corner of the Little Cloisters, next to the main entrance. This leads us into a series of rooms covered with paintings by Lanfranco, Giordano, Solimena, Stanzioni, Arpino, Reni, as well as by Ribera, Corenzio, and Caracciolo, the triumvirate who drove away from Naples all capable competitors. The mercenary monopolists compelled the Cavaliere d'Arpino to leave the ceiling of the choir here unfinished, as they forced Guido Reni also to flee from Naples and assassinated Domenichino (*see* p. 137). We come first to the Chapter House, an oblong hall panelled with *intarsia* work. Beyond is the Treasury, in which are two very remarkable pictures. The first is Ribera's masterpiece, the Descent from the Cross (1637). The exaggeration of light and shade, the daring foreshortening, the self-conscious cleverness of the whole thing are apparent. But it strikes the true tragic note by its effective and unforced realism. It should be compared with his St Jerome and St Sebastian in the *Museo Nazionale*. On the ceiling is the Judith by Luca Giordano, which was painted by him in forty-eight hours, at the age of seventy-two (1703). For a *tour de force* it is a *tour de force*. An amazing feat certainly, and typical of a painter of such marvellous facility and speed that he could turn out at a moment's notice a picture in the style of any master so as to deceive a connoisseur. But the criterion of art is not m.p.h.

Next is the Sacristy, with magnificent *intarsia* stalls by Bonaventura Presti, and paintings by Stanzioni (Hall of Pilate), Cavaliere d'Arpino, Saraceni and Caravaggio (Peter denying Christ—a fine picture).

The church itself is a remarkable example of baroque ornamentation. Walls and arches have been inundated with a torrent of paint and a deluge of multi-coloured marble. Massive, shapeless piers are crowned by capitals that are no capitals, but simply applied ornamentation, mere excuses for carving and scroll work, with only the barest pretence to any constructional use or meaning. An effect of overwhelming sumptuousness is achieved by the cynical sacrifice of the last atom of architectural consciousness or artistic sincerity. The lighting and the construction are wholly subservient to the display of the painters. The whole effect is not brilliant but dazzling. Excuses in plenty have been made for this style by writers from Goethe downwards. The brilliancy of the Neapolitan climate and sunshine, it is urged, had to be surpassed; the poverty-stricken people must be provided with luxurious palaces in the House of God, and so forth. The fact remains that it is a monument of vulgarity and bad taste.

Ribera ("Lo Spagnoletto") shared the task of decorating the Chancel with Lanfranco. In the vaulting are the strong, nervous figures of his Twelve Apostles on the roof. Over the main doorway is the Descent from the Cross, by Massimo Stanzioni, notable for its grace and gentleness, which is said to have inspired Ribera to outrival it by his picture in the Treasury.

In the Choir the frescoes are by Arpino. Here are other pictures by Caracciolo (Washing of the Disciples' Feet), Ribera (Last Supper), and Stanzioni (Last Supper), whose work shows plainly the influence of Vandyke and the Flemish school. They are quite eclipsed by the genuine feeling, simplicity and masterly composition of the Nativity by Guido Reni (at the back of the Choir), who died before it was completed. The exceeding beauty of the Madonna is unforgettable.

A doorway in the Little Cloister, close to the entrance to the church, leads to the Refectory, which contains some of the furniture and vestments, etc., belonging to the old monastery. At one end of the hall is a painting of the Marriage at Cana, at the other a portrait of Christ and some magnificent illuminated Missals.

The Great Cloister is reached by a corridor in the far side of the Little Cloister. Sixty columns of white marble carry this charming and dignified composition by Fansaga. Its simplicity and severity are only spoilt by clumsy baroque sculpture about the entrances at the four corners. The upper recessed story is surmounted by a balustrade. The centre is relieved by the softness of a green, formal garden, in one corner of which is the monks' cemetery, enclosed by a Renaissance balustrade, decorated with carven skulls. The dial of a large clock recording six hours only will be noticed in the south-west corner, in which is the entrance to the monastic dwellings, now used as a museum.

The first room of the *Museo* contains specimens of Neapolitan and Capodimonte ware. In a room to the right is a very curious *Presepe* (*see* Chap. I.). All the actors in this scene of the Nativity are dressed in old Neapolitan costumes.

In the right-hand corner of the second room on the right, there is an interesting group of relics and mementoes of Masaniello's insurrection (*see* Chap. XIII.). They include a picture by Micco Spadaro, the seventeenth-century *genre* artist, of the final scene in the Piazza del Mercato (9729), a medal and a mask of the Peasant Duke (2474), portraits of himself, of Bernadina Pisa, his wife, and Grazia, his sister (5849, 5850, 6829, 9728). Next to them are some remarkable pictures of eighteenth-century Naples, notably—

(1) Charles III. and Maria Amalia driving in pro-

cession to the Feast of the Piedigrotta ; (2) Charles III. leaving Naples for Spain, October 6, 1759. (3) Portrait of Charles III. (4) Charles III. renouncing the Kingdom of Naples to Ferdinand IV. (Michele Foscini). (5) Accession of Ferdinand IV.; his portrait (9789); and a water-colour sketch of that monarch dressed and posing as a Neapolitan fisherman (5769). (6) Naples in Carnival time.

For the rest, there are several other rooms of relics and records of the Bourbons and the Risorgimento—Murat's cloak, Bomba's *kepi*, Ruffo's hat, Garibaldi's coach, Ferdinand's repulsive mask, and so on.

CHAPTER XIII

Masaniello and the First Parthenopean Republic

> "Con l'ampia monarchia pugna il Mercato,
> E contro il summo si solleva il vile. . . .
> Dal Mercato alla forca il pass' è breve."

NAPLES was now a mere province of Spain, and was administered as such. Ferdinand rewarded Gonsalvo by making him his first Viceroy. But his conduct soon gave rise to suspicion that the Great Captain might play the traitor or usurper. Ferdinand therefore paid a hasty visit to Naples (1506), and fetched him back to Spain. Ferdinand refused to pay tribute to the Pope, and disappointed the people who clamoured for relief from taxation. For he was himself hard put to it to compensate his own supporters, whom he was obliged to deprive of their lands in order to restore the property of the Angevin nobles, in accordance with the treaty.

His successor, Charles V., came to terms with Francis I., who assigned to him the French part of the kingdom of Naples, as the dowry of his daughter. But the election of Charles to the Empire roused the jealousy both of the French King and the Pope. Leo X. did indeed grant him a bull dispensing with the investiture of Naples. But Francis began to reassert his claim. Taken prisoner at Pavia, he renounced his pretension. But ere long France and the Papacy formed an alliance with Venice and Milan against the Emperor. Sicily and Naples were to be the Pope's share of the booty (1526). Matters, however, did not go according to plan. Pope Clement invited Prince Vaudemont into Italy to press his claim as heir to the House of Anjou. He appeared off the coast of Naples, and co-operated with the Papal troops. But the advance of the Duke of Bourbon upon Rome changed the situation. Clement was captured and compelled to come to terms with the Imperialists (1527). Two months later Lautrec, marching to his relief, invaded Naples. The greater part of the country declared for him. Reinforced by the Florentines, he compelled the Prince of Orange, who had succeeded the Duke of Bourbon in the command, to withdraw into Naples. On 30th April 1528 Lautrec sat down before the city, determined to starve it into submission. The people suffered terribly from plague and famine, and were in the utmost despair, for the blood of S. Gennaro had refused to liquefy. In spite of the efforts of the Viceroy the French fleet commanded the sea and intercepted all supplies from Sicily. But the unexpected happened. Andrea Doria deserted from the French fleet with his Genoese galleys, and some plague-infected Neapolitans carried the epidemic into the besiegers' camp and devastated their army. Lautrec himself died of it. His memorial by Caccavello is in the chapel of Sta Maria la Nuova, founded by Gonsalvo in 1504. It was chivalrously erected by the Great Captain's nephew, a later Viceroy, " mindful of human misery," to his uncle's foe. The siege was raised on 28th August, and Francis, by the Treaty of Cambrai, was forced once more to renounce all claim to Naples (1529).

The Regno had now to pay for the Spanish occupation and the wars of Charles V. Enormous contributions in taxes and subsidies were exacted. The Prince of Orange bled to the bone those barons who had supported the French, whilst those who had favoured him were allowed the utmost licence. Living in their palaces and surrounded by vassals who did their every bidding, they behaved as if they were entirely above the law, oppressing the people and defrauding tradesmen with impunity.

At the same time the commerce of the country was cruelly injured by the depredations of the Moslem pirates. Chief among them was Chairredin Barbarossa. Charles earned the gratitude of the Neapolitans by carrying the war into the enemy's country. His return from Africa (25th November 1535) was celebrated, after a triumphal progress through the Porta Capuana, by feasts and tournaments, and he was granted a subsidy of a million ducats towards the expenses of the war against the corsairs. He was, indeed, offered a million and a half by the Marchese del Vasto and the Prince of Salerno, leaders of the nobles, who hoped thereby to induce him to remove the new Viceroy, Don Pedro de Toledo (1532-54). But Charles recognised that in him he had a great Viceroy, whose stern and just administration and repression of the lawlessness of the nobles were the real reasons for their resentment. He had made his intentions clear by beheading a couple of nobles in the Piazza del Mercato for harbouring some criminals. Severe punishment was meted out to all offenders against law and order, and many good measures were introduced for safeguarding the lives and properties of the citizens. Don Pedro banished Jewish usurers from the kingdom (1540), substituting for them a Monte della Pietà. Glimpses of court life at this period are revealed in the poems of Luigi Tansillo, a Spaniard whom the Great Viceroy patronised whilst he closed the Academies as being hot-beds of anti-Spanish feeling. Tansillo's sonnets are full of fire and passion. His ardent temperament, indeed, led him into literary indiscretions, which brought some of his works into the *Index Expurgatorius* and the author into prison.

We have seen (Chaps. I. and XII.) how Don Pedro paved and widened the streets, built new walls, and introduced many sanitary improvements into the city. He built the Church of S. Giacomo degli Spagnoli. His cenotaph there was wrought for him during his lifetime by Giovanni Merliano da Nola. It was one of the artist's latest works. The bas-relief representing the Viceroy's entrance into Naples, and the statues of the Viceroy and his wife are very good, but most of the rest is mannered and formal, and devoid of that simplicity and sincerity which distinguished him at his best. There are many far more beautiful works of Nola's in the churches we have visited, the altar at San Domenico, for instance, or the Cicara tomb in S. Severino.

The Great Viceroy vigorously defended the coast against the attacks of the Barbary corsairs, who seized and sacked Capri, Ischia and Procida, but were defeated in an attempt to raid Pozzuoli. But so long as the Moslems retained supremacy in the Mediterranean, Turkish raids upon the coast continued. A memory of them remains in the little tower near Mergellina, the "Torretta," built to protect that district, and in the name of the Punta di Campanella, where Charles V. hung a bell to give warning of the approach of pirates. It was not till 1571 that the victory of Don John of Austria at Lepanto restored the supremacy of the Mediterranean to Philip II.

Mus. Naz.] [*Alinari*

CUPID SLEEPING

Naples was then relieved by the Spanish dominion from this pest, as she had already been relieved from the pressure of the French. The popularity of his victory turned the head of Don John, whose conduct presently roused the jealousy of his brother, Philip II. So popular, however, was he that, as a protest, the Neapolitan nobles began to form a league for demanding provincial assemblies and the withdrawal of the Spanish garrisons.

The objects which Don Pedro had set before him were to suppress the licence and disorder of the nobles, to render Naples a city worthy of its great position as the metropolis of the whole kingdom, and to extend the power of his royal master. In spite of his exertions he had not succeeded in eliminating the disorder and brigandage which were rife throughout the Regno. It was an evil which grew gradually worse under the less honest and capable viceroys. Throughout the century bands of roving brigands wandered through the country and the neighbouring Papal states, openly waging wars of plunder, pillaging towns, and carrying ruin and desolation everywhere. Meanwhile the kingdom was drained of money by the enormous contributions exacted by the Spaniards both for the service of the Crown and their satellites. For Don Pedro was succeeded by a series of proud and ambitious Spanish satraps, who were got rid of from Spain by the Habsburgs and planted out as viceroys, subject to very little control from Madrid. Of these perhaps the most arrogant and ambitious was the Duke of Ossuna, who actually waged war upon Venice under his own flag. Rightly or wrongly, he was accused of conspiring to make himself an independent sovereign (1619).

About this period we have the first beginnings of that Neapolitan dialect literature, of which Salvatore di Giacomo is the great modern exponent. It arose partly no doubt from the itch of the era for something new and strange, but largely, too, from a genuine patriotic preference for the native things of Naples. One may see in it something of the underlying unrest beneath the Spanish yoke which found momentary expression in the rebellion of Masaniello. The slightly satirical lyric and descriptive poems of Giulio Cortese are filled, too, with a passionate love of Naples. They have just the same native touches of vehemence and realism and exuberance as distinguish the *Pentamerone* of Giovanni Basile, Count of Morone. These fairy tales reek, indeed, of Rabelais and the Neapolitan streets; but they have more than a local interest. For here the folk-lore favourites, Puss in Boots and Cinderella and many another first made their appearance in literary form.

Even Don Pedro had caused disaffection and riots by the heaviness of the taxation he was obliged to impose in order to defray the demands of Charles V. and his own improvements. Since then, Spanish exactions had been continuous and increasing. Apart from enormous subsidies on every occasion, the annual revenue extracted from the Regno had risen from two and a half million ducats in 1501 to seven million in 1641. *I Bisogni* the Neapolitans termed these extortionate foreigners, who were always increasing their demands for "the needful." Their discontent was increased by the knowledge that part of the money wrung from them went merely to enrich the needy adventurers, who came to batten upon their misery and returned to enjoy their wealth in Spain. Even more bitterly did they hate the tax-collectors, usually Flemings or Genoese, to whom the taxes were farmed out.

The ruined peasantry flocked into Naples and

swelled the ranks of the naked, starving beggars there, who about this time received the name of *lazzaroni*, or joined the roving bands of banditti in the mountains. One of the leaders of the latter, Marco Sciarra, took the title of King of Campagna, and defied the forces of the Pope and Viceroy alike for some years (1587-92). Visitations of plague and earthquake added to the distress caused by the continual calls for subsidies and recruits for the Spanish wars in France and Flanders. Appeals for relief were made in vain to the Court of Spain. The prevailing distress and the rising power of France encouraged the Angevin party to enter into negotiations with the French. The conspiracy was suppressed, and a French fleet which came to support it was beaten off (1640).

The exhaustion of the country was now extreme. Alfonso Enriquez, Admiral of Castile, appointed Viceroy in 1644 with the usual order to raise a subsidy of a million ducats, resigned rather than enforce a new tax upon this impoverished land. He wished, he said, to serve and not to betray his King (February 1646). He was succeeded by the Duke of Arcos, who had no such scruples. Funds were urgently needed. For Mazarin had sent a squadron to attack the Spanish fortresses on the Tuscan coast, and some French ships actually appeared off Naples. They were repulsed, but shortly afterwards the Spanish Admiral's ship was burnt one night in the harbour. Arcos arrested on suspicion and imprisoned the Duke of Maddaloni, the head of the great Caraffa family, and a well-known opponent of the Spanish dominion. It was a sign of the times, too, that when he summoned the militia to Naples they refused to come. Arcos, however, had obtained a vote for the subsidy of one million ducats. In order to raise it, and in spite of warnings and protests, he imposed a tax upon fruit.

That was the last straw. Fruit was, as it still is, the principal food of the Neapolitan poor, and it was the one article which remained untaxed. A previous attempt to impose such a tax had been abandoned by the Duke of Ossuna. Acting in concert with Giulio Genoino, at that time the *Eletto* of the People, his policy had been to curry favour with the crowd in opposition to the nobles. With a dramatic gesture he had severed the cord of the scales in the Custom-house in Mercato, and proclaimed that he would rather die than permit a tax upon fruit!

The Parliaments which used to meet every two years had fallen into disuse. The method now adopted was for the Viceroy to instruct the *Seggi*, or *Piazze*, to assemble and grant a subsidy, and to elect deputies to propose means for raising it. Charles VIII. (1495) had added to the five *seggi* of the nobles a *seggio* of " the People "—that is, of the *popolo grasso*, the rich, middle class—who met in the monastery of S. Agostino, and administered the affairs of its particular class with the aid of a dozen *Consultori*. Their representative, the *Eletto del Popolo*, also joined with those of the five noble *seggi* in S. Lorenzo to conduct the general affairs of the city. These privileges had been soon curtailed by Federigo (1498) in favour of the nobles. Ferdinand restored part of their privileges (1507), but rejected some of their claims, such as those for an equal share with the nobles in the custody of the gates, and an annual income from the public purse.

The policy of the Spaniards, pursued both by Ferdinand and Charles V., was to curtail the political power of the nobles and, by favouring the people rather than the nobility, to maintain a perpetual opposition between the two classes. In 1620 there were living in Naples no fewer than 800 nobles, with

6000 vassals at their beck and call. They were not, of course, a united class with one political aim or interest, except in detestation of the claims of the people. Before long, the Viceroys assumed the power of nominating the *Eletto del Popolo* from six candidates presented to them. From 1548 onwards this officer was merely a tool of the Spanish Government, who lined his own pockets at the expense of his constituents. This being the case, it is not surprising to find that Andrea Naclerio, the *Eletto del Popolo* on this occasion, joined with the other deputies in recommending new taxes on foreigners, tobacco, timber and fruit.

It is evident that discontent had long been simmering. It had now reached boiling-point. Behind the scenes Giulio Genoino, priest and Doctor of Law, had for many years been working for a revolution. He was now in his eightieth year, but neither age nor long experience of Spanish prisons had cooled his ardour. His experiences of the previous attempt to impose this tax showed him that the psychological moment had arrived. Busily and surreptitiously he prepared for a rising, acting in concert with a Carmelite monk. The protagonist in the rebellion was to be a dissolute young dare-devil of a fish-vendor, one Tommas Aniello. Behind the Carmine Church, near the Piazza del Mercato where his business lay, he was now often seen in earnest conversation with the aged priest. Mas'aniello, as his name was pronounced in local speech, was born in the Vico Rotto, near the Mercato, of parents who came from Amalfi. Very poor, a gambler and ne'er-do-weel, he was tall and handsome, and a certain proud recklessness marked him out as a likely leader of men. Moreover he had grievances against the powers that be. One day, when he had taken some fish to the palace of the

Duke of Maddaloni, he had been beaten by the servants of that great nobleman. He had been imprisoned himself for smuggling fish without paying the tax, and his wife, Bernardina Pisa, had been thrown into gaol for smuggling flour. This was the man selected, apparently by Genoino, to be the active leader in the revolt.

Already, on 26th December 1646, when the Viceroy was on his way to attend Mass at the Carmine Church, a crowd had gathered round his carriage, and called upon His Excellency to withdraw the *gabelle* upon fruit. The Duke, in an agony of fear, created a diversion by scattering gold amongst the crowd, and so escaped to the church. Discreetly he returned to the Castel Nuovo by sea. None the less, details of the new tax were published. At the same time came news of a successful rising at Palermo against a similar imposition. The walls were placarded with gibes at the supineness of the people who did not follow the example of the Sicilians. On 6th June a toll-house in the Mercato was burned down. Masaniello afterwards confessed that he was the author of this outrage. Meanwhile the strength of the garrison was seriously diminished by drafts sent north to oppose the French.

It was the custom at this season of the year to erect a little wooden fort in the centre of the Mercato, round which scenes of mimic warfare were waged by the rabble of the district, representing Turks and Christians, on the Feast of the Madonna del Carmine (16th July). Genoino seized the opportunity. Masaniello was chosen as captain of one of the bands of the Alarbi, as the combatants were called, and his friend Pione of the other. They were armed with sticks, and (ostensibly in preparation for the Festa) were drilled by their captain, who invented, or more probably was given, a catchword which he taught them to repeat—"Long live the King, and down with bad government." An unforeseen incident led to an outbreak before the day of the Festa.

On Sunday, 7th July, the Mercato was filled by crowds of holiday-makers and sellers and buyers of fish and fruit. Masaniello was there, too, with his band of Alarbi. Suddenly a dispute arose between peasants who had fruit to sell and stall-holders who wished to buy it. Which of them was to pay the tax? The *Eletto* of the People was consulted. He decided that the producer must pay. Thereupon a peasant angrily flung his basket of figs on the ground and declared that he would neither sell nor pay. "God gives plenty, and the Government makes famine," he cried. He was beaten by the guard. Masaniello and his ragamuffins rushed to the rescue, brandishing their sticks and shouting their slogan. The guard gave way, and the *Eletto* fled to the beach, pursued by showers of fruit and stones. Masaniello now assembled his followers on the site of Conradin's execution. He called upon them to follow his example in burning the office of the *gabelle* in the Mercato. The outbreak spread rapidly. The insurgents were quickly organised by Masaniello and the other leaders of the rebellion, who sent them into different quarters of the city to break up the stalls of the tax-collectors, and shout for the King and the abolition of the tax.

Clad in the loose white shirt and drawers of a fisherman, Masaniello now mounted a horse and led a huge crowd to the Viceroy's palace. Arcos, terrified, appeared on the balcony and began to offer them everything they asked for. But he could not be heard for the din. The mob was already breaking into the palace when he made his escape by a back door. He was quickly overtaken and dragged out of his coach.

His whiskers were pulled by the mob, but he again managed to create a diversion by throwing handfuls of gold amongst them, and so gained refuge in the Convent of S. Luigi. There the Cardinal Archbishop, Ascanio Filomarino, persuaded him to sign a document abolishing all taxes on provisions. While the Archbishop drew away the crowd by entering his coach and waving this paper in the air, the Viceroy escaped to St Elmo in a sedan chair. The riot, however, continued unabated.

Throughout the night Masaniello remained in the Mercato exhorting, directing, organising. A strolling players' stage which had been erected there served as the seat of his government. Under his direction the houses of all the tax-gatherers and farmers and authors of the *gabelle* were burnt to the ground. A Sicilian refugee led an attack upon the armoury. The prisons were broken open and all the gaol-birds set free. Masaniello was now master of the city, for the few Spanish and Swiss guards remaining appear to have been quite useless. He called upon the Viceroy, who had withdrawn to Castel Nuovo, to abolish all taxes and to deliver up the grant of privileges by Charles V., which Genoino declared he had seen written in letters of gold. Arcos made a cunning move. Having failed to bribe Masaniello, he released the Duke of Maddaloni from prison, and sent him to the Mercato with a false copy of the charter.

The trick was discovered. Maddaloni was sternly denounced as a traitor by Masaniello, and was hounded back to the Viceroy. There was an end of any fear of a combination between the nobles and the people. But the head of the House of Caraffa could not leave such insults unavenged. Whilst the Archbishop took up his residence at the Carmine and exerted his influence over Masaniello to negotiate a settlement, and persuaded him to desist from reprisals upon the nobles, Maddaloni and his friends introduced 300 bandits into the city. On 10th July, as he was entering the Church of the Carmine, Masaniello was greeted by a discharge of arquebuses. He was not touched, but 150 of Maddaloni's men paid for the attempt with their lives.

Hitherto Masaniello had acted with great moderation and good sense. But the stress of excitement unbalanced him. He quarrelled with Genoino, who began to plot for his overthrow. At the bidding of the Archbishop he discarded his rough fisherman's dress and put on garments of silver cloth, in order to attend the Viceroy, who was now forced to accept his terms. He made a royal progress to the castle, and there received the charter of Charles V. and an undertaking that all taxes imposed since should be abolished. To preserve some shadow of authority, the Viceroy hung a gold chain about his neck, and appointed him Captain General. Returning to the Mercato, he now began to exercise all the functions of an arbitrary sovereign, whilst always professing his devotion to the King. The Archbishop lived at his side.

But the strain of judging, organising, negotiating ceaselessly and without sleep was already telling upon the youth's excitable brain. He was haunted by fears of assassination. He thought that he had been poisoned by a cup of wine handed to him by the duchess. His attempts to maintain order and to put a stop to pillaging by wholesale executions lost him popularity with the crowd he had excited. On the Feast of the Madonna del Carmine he attended Mass, and mounting the pulpit, recounted his services and reproached the vast crowd for their waning loyalty. Lashing himself into a delirium of passion, he tore off his clothes and threatened to hurl himself from the pulpit. He was forcibly restrained, and by order of the Archbishop led to the dormitory of the monks and left alone. There he heard the voice of a former friend calling him. He opened the door, and was riddled by a volley from a band of assassins (16th July). The fisherman-prince had reigned for just a week, and died at the age of twenty-four. The people had already tired of him. The fickle mob hailed his fall as they had hailed his rise. His body was thrown into a ditch. His head was stuck on a pike and carried in triumph to the Viceroy, to whom the Archbishop and others offered their congratulations. The duke confirmed the concessions he had made. But next day the price of bread was raised. The mob changed sides again. Masaniello was once more their idol. They advanced upon the Castel Nuovo, with tiny loaves fixed upon the points of their pikes, and demanded the punishment of the rapacious bakers and permission to bury Masaniello. His body was picked out of the gutter and he was buried with pomp in the Carmine Church, bewailed by the crowd as their martyred benefactor.

There was a momentary lull. Meantime the Provinces too had taken up arms, and Philip had sent his handsome son, Don John of Austria, with a fleet to suppress the revolt. The people refused to lay down their arms, which they had been allowed to retain, until their privileges were confirmed. Don John therefore delivered an assault upon the city, conducted with furious cruelty. But after the first shock the people turned upon the Spaniards, repulsed them, and, declaring their allegiance at an end, appointed Gennaro Annese, an illiterate ruffian, as their leader. But a new claimant had appeared in the field. Henry, Duke of Guise, who was at the

Papal Court, revived the old claim of the House of Anjou, and offered himself as their head. A French fleet appeared in the Bay, and he was elected Doge of the First Parthenopean Republic (15th November 1647). The nobles however held aloof. It was evident that a large part of the citizens still favoured the Spaniards. Guise's military position was weak. Mazarin did not favour his enterprise, and the French fleet failed to co-operate with him. On 6th April 1648 the Spaniards recaptured the city by a *coup de main*, after Guise had been enticed to Posilipo by a feint. Popular Government ceased amidst the cheers of the mob, who had had their fill of disorder, and the Spanish regime was re-established. Severe reprisals were made upon the ring-leaders of the rebellion and the banditti, who had declared themselves earnest Republicans. The Duc de Guise made another attempt in 1654, and seized the Castel dell' Ovo. But the appearance of an English squadron under Blake caused the French to beat a hasty retreat.

The revolution of Masaniello caused a great stir in the world. The story of the Neapolitan fisher-lad was handed up and down Europe for two hundred years as very stirring Republican propaganda. The English spoke of it with admiration during the Commonwealth, and when the tide of revolutionary feeling was flowing strong about a century ago, Masaniello became once more the hero of the people and the stage. In 1828 the music of Daniel François Auber made famous the opera written about him by Eugène Scribe and Germain Delavigne, *La Muette de Portici*. Indeed, the performance of this opera in Brussels in August 1830 roused the Belgians to the outburst of enthusiastic patriotism which ended in the reassertion of their national independence.

There are several accounts of the Revolution by

eye-witnesses, notably the Archbishop Filomarino and Gabriele Tontoli. It has been treated romantically by Dumas and Miss Hay (Mas'aniello), and in a scientific historical spirit by Michelangelo Schipa (*Masaniello*, 1925).

Dumas, following a popular tradition, represented the painter Salvatore Rosa as an intimate friend and associate of Masaniello. No contemporary chronicler mentions him in connection with the Revolution. We know, from his letters, that he was at work in Tuscany at that time. But at least he could praise him from a distance; for does not the Court painter of the Grand Duke of Tuscany in his satire, *La Guerra*, bid us admire " the lofty soul of the low-born Fisherman, who abased the heads of the mighty and gave laws to Kings "?

CHAPTER XIV

Baroque and Rococo

The coming of Baroque—The Reformation and the Catholic Reaction—The Jesuit Style—Marini—Neapolitan thinkers and martyrs—Spanish influence—Baroque Art and Neapolitan Churches—Painters of the *Seicento.*

THE great revival of arts and letters which we term the Renaissance culminated as to art and architecture in the works of Michelangelo and Palladio.

That period was followed by an age of anarchical reaction. There was a determined revolt against classical formalism and rules that were deemed pedantic. Rebelling against restrictions which seemed to cramp imagination and put a stop to experiment, artists soon went to the opposite extreme. They surrendered themselves to the cult of the fantastic and bizarre. Architecture followed the decadent example of the painters and craftsmen; Bernini succeeded to Bramante; Borromini, Guarini, Pozzo and Fanzaga to Peruzzi. Much of Bernini's work, of course, is of the classic type and classic grandeur, but his rich and tireless invention and his love of colour effects and theatrical decoration led him more and more into the mazes of the Baroque. It is in his contemporary, Francesco Borromini (1599-1667), that one finds its first high priest. The innovations introduced by him will explain more fully than a definition the meaning and the aims of the Baroque artists. Intoxicated by the exuberance of their own unbridled imaginations, running riot in curve and scroll, straining after originality, and revelling in decoration for decoration's sake, the artists of the seventeenth century degenerated with startling rapidity from the standard of the simple and severe. Caprice became the only accepted guide and affectation ceased to be regarded as a vice. The contemptuous word *barocco*, which Italian jewellers used to describe a misshapen pearl, was borrowed to express the fantastic and decadent quality of this new seventeenth century art. A contemptuous word rightly applied to a decadent quality; for the meaningless contortions and involutions of this fussy, restless style are essentially ignoble and debased in so far as they lack sincerity and reserve, and in so far as they offend against that simplicity which, the Greek historian observed, is so large an element in all noble natures.

It is not easy to define Baroque. The term denotes, not a style of architecture, but a tendency in art. It describes an excess, an aberration, a perversity in forms of decoration. It denotes an indulgence in ornament for ornament's sake, which ignores architectural construction, perverting, concealing and distorting the meaning, the history and the use of architectural features. In that sense Baroque is a negation of style in architecture. It is a method of treating detail with a wilful whimsicality, in such a way as to cause a sensation at all hazards, whether by dramatic appeal, violent distortion or startling novelty. To define it, therefore, is not easy, though it is easy enough to recognise. By date, it is the style of the *Seicento*. For the period in which it flourished was roughly from the middle of the seventeenth to the middle of the eighteenth century. It coincided with the domination of the Spaniards and the Jesuits, and lasted in Naples until the time of the Bourbons, when, under French influence, its extravagances began to give place to the refinement and graces of Rococo—the style of the *Settecento*.

The normal desire of artists is to create and to re-create, to develop and improve. When the bounds of perfection have been reached in one form of literature or art, the new generation tries back or reaches forward. Endeavouring to improve on the unimprovable, or groping blindly for a new form of self-expression, it either over-elaborates the old, or destroys it in the rapture of creating a new-found style. Art, like cities, is always being refashioned. Even Michelangelo thought nothing of destroying priceless Roman temples in order to recreate the material in a new form of art. At Naples the Spaniards and the Jesuits substituted Baroque for Gothic. They were probably actuated in some degree by the natural desire of newcomers to obliterate former civilisations and the triumphs of their predecessors. The Christians deliberately superseded the practices and local habitations of persistent Paganism, substituting saints for gods and baptisteries for baths. So the Jesuits and the Spaniards reconstructed almost every Neapolitan church and building in their new style. Most of us regret it. But there is this to be said. Angevin Gothic was not a national style, or even one suited to the climate and the temperament of the people. Palermo had that to offer, the rounded arch, the dimly-lighted space, the cool mosaic. Events forced its rejection. The florid interiors of the Gesù Nuovo, the Duomo, Santa Chiara, de' Gerolomini, S. Gregorio Armeno, S. Paolo, S. Domenico, SS. Severino e Sosio, Sta Maria del Carmine, S. Martino, and a dozen others are there to commemorate the

Spanish triumph and the Jesuit at large. They must be seen to be believed.

For two other influences, besides those more general ones we have suggested, worked hand in hand to promote the development of the pretentious and artificial style known as Baroque. The first was religious, the second social and intellectual. The first was the triumph of the Jesuits; the second the triumph of Spain. Baroque has been called the Jesuit style. For it was through the rigorous system of the Jesuits, and their elaborate scheme for forming the minds and directing the energies of the rising generation, that the victory of the Catholic Reaction was achieved. And it was under their regime and under the direction or inspiration of Pozzo, the Jesuit architect, that the greater part of the characteristic Baroque buildings was erected.

The amazing profusion with which they then decorated their churches seems to have been intended to demonstrate the splendour and power of a Church Triumphant, which has overwhelmed all its enemies, and extracted from vanquished foe and faithful follower alike rich tribute of marble, porphyry and precious stones. Certainly they compelled Art to become once more the handmaid of Religion, whereas, during the Renaissance, Religion had been very much the servant of Art.

The Catholic Reaction was the successful answer of the Roman Church to the challenge of the Reformation, and the whole spirit, the joyous, pagan, undisciplined, democratic spirit of the Renaissance.

The Society of Jesus, inaugurated by Ignatius Loyola in 1540 to enforce a rigid orthodoxy, was approved by Paul III. in 1543. Their theory that to suppress heresy and to ensure absolute moral and intellectual obedience, the end justified any means, was

[*Alinari*

LA GUGLIA DEL GESÙ

(A typical Baroque Monument, 1750)

reinforced by the weapon of the Inquisition. Art, science, literature, politics and morality suffered alike from this deadly system, which put everywhere a premium upon artifice, subterfuge and sham. The system of the Jesuits was successful, until the very success of its tyranny brought about its downfall.

The doctrines of the Reformation had made considerable headway in Naples, chiefly amongst the upper class. The central figures of the movement were Juan de Valdès, who came from Spain with Charles V., Vittoria Colonna, and Giulia Gonzaga, widow of Prince Fondi. The latter was reputed to be the most beautiful woman in Italy. Barbarossa, the corsair, is said to have raided Fondi in order to capture her for the Sultan's harem. She was warned in time, and fled, almost naked, on horseback. The story goes that she caused the servant who had warned her, and thereby beheld her charms, to be killed.

An attempt to introduce the Spanish Inquisition into Naples provoked a brief but violent resistance, as much political as religious. A papal brief, in which Paul III. hinted at its establishment, was torn down from the Duomo. Spaniards were seized and murdered by the crowd. The position of the Spanish garrison became critical. The situation was saved by Toledo's judicious handling, and by the substitution of the milder form of Roman Inquisition. But by 1600 the Jesuits had triumphed, and heresy was stamped out.

The triumph of the Catholic Church over Humanism was celebrated by an outburst of profuse and unbridled magnificence in every direction. Whilst dogma reasserted its sway over freedom of inquiry, virtuosity in Art echoed virtuosity in Literature. Emptiness of intellect was concealed beneath a display of luxurious living, of extravagant writing, and of art which aimed at the marvellous and the grandiose. Rich colouring took the place of chaste design in painting, coloured marble, gilt plaster and theatrical effects the place of outline in architecture, extravagant inventions and strained conceits the place of thought in poetry. For in literature precisely the same ambition to dazzle and astonish at any cost is seen in the poems of Giovanni Battista Marini (1529-65). His descriptive poem, *Adone*, consisting of some 50,000 lines of brilliant word-painting, is essentially sweet and musical, but intolerably overladen with conceits and far-fetched imagery. Its reverberating success was necessarily followed by oblivion when taste revived. Yet Marini was a genuine lyric poet, gifted with all the spontaneity and fervour of his race and an eloquent devotion to his native city, which make one wish he had been born in a happier epoch. His worst fault, apart from the licentious character of much of his writing, is that he inspired a host of imitators in France and England, as well as in Italy, who exaggerated his faults and seldom shared his genius. He is buried in S. Domenico.

Yet even so, the tyranny of the Church and the terror of the rack and stake could not banish from some rare spirits the love of truth or deter them from the pursuit of scientific inquiry. Perhaps it is due to the Greek blood in their veins that the Neapolitans have always displayed a peculiar genius for abstract thought and philosophical research. In this era of persecution the chief Italian thinkers before Galileo all came from the kingdom of Naples. Of these Bernardo Telesio, praised by Bacon as the first experimental observer of nature, escaped martyrdom. But Cesare Vanini was burnt at Toulouse, and Giordano Bruno at Rome, whilst Tommaso Campanella spent the greater part of his life in prison. Bruno's crime was his intuitive recognition of the unity of all existence and the importance of the Copernican theory. The vehemence and metaphysical instinct characteristic of the Neapolitan writers combined to make of him a poet-philosopher "as incoherent as if he had just emerged from the Sibyl's cave, but full of the most surprising intuitions, instinct with the germs of modern thought and discovery."[1] Campanella's creed, like that of Vanini and Bruno, was pantheistic. His rough-hewn, Michelangelesque sonnets are more remarkable than his prose, of which the best known piece is the *Città del Sole*, in which he describes an ideal community. His offence was political as well as religious. For he dared to dream of a perfect republic in Naples some years before the rebellion of Masaniello, and to look to the Turks for the deliverance of his country from the Spanish yoke.

The social changes introduced by the ascendancy of the Spaniards were of the most marked character. Aristocratic hauteur and reserve took the place of that joyous, open-hearted delight in life and beauty in all its many-sided manifestations which characterised the free citizens of the Italian city states. Competition in display supplanted competition in achievement of art or craft. Instead of pride in excellence of work, false shame of labour was substituted. The burgher was no longer content to share in the lives and amusements of the common people, but strove by ostentatious display of wealth and retinue to differentiate himself from them. Society was ruled by an elaborate code of etiquette. A stiff and formal tone became the mode in place of the easy manners and open speech of Renaissance days. Stateliness and Spanish hauteur succeeded to native frankness, flattery to sincerity, hypocrisy to shamelessness. These char-

[1] Richard Garnett, *Italian Literature*.

acteristics are reflected in the fashions of art and apparel. The gorgeous fabrics worn by the Renaissance princes and burghers were now discarded in favour of the black garments of the Spanish hidalgo; the free manners and unrestrained enjoyment of life which characterised the Renaissance ladies were exchanged for cloistered seclusion or secret amours. And in art the same influence is traceable in over-elaboration and love of display, excessive ornamentation, and an utter lack of sincerity whether in decoration or in design. How could it be otherwise? In the stifling atmosphere of repression, corruption, and tyranny of alien domination and debased priestcraft, genius, so far from being nurtured, was necessarily repressed.

There, as under the Empire of the Neros, all that was noble in emulation was forbidden. Ambition, in the regions of a despotic and luxurious Court, was reduced to a contest of flattery, craft and insincerity. Poverty was enforced by taxation and relieved by pauperisation. Originality or effort in any direction, except in that of fatuous inanity, was repressed as an offence against the ruling powers. It is not in such surroundings that genius in art is encouraged.

The function of art, as conceived by the artists of the seventeenth century, was, as we have said, to startle and amaze. The obvious way to startle a man is to shriek unexpectedly in his ear. In terms of architecture, the equivalent of a shriek is to do a thing in a way that it has never been done before, not from the point of view of fulfilling an architectural function or constructional purpose, but simply and solely with the object of attracting attention to its eccentricity and, presumably, to the cleverness of its perpetrator.[1] If these are his ideals, the artist, whether in architec-

[1] See in this connection Sir Reginald Blomfield's article in the *Quarterly Review*, 1926.

ture, sculpture, or literature, will easily fall a victim to the temptation to indulge in pretentious and utterly insincere ornamentation. He will be led into imposture and bad taste, because he is concentrating his efforts upon catching the eye by surprising novelties or striking abnormalities. Baroque is essentially meretricious.

Having once accepted this ideal of being clamorous and original at all costs, the Baroque artists, being perfectly reckless as to the meaning and use of the architectural features which they were disguising, were able to apply their ingenuity—and it was often immense—to the handling of curves and ovals, the development of sinuous planes, the manipulation of involutions and scroll work, the alternation of curves and the introduction of spirals. Much of this work is in itself as beautiful as it is capricious, for curves are essentially beautiful, and these artists delighted in curving lines, wandering scrolls and meandering waves. But their chief object being to surprise by some bold innovation, they were naturally led into covering their buildings with preposterous ornamentation in marble, paint or stucco. Inversion of the normal method is the easiest way to achieve a daring innovation. Pediments, therefore, which should protect openings were broken in half or turned back to back. Columns were placed in front of pilasters. Angles of buildings which should be square were now rounded, cornices were waved. It was Borromini who furnished the first examples of broken tympana with scroll-like outlines, and of multiple mouldings, Borromini who devised the lines upon which the profuse and fanciful ornamentation of the seventeenth century was to be developed, now giving to a console the form of a flexible branch, now decorating a balustrade with reclining cherubs, or applying to a pilaster a group of angels ensconced in a shell, now twisting the centre of a candelabra into the likeness of a spiral campanile.

The work of such artistic acrobats appeals and can only appeal to those who are ignorant of the principles of great art, who think the part greater than the whole, or whose uneducated and vitiated taste prefers the bizarre to the beautiful and the cheap paradox to truth. Yet this style has its virtues, as it has its modern defenders. The desire for self-expression rather than mere uninspired and lifeless copying is essential for the production of good art. The Baroque artists had this merit at least, that they were breaking away from pedantic austerity, and seeking after originality. If they broke away in the wrong direction, still they often succeeded in achieving effects that are both interesting and occasionally full of charm.

Whatever the causes and motives of the change, certain it is that at this epoch churches, palaces, gardens, and pictures designed in this style covered Italy from Rome to Venice, and from Genoa to Naples. Baroque spread through Europe like an epidemic. It had comparatively little success in France. But in Southern Germany and, above all, in Spain and Portugal, it reached a pitch which even one of its most recent, but judicious defenders describes as the point of insanity.[1] Naples, permeated by Spanish influence, became not unnaturally a *locus classicus* of the florid ornamentation and excursions into the bizarre which distinguish your true Baroque.

Eagerly encouraged by the Viceroy Barrionuevo, Baroque artists set themselves to hide or to destroy the traces of their predecessors. They did not build new churches, they obliterated the old ones. Gothic ogees, lancet windows, Renaissance arches alike disappeared.

[1] Martin Shaw Briggs, *Baroque Architecture*, p. 23.

Stucco, volutes, ornamentation and marble draperies concealed the cold bare stone, or frescoed walls. Where once a slender column, that seemed like the chalice of a flower, rose towards a vaulted ceiling, crowned by a delicate capital, now huge columns appeared covered with garlands and flutings. The vaulting itself was converted into a flat background, square or oval, for anecdotal pictures. The roof, if it was not a dome, was covered with barrel vaulting, or flat, coffered ceilings, the coffering sometimes coloured, sometimes gilded, but the whole always a mere series of frames for pictures. The windows, square or harp-shaped, and surrounded by sculptured garlands, or surmounted like the arches by bands of plump cupids, were designed solely to throw light upon the painters' work on the ceiling or pendentives. Marble, stucco, gilding filled every corner from floor to ceiling, producing a polychromatic effect so dazzling as to destroy the very beauty of the rich material used. Brilliantly polished and multi-coloured marbles paved the floors with exuberant designs.

DETAIL OF CHURCH WINDOW
STA MARIA DEL CARMINE

"Our attention," writes Salvatore di Giacomo enthusiastically, "claimed on all sides by such abundant and varied decoration, has no time to fix itself; statues, mausoleums, pictures, medallions, rich lamp holders, enormous sculptured candelabra, precious and triumphal altars, balusters leave us incapable of doing aught but gaze in an ecstasy of wonder at such lavish riches."

There you have it! To dazzle one into an ecstasy

of admiration, that was the object of these artists and their employers. They became so engrossed in the business of ostentatious display and the parade of their own ingenuity, that they would treat the façade of a church as if it were the canvas of a picture or the drop-scene of a theatre. They would plaster it with richly coloured marbles and pillars and columns and niches, entirely ignoring its structural relation to the interior, or to the sides, which were allowed to remain of bare brick in the hope that they would not be seen. For the most part, however, the exteriors of the churches are very plain. The contrast between the plain exteriors and the interiors with their riot of colour and ornamentation is again dazzling. Was it intended to tempt the wretched, starving, half-naked denizens of the Neapolitan slums within, and that the "House of God" should be the Palace of the Poor? Was it the design of the Jesuits that those who could not enjoy the wealth and luxury of art and furniture and gorgeous raiment which were the lot of those who dwelt in courts should find them, in glorious contrast to the squalor and emptiness of their homes, in the gilded halls of God?

As with architecture and sculpture, so with painting. The characteristics of the Baroque school were, roughly, violent and arresting effects of light and shade, rich colouring and groups of figures, nude or gorgeously apparelled, in poses which were striking and proclaimed the artist's skill in anatomy, but which bear, as a rule, no conceivable relation to the whole composition. It has been well remarked by Mr Briggs that the strong shadows and bold composition of the Bolognese artists, or of Ribera and his contemporaries, were specially adapted to the strong lines of Baroque churches.

The subjects were taken mainly from the lives of the Saints. They were treated with intense realism.

Here, as in sculpture, an extraordinary mastery in modelling and portraying the human form was achieved. Such mastery enabled the Baroque artists to apply and display statues and paintings in the most difficult corners, above altars or in the vaultings of ceilings.

The chief creators of the Baroque school were Caravaggio, the Lombard, and Pellegrino, and the Caravacci, the Bolognese painters. Domenichino (1581-1641), and Guido Reni (1574-1642), who worked at Naples, were pupils of the latter. Foremost among painters who covered the interiors of the Neapolitan churches with so brilliant a pageant of pictures is Giuseppe Ribera, nicknamed Lo Spagnoletto (1588-1656). Born in Southern Italy, he studied under Caravaggio and in Spain, then came from Rome to exploit the demand for brilliant painting under the Viceroys. We have seen how he and his followers crushed the competition of Reni and Domenichino. Belisario Corenzio (1585-164 ?) was with him; Giovanni Battista Caracciolo (1570-1637), and Giovanni Lanfranco (1581-1643) and Massimo Stanzioni (1588-1656) were for him. With them and Micco Spadaro (1612-79), Aniello Falcone (1600-65), and Salvatore Rosa (1615-73), and some others, Ribera monopolised the decorating industry and divided the spoil, performing with brilliant ability the allotted task of producing dazzling effects of colour, richness and virtuosity.

Their mastery of light and shade earned them the soubriquet of *Tenebrosi*. An excellent example of this quality with its weakness and its strength, combined with the brilliant colouring and movement characteristic of this school, is afforded by the works of Luca Giordano (1632-1705). Giordano was nicknamed *Fa Presto* in token of the rapidity with which he worked. A painter of inexhaustible fertility and invention, he was more than a facile copyist of the great masters, any one of whom he could imitate so as to deceive an expert. An example is his Christ before Pilate in the *Museo*, after the manner of Durer, or his Marriage of Cana there, and his St Michael in SS. Ascenzione, after Veronese. He painted the two angels on the right of the altar in Sta Maria la Nuova at the age of eight, and at seventy-two performed his *tour de force* in S. Martino (Chap. XII.). His Christ driving the money-changers from the Temple in the de' Gerolomini (S. Filippo Neri) is a characteristic piece, full of life and movement, where life and movement are a true part of the theme.

In the next generation Francesco Solimena of Nocera (1657-1743) stands almost alone. We have mentioned his brilliant painting in S. Domenico and his Heliodorus in the Gesù Nuovo. Some of his best work is in S. Paolo Maggiore. His work is full of fire and life, his colouring bright and joyous, but the wild display of whirling arms and sprawling legs in which he delighted spoil compositions sometimes masterly. His chief pupils were Sebastiano Conca, Francesco di Mura and Giuseppe Bonito.

Attempts have been made to establish the existence of a distinct and original school of Neapolitan painting. Writers, fired by local patriotism, even invented the names and lives of great Neapolitan painters and architects, and strengthened their argument by falsifying dates. A crushing answer to these claims by De Dominici (*Vite de' pittori*, etc.), Sannazaro and the architect Summonzio was delivered by Signor Frizzoni (*Archivio Storico Italiano*, 1878). The fact is that almost every artist who worked in Neapolitan territory was a foreigner, or, if not a foreigner, was the pupil of a foreign artist and an imitator of a foreign school. Giotto came to Naples and inspired a few followers, but his influence soon died out. There followed a period when Flemish influence predominated, when many works were produced either by native artists under that influence or by Flemish painters who were brought to Naples. Thus the picture of St Jerome in the *Museo Nazionale*, representing St Jerome extracting a thorn from the paw of the lion, was ascribed to an early Neapolitan painter named Colantonio del Fiore. It is now ascribed to the school of Roger van der Weyden, and Colantonio is shown to have existed only in the lively and patriotic imagination of Summonzio. Others there attributed to Simone Papa have the same marked Flemish character. What is more deplorable is that where such foreign influence is absent, the works of native artists are utterly crude and uninspired.

After this period Tuscan and Umbrian influences predominated. Antonio da Solario (Lo Zingaro) is supposed to have married the daughter of another imaginary Neapolitan painter, Colantino. But not a single authentic work of his exists amongst those of varied style and date with which he has been credited. During the Spanish supremacy hardly any of the painters, sculptors or architects who worked at Naples were native born. There was no definite Neapolitan school, although the artists from Spain, Bologna or the neighbourhood who came here did work in a certain unison of spirit and ideas.

CHAPTER XV

The Bourbon Rule

Eighteenth Century Writers—The Bourbon Restoration—Charles III.—Reforms of Tanucci—Vanvitelli—Caserta and S. Marcellino—Sanfelice—Villa Nazionale—Cappella S. Severo and the Dead Christ—Ferdinand IV.—Nelson at Naples—Lady Hamilton—The *Lazzaroni* and the Parthenopean Republic—Cardinal Ruffo and the Capitulation—Execution of Commodore Caracciolo—The Napoleonic Kingdom—Return of Ferdinand—The *Carboneria*—Ferdinand grants a Constitution—Is Restored by Austria—His Revenge—Bomba and Gladstone—Garibaldi.

FOR Italy the eighteenth century was a period of regeneration, rendered possible by the disappearance of the Spanish dominion. Not that political and spiritual tyranny disappeared with it. But oppression was relaxed for a while, and when the Spanish Bourbons re-established themselves in 1734, they acted as Italians and through Italian ministers, not through viceroys. Music, and through music, Italian opera and drama, rose to unexampled heights, and for the first quarter of the century Naples, thanks to the genius of Leonardo Leo, Niccolo Porpora, Alessandro Scarlatti, Giambattista Pergolese and Niccolo Jommelli, led the way. In Literature men's thoughts turned with a new freedom to criticism and reform. The study of history, philosophy, jurisprudence and political economy revived. It says much for the liberal government of Charles III. and the national trend of Neapolitan genius, that of the distinguished Italian legists, economists and philosophers of this period, Giovanni Battista Vico (1668-1744), Pietro Giannone (1676-1748), Gætano Filangieri (1752-87), Cesare Beccaria (1738-94), Antonio Genovesi (1712-69), and the witty Abbate, Ferdinando Galiani (1728-87), all but one were Neapolitans. The piercing intellect of Vico placed him in the highest rank as a philosopher and literary and historical critic. Giannone, in his great *Civil History of the Kingdom of Naples* (1723), refuted the claims of the Papacy to jurisdiction over Naples, for which he was hounded into exile and imprisonment by the Church. Its great learning renders it the foundation of all Neapolitan history as well as a lasting authority on mediæval law. The others are famous for their advocacy of juridical and legislative reform and of free trade.

The Neapolitans welcomed the French in 1700, when Philip of Anjou succeeded to the throne bequeathed to him by Charles II. of Spain. They welcomed the Austrians in 1707 with the same joyous enthusiasm when they turned out the French; and they welcomed the Spanish Bourbon, Charles, Duke of Parma, when this coveted morsel of the Austrian possessions fell to his share in 1734. The two Austrian banners which hang before the high altar in the Duomo are his votive offering to San Gennaro for his signal victory at Velletri (1744). Son of Elizabeth Farnese, Charles brought from Parma all the treasures of the House of Farnese, and so formed the beginnings of what is now the *Museo Nazionale*.

All this time Naples and Sicily were factors in the European situation in so far as the possession of them added weight to one scale or the other in the balance of power which England was endeavouring to maintain between Austria, France and Spain. As for the Neapolitans themselves, such changes were always the occasions for the pageants and festas that the people loved. Economically, they could hardly be for the worse; politically, they sometimes proved the occasion of concessions and privileges. They were needed. The condition of the country, after all these years of feudal anarchy, Angevin absolutism and Viceregal exactions, was deplorable. Roads, bridges, manufactures, trade had almost disappeared from the land; agriculture was overwhelmed by a multitude of mediæval impositions; priests and monks monopolised a large part of the produce, paying no taxes and claiming immunity from civil courts. Smugglers and brigands preyed on the countryside. Disastrous interference with the coinage had paralysed commerce.

The people were right in welcoming Charles. For the Infante Don Carlos, as he then was, aided by his enlightened Tuscan minister, Bernardo Tanucci, proved a good ruler. Between them they curtailed the privileges of both nobles and clergy, and did much to suppress brigandage. Charles built and endowed the famous opera house of S. Carlo. But his chief delight was in hunting and in building the great palaces of Capodimonte (*see* Chap. XII.), Portici and Caserta as hunting boxes and summer residences. Capodimonte he chose because it was a good spot for shooting *beccafichi*. The amazing palace at Caserta, some twenty miles north of Naples, with its immense gardens and cascades adorned with white marble statuary, is the standing monument of the genius of Luigi Vanvitelli. It was begun in 1752.

We have already mentioned some of Vanvitelli's work in Naples. Besides altering the Annunziata and the Palazzo Reale (erected in 1600 by Domenico Fontana and built for the Viceroy, Conte di Lemos), he built the fascinating convent of S. Marcellino, opposite the Church of SS. Severino e Sosio. Part of the old buildings has been appropriated by the University. The cloister and garden demonstrate Vanvitelli's genius for design and his determination to break away from the cruder extravagances of Baroque and the fanciful elegance, the twirls and love-knots of Rococo, and to restore the chaste simplicity of classical lines.

The cardinal vice of ostentation and display inherent in the ideals of the Baroque and Rococo age led artists to aim at creating an impression that a building was larger than in reality it was. To promote this illusion, a blank wall would be decorated with a fountain or a clever representation of a colonnade in perspective, exactly after the manner of the artists of Pompeii. A similar motive inspired the design of the magnificent double staircases which Ferdinando Sanfelice introduced into the palaces with which he, as well as Vanvitelli, enriched Naples (*e.g.* Palazzo Spagnuolo, Palazzo Majo, Palazzo Serra Cassano). Vanvitelli also designed the *Villa Reale*—now called *Nazionale*—which was begun in 1778 as a promenade for the nobility. The common people were rigorously excluded from it. A map printed about 1680 shows the site as simply part of the Neapolitan beach, and a map of 1845 that it was still the extreme limit of the town. The Strada di Chiaia had been constructed by the Viceroy Medinacœli in 1697. Its name—for Chiaia is derived from *plaga*—recalls the beach, the *plaga Olympica*, upon which the great festival of Jupiter used to be held. That filthy old beach, reaching to the Point of Mergellina, was finally reclaimed by the modern magnificent Caracciolo embankment. Between it and the Riviera di Chiaia, the extended garden of the Villa Nazionale now stretches from the Piazza Vittoria to the Piazza Principe di Napoli. In it was placed a wonderful porphyry basin from Pæstum. Temples to Vergil and Tasso and copies of some of the finest classical statuary also adorn the park, and also a charming fountain, attributed to Giovanni da Nola, but more probably the work of Geronimo d'Auria (1606). The theme of the arch is the fisherman's calling, which reminds us that it was first erected in Sta Lucia. Fishy, too, is the aquarium in the centre of the park. It was founded by Anton Dohrn in 1874, and ranks with

FOUNTAIN IN VILLA NAZIONALE

those of Monaco and London as one of the chief zoological stations in the world. (*Entrance*, 5 *lire*, *daily*, 8-5.)

The development of eighteenth-century Art after Vanvitelli is exemplified by the statues in the Cappella San Severo. They are by no means the things most worth seeing in Naples, but they are triumphs of technique, and they have the fascination of a grisly realism.

No. 19 Salata San Severo, low down on the left-hand side as you descend that street from the Piazza Luigi Miraglia (which it leaves almost opposite to the Via del Sole and Pontano's monument), is this chapel of the princes of Sangro di San Severo. It is sometimes referred to as Santa Maria della Pietà (1690). Two lire is the charge for admittance.

Mus. Naz.] [*Alinari*

PSYCHE

The chapel is filled with monuments and frescoes. Over the doorway is the monument of Cecco di Sangro springing out of his tomb fully armed, of which many a tale is told. Legends, too, have gathered round the name of Raimondo di Sangro, who enlarged the chapel in 1766. He was a chemist and inventor, who made interesting experiments in colour-printing. Needless to say, his printing presses and his crucibles quickly earned him the reputation of a magician with the Neapolitans. But the three famous statues which we have come to see are, first, *Il Disinganno*, by a Genoese artist, Francesco Queirolo. It represents a man struggling, like an enmeshed fish, in a network of vice, or to free himself from the temptations of this world. The net is carved with amazing skill. It is a monument to Raimondo's father, who became a monk. The second, a monument to his mother, is a draped figure by Antonio Corradini representing *Modesty*, a clumsy, showy piece of clever carving. The last is the *Dead Christ*, by Giuseppe Sanmartino, the Neapolitan sculptor who died in 1800. The technical skill, with which the dead and agonised body of the Saviour is rendered visible through the sculptured folds of the transparent burial shroud, is immense. You feel you are in the presence of a triumphant *tour de force*; but beyond that, genuine feeling and pathos are expressed which do not fail to produce a great impression upon the beholder. The treatment of the drapery speaks of a time when the tyranny of baroque frivolity was at length overpast, and a return to severe realism, grisly though it be, was combined with purity of line and delicacy of treatment.

When Carlos succeeded to the Crown of Spain as Charles III. (1759), his son, Ferdinand IV., was only eight years old. Tanucci was therefore able to continue his policy of retrenchment and reform, reducing the feudal privileges and exactions of the nobles and the enormous wealth and power and numbers of the clergy. Allegiance to the Pope and the ecclesiastical right of asylum were suppressed; marriage and education passed into the hands of the civil authorities. The Inquisition was excluded and the jurisdiction of the ecclesiastical courts curtailed. The framework of a modern State was, in fact, at length created. It was not to survive long.

Ferdinand inherited from his father a love of sport and the prodigious family nose, but of brains and character not a tittle. The nose, which would have put that of Cyrano de Bergerac in the shade, earned him the nickname of Nasone; the love of sport, combined with a taste for low company, that of *Il Rè Lazzarone*. He spent his days in fishing and shooting; he talked only dialect, refused to write, and was never so happy as when he was selling the fish he had caught in the market-place, or acting the part of a publican. A magnificent shot and brave enough as a hunter, this hobbledehoy of a King was to prove himself in political crises a savage tyrant, a shameless liar and a contemptible poltroon. At the age of sixteen he married the Austrian Princess, Maria Carolina, the beautiful and high-spirited sister of Marie Antoinette. As soon as she had borne him a son she claimed the right to sit in Council. For she was ambitious, and had determined to govern in his stead. Nothing could have suited Ferdinand better. But Tanucci objected, probably foreseeing her reactionary and Austro-phil policy. He was dismissed and replaced by the Queen's favourite, an Irish adventurer, John Acton, who quickly became all-powerful. The internal reforms of Tanucci were continued for a while. Then the excesses of the French Revolution produced a reaction of panic and savage repression.

The execution of Marie Antoinette confirmed Maria Carolina in her determination to stamp out any tendency towards such Liberty and Equality in Naples.

The *Lazzaroni* were armed and drilled into the semblance of a military force. A system of police was organised under Medicis, which became a terrible instrument of inquisition and intimidation. It was death to read Voltaire, death, imprisonment or torture to fraternise with the French or to show any inclination towards liberalism. The prisons were soon filled to overflowing. For had not the French butchered the Queen's sister, and were not the Revolutionary maniacs threatening all the crowned heads of Europe? Ferdinand was in terror for his own skin; Maria Carolina alternated between fits of fury and despair. Neapolitan policy accordingly blew hot and cold. Its neurotic indecision proved of little use to allies opposing the organised enthusiasm and military strength of the Sanculottes.

Alarmed by the preparation of a great French armada, the British Government sent a powerful fleet into the Mediterranean, under Sir Horatio Nelson, to destroy it. It was at first supposed that an attack on Naples was intended. Nelson, sailing in that direction, got upon the track of the French fleet, followed it to Egypt, and achieved the dazzling victory of the Nile (August 1798). He returned at once to Naples in obedience to his orders to protect that kingdom. Naples had already had one experience of British sea-power. When in 1740 Charles was about to help his father, Admiral Martin entered the palace, and placing his watch upon the table, gave him two hours to make up his mind. He chose neutrality for the time being, but the Spaniard never forgave the English for this blow to his pride. Very different were the feelings with which the British fleet was received when Nelson arrived on 22nd September 1798. The whole city went mad with joy. The King and Queen and all their ministers went on board the *Vanguard* to welcome " our Liberator."

They were accompanied by the British Ambassador, Sir William Hamilton, an old man now, a scientific investigator, a connoisseur of art, a thorough Neapolitan, and immensely popular in Society. He had lately married Emma Hart, his nephew's discarded mistress, whom the latter had picked out of the gutter, and whom Romney had painted, enthralled by the beauty of her features, form, and eyes, and the wonder of her long auburn tresses. Her beauty, vivacity and a certain naive charm of manner captivated the crowd and Queen alike. The crowd mobbed her carriage, exclaiming at her loveliness and half believing that she was the Virgin come to life, which was indeed very far from being the case. The Queen doted on her, shared her bed, and used her influence to further her policy. Lady Hamilton was an accomplished actress, to whom admiration was the breath of life, and whose ruling passion was ambition. She accompanied her husband to welcome Nelson, and fainted with emotion into the hero's arms. Nelson lodged with Sir William in the Palazzo Sessa. The inevitable happened. Nelson was ill, and Lady Hamilton nursed him ; he was victorious and avid for adulation, and she praised him ; she was the loveliest daughter of Eve, and he admired beauty ; she had a warm heart and kindly nature, and his wife was cold and reserved ; he was starving for passion and romance, and she was all ardour, gaiety and sparkle. So began the great sailor's lifelong devotion.

The victory of the Nile stirred the enthusiasm of the war party in Naples, which was fanned by the

Queen, Lady Hamilton and Nelson. With Buonaparte shut up in Egypt, the moment seemed propitious for a break with France. When Malta declared for the King of Naples, Ferdinand aided Nelson in blockading the French garrison. There had been delay in forming the second Coalition against France, for the Austrians were waiting for Russian aid. The Neapolitan Court in vain endeavoured to induce the Emperor Francis to strike the first blow. They were warned by Grenville (3rd October) against taking the offensive unless supported by Austria. But they were confident in the deceptive military reputation of General Mack, whom they had borrowed from Austria to lead their ill-disciplined army of brigands and *lazzaroni*. They occupied some Papal fiefs, and on 22nd November an army of 40,000 men marched against the French commander, Jean Étienne Championnet, and occupied Rome. At the same time Nelson sailed for Leghorn with 5000 Neapolitan troops to raise Tuscany against the French. But Championnet easily out-generalled Mack and smashed his army. Ferdinand escaped in disguise.

Whilst Mack made a truce with the French and sought refuge in their camp, the peasants of the countryside, roused by their priests, harassed the French divisions, and the *lazzaroni* of the city prepared to resist them to the last.

Their devotion to the reigning House was only surpassed by devotion to S. Gennaro. They hated the French and their atheistical Republican ways. The aristocracy might dabble in new-fangled ideas of revolution and reform, but such notions were hateful to the rabble. They demanded to be armed, slaughtered an Austrian courier under the eyes of the King, and extracted from him a promise not to desert them. Ferdinand showed his valuation of a royal pledge by packing every penny he could raise on board Nelson's fleet (21st December) and fleeing to Palermo.

The astonishing loyalty of the masses to their King and Fatherland is to be explained partly by natural patriotism and religion, partly by the personal popularity of Ferdinand, who had rowed and raced and fished with them as one of themselves, but largely also by the economical and agricultural reforms which had been effected by Tanucci and Acton, under the inspiration of men like Filangieri and Galiani, to the detriment of the landlord classes. These reforms had enlisted on behalf of the Monarchy the devotion of the *lazzaroni* of the city and the *cafoni* of the rural districts, who looked to the Crown as the only bulwark against the tyrannical exactions of the landed aristocracy and the nobles and *bourgeoisie* of the city. And it was amongst these latter classes, the *galantuomini*, consisting of landlords, lawyers and professional men, that the supporters of liberal ideas and revolutionary principles were found. They and their doctrines were bitterly hated by the *popolo*—labourers, fishermen and peasants. For they were mostly new men, who had taken the place of the old landowning aristocracy, and proved, as is usual, more greedy and oppressive than those whom they supplanted.[1]

When, then, the King fled to Sicily and Prince Pignatelli was left in nominal command, it was the *lazzaroni* who really took charge, and prepared to defend the city to the last. The reformers within the gates urged Championnet to advance quickly. The *lazzaroni* swarmed out to fight him, disputing every inch and making use of every farmhouse or village to hold up the invader. Championnet's trained

[1] This subject has been elucidated in a recent work by Niccolo Rodolico, *Il popolo agli inizi del Risorgimento*, 1926.

battalions advanced indeed, but suffered very heavy losses. They succeeded in capturing the Castel St Elmo by a ruse. But still the people fought from house to house, from street to street. There were two days more of terrible slaughter before disciplined valour defeated fanatical bravery. Championnet helped to win the day by promising the people the freedom of their city and respect for S. Gennaro. He was welcomed by the democrats with an ovation at the Theatre, and the "Parthenopean Republic" came into being on 23rd January 1799.

Five eminent men were appointed as Directors. Councils took in hand the abolition of tithes and feudal abuses. But 60,000,000 francs were demanded from the conquered territory, whilst French Commissioners came to gorge upon the city and carry off its art treasures to Paris. Championnet expelled them, whereupon they secured his disgrace. He was replaced by Macdonald. This was hardly the way to shake the loyalty of the *popolo*.

Suvoroff's victories brought about the fall of the Parthenopean Republic. Macdonald retired in April. A British squadron under Troubridge co-operated with a band of Royalists collected by Cardinal Ruffo, and reinforced by some Russians and Turks from Corfu. Ruffo's "Santa Fede" crusade was conducted with appalling savagery by the Calabrian peasants he had raised. They advanced in triumph upon Naples, slew the garrison of the Castel del Carmine to a man, and shut up the rest of the Republican forces in the castles of St Elmo, dell' Ovo and Nuovo. Days of hideous slaughter and pillaging by the Sanfedisti ensued. An armistice for negotiation was arranged with the Republican garrisons of the lower castles on 19th June, and a capitulation was signed on 23rd June, by which Ruffo granted them the honours of war and liberty to remain at Naples or a safe-conduct to Toulon. In this he clearly exceeded the instructions sent to him by the King (1st May), not to treat the rebels with leniency. The agreement was signed by Ruffo, the Russian and Turkish commanders, and by Commodore Foote, of the *Seahorse*, the British naval officer in command of the Bay of Naples. But before the capitulation could be put into execution, Nelson arrived from Palermo with the Crown Prince and the Hamiltons on board (24th June). He immediately made a signal annulling the truce. Acting with full powers as the representative of the King, Nelson repudiated the capitulation, which he regarded as infamous. For St Elmo, still in the hands of the French, dominated the lower castles of Ovo and Nuovo. Surrender of the latter without the former was therefore of no such importance as to justify leniency contrary to the King's command. The only admissible terms were unconditional surrender until the King's pleasure should be known. The garrisons came out of the castles, Nelson says, " with this knowledge." Those who wished to go to Toulon were allowed to embark, and were then detained under the guns of the fleet till the arrival of

CARDINALE RUFFO MEMORIAL, A.D. 1799

Ferdinand.[1] Nelson landed some marines to attack St Elmo in conjunction with the Royalists and Russians. The castle surrendered three days after Ferdinand arrived from Palermo. He made Nelson's flagship, the *Foudroyant*, his seat of government (10th July). Vengeance was now wreaked upon the rebels. Many of the leaders were taken out of the transports at the instance of the Queen. One hundred and twenty found their way to the scaffold in the Piazza del Mercato, meeting their death with heroic defiance.

Amongst those who had taken part in the rebellion was the former commander of the Neapolitan Navy, Commodore Francesco Caracciolo, member of a famous house. He had fired on British and Neapolitan vessels and inflicted considerable damage on the *Minerva*, a Neapolitan frigate. He had taken refuge in the castles, and fled from them in disguise before the capitulation was signed. Captured in the country, he was brought on board the *Foudroyant*, where Nelson had him tried for high treason by a Court-martial of Neapolitan officers, and hanged from the yard-arm of the *Minerva*. That was on 29th June, a fortnight before the surrender of St Elmo. This has been called " the shame that tarnished Nelson's name." The only possible criticism is, that he might have left the job to Ferdinand. But it was not Nelson's way to shirk responsibility, least of all in dealing with Republican rebels and naval deserters. It is said that after the King arrived, the dead body of Caracciolo rose half out of the water into which it had been cast, and was driven towards his ship by the wind. Ferdinand asked what the dead man

[1] The account of these events by Dumas and others is a travesty of the facts. *See* Mahon, *Life of Nelson* (2nd ed.), and Documents of the Navy Records Society.

wanted, and when a chaplain suggested Christian burial, he directed that he should have it.

After staying a fortnight, Ferdinand retired to Palermo without having set foot ashore. He did not return until after the Peace of Amiens (1802). In 1805 Naples signed a treaty of neutrality, but denounced it in the following month, and called upon the Allies for aid. Austerlitz enabled Napoleon to take his revenge upon Queen Carolina. His army entered Naples on 4th February 1806, and he set his brother Joseph on the throne. Joseph continued the work of reform which Tanucci had begun. The Code Napoleon and many beneficial measures were introduced; the finances and taxation were reorganised; monasteries dissolved; schools set up, and an impetus was given to the reform movement which was at long last to come to fruition. Joseph, called to rule in Spain, was succeeded in 1808 by Napoleon's brother-in-law, Joachim Murat, who repressed the democrats and ruled despotically. All this time a ferocious guerilla warfare was carried on against the French by the brigands of Calabria, supplied with money and arms by the Queen in Sicily and with military help from the British. When Napoleon escaped from Elba, Murat called upon the Italians to rise. But the Austrian army and the threat of bombardment by the British drove him from Naples. The Austrians brought back the Bourbons. After Waterloo, Murat landed in Calabria and tried to raise the country against them. He was seized and shot.

When Ferdinand came back he was greeted with the enthusiastic cheers of the *lazzaroni*. He had been warned by the Powers that there must be no executions and confiscations after the manner of 1799. He now styled himself Ferdinand I. of the Two

Sicilies, and issued a resounding declaration, proclaiming the liberty of the subject, security of property and equality of opportunity for all (May 1815). But with characteristic perfidy he agreed to a secret article in the treaty with Austria, by which the Neapolitan Government was bound not to introduce any constitutional changes other than those allowed in the Austrian dominions in Italy. In other words, he was to maintain the Austrian principles of government, which were corruption, repression, force.

The natural answer to the systematic repression of all liberal ideas by an administration, which itself worked hand in glove with bands of brigands who terrorised the country, was the formation of secret societies. Of all those which were formed in Italy at this period, with the object of securing national independence, the most important was the *Carboneria*. Its headquarters were in the kingdom of Naples. It had come into existence under the Napoleonic rule, and was composed mainly of middle-class liberals, landowners, soldiers and lawyers, who aimed at improvement in civic and political conditions. Naturally, it throve upon the mass of suppressed discontent, disappointed ambition and righteous indignation generated by the present era of tyrannical absolutism and corrupt misgovernment.

The success of the Spanish Revolution gave the signal for an outbreak. On 2nd July 1820 a couple of young army officers rode into Naples at the head of a few score of cavalry, waving the tricolour banner of the *Carbonari* and proclaiming God, the King and the Constitution. The vacillation of the Ministry and the abject cowardice of Ferdinand played into their hands. The revolt spread. The General of the Army, Guglielmo Pepe, slipped out of Naples and put himself at the head of the rebels. Early in the morning of 6th July Ferdinand, weeping with terror, granted a Constitution after the Spanish model. Ardent patriots, like Gabriele Rossetti, proclaimed in ringing verse to the excited crowd outside the palace that Italian slavery was at an end. Shelley, in an ecstasy of delight, indited his magnificent *Ode to Naples*.

But, in fact, Metternich was not so easily disposed of, and Ferdinand was as ready to repudiate a document as to break his royal oath. Whilst the new Constituent Assembly was meeting at Naples, and repressing a demand from Palermo for a separate Constitution, Metternich summoned a Congress of the Powers. Ferdinand induced his people to allow him to attend it, in order to obtain the sanction of the Powers for their newly acquired liberties. At Laibach he denounced the Constitution he had sworn to defend. The Powers agreed that the kingdom of the Two Sicilies was a danger to Europe. By the secret article of the Treaty mentioned above, Austria was entitled to intervene, for no attempt at self-government was permitted in her dominions. An Austrian army, therefore, marched upon Naples, scattered General Pepe's undisciplined troops near Rieti, 7th March 1821, and entered the city on the 23rd.

When all was safe, Ferdinand returned. He was free at last to exact vengeance on all who had dared to limit his divine absolutism, free to inflict death, imprisonment, flogging or exile upon all who had caused him to fear. The militia was dismissed and replaced by Swiss Guards and 35,000 Austrians; the schools were closed, and the will of the King became the only law. He died peacefully in his Villa Floridiana on the Vomero in 1825. But his son, Francesco I., and Ferdinand II. (1830-59), continued the appalling era of corruption, violence, cruelty and persecution which he had inaugurated. Of the latter it has to be said that he began well, and lived simply, and built the first railway in Italy, to his villa at Portici, in 1834, whilst Naples was lit with gas five years later. He struck a bargain with the Pope to abandon the old claim to the investiture.

But the revolution in Sicily revealed his real character. He earned the sinister title of Bomba by his cruel bombardment of Messina. Naples, too, rose in 1848, and Bomba granted a Constitution. It lasted till the Austrian guns at Novara relieved him of all fears. Then began that shocking epoch of persecution which filled the filthy dungeons of the Vicaria with 20,000 political offenders. Men of the highest character and intellectual attainments, like Luigi Settembrini, Sigismondo Castromediano, Francesco de Sanctis, and Carlo Poerio, were either driven into exile or herded into these noisome dens alongside with the lowest criminals, kept there without trial, or tried with scarcely a pretence of justice. "Castigate, Fertinante, Castigate!" was the constant advice of his Austrian Queen, and Ferdinand obeyed her with a will. As for the administration of the city, it is hardly an exaggeration to say that, under the King and the police, it was in the hands of the *Camorristi*. The *Camorra* was an organisation of criminals for blackmailing others. It had its origin in the crowded prisons, and established itself by giving protection to the poor, the criminals or the vicious, from whom it levied contributions. The details of this organisation were given to the world by Marc Monnier, a Neapolitan hotel-keeper.

Settembrini's *Memoirs* and his *Protest of the People of the Two Sicilies* (1847), and the writings of Poerio are the classic records of this perverse Government, based solely upon brute force.

"Reaction," says Poerio, "having become government, was organised into a party, dismounted all the social machinery, took possession of all employments, reduced the nation to helots, brutalised the people by keeping them in ignorance and fomenting superstition, terrifying them by tortures, impoverishing and exhausting them by extortion."

Poerio and Settembrini, after a brief period in the Ministry of that Constitutional Government which Ferdinand had guaranteed with a Bourbon oath, went back to prison. Their trial, a travesty of justice, lasted six months. It happened to be attended by an Englishman, the hope of the Tory Party at that time, Mr W. E. Gladstone. He listened to the obvious perjury of the witnesses; he was shown the dungeons where political prisoners were chained to felons and where doctors refused to penetrate. In his famous *Letters to Lord Aberdeen* he roused English sympathy for Italy, denouncing the Bourbon regime, in a phrase borrowed from an Italian, as "the negation of God erected into a system of government." "What we find here," he said, "is not simple imperfection, nor even occasional corruption or severity, but incessant, systematic and deliberate violation of the law." France and England withdrew their Ministers. Three years later Ferdinand died, and was succeeded by his degenerate son, Francesco II. (1859).

After he had disbanded his father's Swiss mercenaries, and Garibaldi, with his thousand Red-shirts, had captured Palermo, Francesco was compelled to grant a Constitution, and offered to ally himself to Piedmont. It was too late. The new Ministers kept order by enrolling the *Camorra*. On 20th August 1860 Garibaldi landed in Calabria and began to march northwards. His standard was joined by thousands of patriots, who regarded him almost as a demi-god. The King and Queen fled to Gæta, leaving Garibaldi free to enter Naples as a conqueror (7th September), where he addressed the enthusiastic crowd from the Palazzo d'Angri (Vanvitelli) in the Toledo. In gratitude for their prolonged support of the cause of Italian unity and independence he presented to the English the site of their present Church. In spite of the exhortations of Mazzini, Garibaldi remained loyal to Victor Emmanuel, who was now marching into Neapolitan territory. Garibaldi attacked the Bourbon army, which was massed on the banks of the Volturno. There, after a desperate battle lasting ten hours, he won Naples for Italy. At Teano, on 26th October, he saluted Victor Emmanuel as her first King. On 7th November they drove through Naples in triumph, side by side. Next day Garibaldi handed to the King the plebiscites of the Two Sicilies. They had voted almost unanimously for union with the House of Savoy (Piazza del Plebiscito). Two days later, unattended, almost secretly, Garibaldi sailed for his island home of Caprera, as poor as he had left it, " to dig up the potatoes he had planted in the spring." And Naples, erstwhile the capital of the Two Sicilies, became the chief town of the smallest province in Italy.

APPENDIX I

MUSEO FILANGIERI

THE *Museo Civico Filangieri* is in the Piazza Filangieri, in the section of the Via del Duomo between the Via Biagio and the Rettifilo. It occupies the fifteenth-century Florentine Palazzo Cuomo, which was removed piecemeal to its present site when the road was widened in 1822. The street at the S.E. corner of the Piazza leads to the fine Renaissance Church of S. Agostino Maggiore, the chapter-house and cloister of which were recently destroyed to make room for a new road. In the arches beneath the imposing raised forecourt typical *bassi* (workshops) are installed (*see* p. 29).

The Museo contains the collection of Gætano Filangieri, Principe di Satriano (*d.* 1788, *see* Chap. XV.). Portrait by Domenico Morelli (1885). An elaborate *catalogue raisonné* is lent by the attendant. Besides many pictures of inferior worth are a portrait on wood of a gentleman of the fifteenth century by Ghirlandaio (*No.* 1506); Madonna and Child (1489), and S. Prassede squeezing the blood of Christ from a sponge (1470), by Bernardino Luini; Portrait of a beardless young man with a mop of chestnut hair beneath a black cap, doubtfully attributed to Botticelli (1513 *bis*); two fourteenth-century paintings, Madonna and Crucifixion by (?) Simone Martini, brought from S. Lorenzo; paintings by Salvatore Rosa (1491), Domenichino, Woickert and Jan Steen (1439), and paintings of his daughter by Ribera, one in her youth and one when death was approaching. Her seduction by Don John of Austria is said to have broken the painter's heart. There is a remarkable death-mask of Ferdinand IV.—"Nasone." The picture by Fragonard of a young girl reclining upon a couch, "Sogno e Sorpreso," was stolen some years ago. In the gallery above are a Crucifixion by Van Dyck and two panoramas of Naples in the eighteenth century. In this gallery and a large room with Renaissance panelling upstairs are notable collections of arms and armour, terra cotta, and majolica (Castelli di Abruzzo), and china ware from Greek vases (1717–26) to Sèvres. In the library an autograph leaf signed by Torquato Tasso.

APPENDIX II

MUSEO NAZIONALE

(Reached (1) by tram No. 18 from Piazza Vittoria, E. end of Villa Nazionale.

(2) By tram No. 6 from Via di Piedigrotta at W. end of Riviera di Chiaia. This route winds round the heights under Castel St Elmo, by way of the Corso Vittorio Emmanuele and Via Salvatore Rosa, yielding glorious bird's-eye views of the Bay, Posilipo, Vesuvius, and the city and harbour beneath.

(3) A quicker method from Chiaia is by the Napoli-Pozzuoli underground railway (50 *c.* 3rd class) from the Stazione di Chiaia to the Stazione di Piazza Cavour. The entrance to the Stazione di Chiaia is just above that to the Grotto Vecchia at the end of the Via Piedigrotta.)

Open, 10–4. *Admission* 5 *lire*. *Sunday*, 10–2, *admission free*.

In this magnificent Museum are stored the works of art and objects of interest discovered at Herculaneum, Pompeii, Baia, Cuma, etc., as well as the famous Farnese Collections and the Borgia Collection from Velletri. It is of unsurpassed importance, therefore, for the study of Greek and Roman sculptures and antiquities. The Picture Gallery contains a few works of first-rate excellence.

These treasures are housed in a Palazzo at the west end of the Piazza Cavour, originally built for barracks in 1586. The arrangement of the Museum is exceedingly good. The various objects of art are set out in such a way that they can be seen to the best advantage. But unfortunately the labelling of the exhibits is chaotic in the extreme. Some of the exhibits are numbered, some are not; some have more than one number, and the numbers themselves bear no relation to one another, so far as any present consecution is concerned. A few have inscriptions in Latin; more have labels in Italian; many have none at all. Catalogues have been published, but are no longer obtainable (1926).

The following list aims at calling attention to the most important works of art.

The general scheme of the arrangement is easily grasped. *The Central Hall and East Wing* (*r.*) of the ground floor contain marble sculptures and the Egyptian collection; *the West* (*l.*) *Wing*, bronzes, inscriptions, and *graffiti*; the *Entresol* (*Mezzanino*) (*r.* and *l.*), mural paintings and mosaics; the *First Floor* (*r.*) small bronzes and mural paintings from Herculaneum and Pompeii; (*l.*) Picture Gallery; *Second Floor*, figured vases, and gold, silver, glass and majolica ware, engraved gems and coins.

The Entrance leads into the *Central Hall* (*Grande Salone*), in which are the statues of Eumachia (6232), and M. Holconius Rufus (6233) (*see* Chap. VIII.), and the pedestal of the statue to Tiberius from Pozzuoli (6780). In the *left Aisle*, (?) Urania (5960), and statues of Romans, amongst whom Cicero may be identified. Roman sarcophagus with Bacchic procession (6776). *Right Aisle and Centre*; equestrian statues of M. Nonius Balbus, father and son (6104, 6211); marble sarcophagus with deep bas-relief representing the creation and death of mankind (6705). [Prometheus is moulding men out of clay in the presence of the Gods of Olympus. Found at Pozzuoli, third-century copy of an older original.] Colossal statue of (?) Alexander Severus (5993); Genius of the Roman people (5975).

East Wing.—The passage on the right of the entrance to the Central Hall leads to three rooms on the right in which are placed masterpieces of sculptures found at Pompeii and Herculaneum. They are for the most part Roman copies of earlier Greek masterpieces. *Hall of the Goddess of Victory.*—Herm of Pallas Athena, ascribed to Cephisodotus or Phidias (6322). Statues of Aphrodite, after that by Alcamenes (5997, 5998). On the left, in the *Hall of Locri*, are fragments and vases, etc., found there, and two marble groups of the Dioscuri dismounting. Fifth century (120,119, 120,120). *Hall of Athena.*—Heads and statues of Athena (6303, 6304, 6024). Beautifully worked copies of fifth century types. Seated statue and head of Apollo. Copies of fifth-century types (6261, 6393). Orpheus, Eurydice, and Hermes (6727). [An exquisite relief, every line of which gives tender but restrained expression to the pathos of parting. Orpheus, wearing a Thracian fox-skin cap and high boots, looks back to see that his half-regained Eurydice is following him, and thereby breaks the condition on which he was retrieving her from the shades. Hermes prepares to lead her back, but shows his sympathy. An Augustan copy of Attic original of late fifth century. Names inscribed above. Portions restored, Orpheus' nose and right hand, nose of Eurydice, left hand of Hermes, etc.] Hebe offering wine to Hercules (6734). [Original

Greek votive relief of fifth century.] Female herm (?), Aphrodite (6369). [A superb example of Greek beauty. Fifth century. The treatment of the hair is particularly beautiful.] Colossal figure of Castor, one of the Dioscuri (131,209). *Cf.* the Doryphoros.

On the other side of the Hall of Victory is the *Hall of the Doryphoros*, so-called from the two Herms (6412, 6164) and the statue of the Doryphoros found at Pompeii (6011). [This is the best Roman copy of the bronze known as the Canon of Polycleitus (*c.* 440 B.C.), because he embodied in it his theory of the proportions of the human figure. The type is that of the massive, thick-set athlete. Called the Spear-bearer, because he carries a short spear in the left hand.] Female statue of fifth-century type (6107), Juno Farnese (so-called). [A colossal head of (?) Artemis. The severe expression and treatment of the hair suggest a fifth-century original (?) by Critius.] Votive relief of three Graces and three nymphs leading a figure which personifies the town of Thelonnesus (62,725). Gravestone of Protarchos (6560). Puteoli base (6715). [A mourning woman represents a province conquered by Rome. The figures are derived from Greek originals of early date.]

These rooms open on a corridor, the *Hall of the Tyrannicides*, so-called from the beautifully balanced group of Harmodius and Aristogeiton, about to slay the tyrant Hipparchus at Athens (6009, 6010). [Roman copies, probably of the copy by Critius and Nesiotes (477 B.C.), of the masterpiece of Antenor erected in their honour (510 B.C.). Found at Hadrian's Villa, Tivoli.] Athena Promachos (6007). [A composite restoration of a Roman copy.] Sepulchral stele (6556). [Early fifth century.] Orestes and Electra (6006). Found in the Macellum at Pozzuoli. [Electra's arm is round the neck of Orestes. She is instigating him to murder Clytemnestra. Copies of statues of different eras; the original of the Orestes probably fifth century.] Herms of Dionysus (6324, 6373, 6484, 6485), "Farnese Artemis" (6008). [She is hunting, and her flowing hair is crowned by a diadem of rosettes. Traces of colour can be discerned. A joyous figure attributed to end of sixth century.] "Farnese Gladiator" (6416). [A warrior wounded in the breast is falling, after the manner of the *vulneratus deficiens* of Cresilas. A wonderful torso. He carries a broken sword in his hand and wears the dazed look of one who has received his death-blow and heard the cry, *Habet* !]

On the right of this gallery is the *Hall of Palestrita*, named after the Pugilist (119,917). [He wears a cæstus, with a herm of the bearded Hercules for a support. A hefty lad, copied from a bronze of the Polycleitus order.] Bearded Dionysus (6308). Wounded warriors (6410, 6411). The *Gallery of Flora* (at right angles to the Gallery of the Tyrannicides) is called after the colossal statue of a woman found in the Baths of Caracalla and known as the " Farnese Flora " (6409). [Clad in a chiton which is slipping from right shoulder and holding some emblem in left hand. The exact significance of this statue is not determined. It is a much restored copy of Praxitelean original.] Æsculapius (6360). [Copy of an original by Alcamenes (420 B.C.). A splendid suggestion of physical and intellectual force.] Ganymede (6351). Paris leaning against a tree (6358). [Restored.] (?) Hector rescuing the body of Troilus (5999). [Restored.] Artemis hunting (6273 and 6276). Dionysus (6316). Demeter (6269). (?) Melpomene (6399). (?) Mnemosyne. From Herculaneum (6378). Venus (6288, 6301, 6295).

On the right of this gallery is the *Gallery of the Farnese Bull* (6002). [Found in the Baths of Caracalla. A late copy of a famous group by Apollonius and Tauriscus, brought to Rome from Rhodes in 4 A.D. Dirce, Queen of Thebes, having captured Antiope, mother of Amphion and Lethus, sons of Zeus, on Mount Cithæron, delivered her to them to be dragged to death behind a bull. At the last moment they recognised their mother and devoted Dirce to the fate she had devised for Antiope. Amphion holds the bull by the head. The " scenery " represents Mount Cithæron. Restored by C. B. Biondi under Michelangelo's direction and by Calì.] Facing it is the *Farnese Hercules* (6001). [A colossal statue found in pieces in the Baths of Caracalla. A copy, as an inscription records, by the Athenian Glycon of an original by Lysippus. Hercules holds in his right hand the apples of Hesperides, and rests upon his club after his labours. The head, bent forward in weariness, is very beautiful. But there is a self-conscious air about the exaggerated muscular development, very typical of the New Attic school of copyists under the Empire.] In this room there are other more beautiful things. In *Bay I.*, Apollo, after Praxiteles or Scopas (6253). A Danaid (?) (6391). Herm of the Bearded Dionysus, with base of Bacchic attributes (6306, 6863). [Copy of original by (?) Cephisodotus.] Winged Eros (6353). [Copy of bronze masterpiece by Praxiteles.] Visit of Dionysus to Icarus and his wife (6713). [The god heads a Bacchic procession.] Colossal Mask of Hercules (6260).

Bay II.—" Farnese Hera " (6027). [Copy of the superbly beautiful Hera of Alcamenes.] Copy of the Ludovisi Ares, a seated torso of an athletic youth. (?) Aphrodite (6035). [Torso after Praxiletes.] Psyche (6019). [So-called, but really Aphrodite looking down at a mirror. Copy of a fourth-century original. A work of extraordinary loveliness. "That Parian face, before which all the beauty of the Florentine Venus is poor and earthly—that aspect so full of harmony—of youth—of genius—of the soul—which modern critics have supposed the representation of Psyche" (Lytton). If this "mutilated, but all wondrous statue," be not a statue of Psyche, but of Aphrodite, it is a manifestation of the Deity in that rare, but not impossible combination of genius and beauty; a spiritual and intellectual Goddess of Love, the incarnation of perfect body and noble mind.] Adonis (6016) after Praxiteles. Paris and Helen (6682). [Aphrodite aided by Peitho, the Goddess of persuasion, tempts Helen to yield to Paris, who is led to her by Eros. A lovely bas-relief derived from a fourth-century original.] Torso Farnese (6034). [Dionysus.] Mask of Zeus (6260). Aphrodite Anadyomene (rising from the sea) (6296). Hercules subjugated by Omphale (6406). Youth leaning against a tree (6016). [After Praxiteles.] Bust of Aphrodite (6361). Nereid on a sea-monster (6026). [Found at Posilipo.] Ganymede embracing the eagle (6355) after Praxiteles. In Bay opposite Psyche, Venus of Capua (Venus Victrix) (6017). [Standing with left foot on helmet of Mars and holding his shield, into which she gazes as into a mirror. Copy of the time of Hadrian from the same original as that from which the Venus of Milo was also derived. Arms restored.] Satyr with child Dionysus (6022). [A satyr dancing to the cymbals smiles up at the boy he carries on his shoulder. Shepherd's crook and pipes on pedestal. A delightful composition, full of gaiety, grace and charm. Copy of a bronze of Hellenistic period. Face and arms of the satyr and child's body restored.] Pan and Olympus (6329). [Pan teaching Olympus to play the pipes. From the original of Heliodorus.] Dionysus and Eros (6307). [After Praxiteles. Arms of figure of Eros restored.]

Bay III.—Bacchic procession (6726). [Exquisitely wrought Roman copy found on the Appian Way.] Relief of Mænad struggling with a Satyr (6724). Marble vessels with Bacchic processions, etc. (6778, 6779). Aphrodite of Sinuessa. [Without head or arms (?) fourth century Greek original.] Roman Sarcophagus of second century, with scenes from the life of Achilles (124, 325). Vase of Gæta (6673). [This beautiful Neo-Attic Krater stood in the Harbour of Gæta. It is signed by the Athenian Salpion. A relief of exquisite delicacy surrounds the bowl representing a Bacchic procession and the infant god being entrusted to the care of nymphs.] Dionysus with panther (6728). Well-head with relief of Satyrs working at vintage (6675). [Very finely executed.]

Beyond Bay III., at S. end of the wing, the *Hall of the Amazons* contains sculptures by which Attalus, King of Pergamum, celebrated his victory over the invading Gauls (239 B.C.). The copies here represent, A dead giant (6013). [Restored.] Wounded Gaul (6015). [In reverse position to that in the Capitoline Museum.] An Amazon (6012). [Wounded in the breast and beautiful in death.] Adjoining is the *Hall of Venus Callipygus* (6020). [Incorrectly named after a statue of a temple in Syracuse. We have here a slim and graceful Aphrodite in a pose as piquant and alluring as it is original. The goddess is removing her chiton in preparation for a bath, and looks over her right shoulder to gaze at her reflection in the water. Self-conscious and *posé*, no doubt, but this good copy of an Hellenistic original is singularly charming. The head, shoulders, left arm, right hand and right thigh have been cleverly restored by Albacini in accordance with replicas of this model.] Eros sleeping (6339). [The little urchin's bow is between his legs.] Aphrodite (?) bust (6285, 6289). Venus of the Medici type (6286). Venus and Cupid in her bath (6293, 6297). [Restored.] *Vestibule at end of Gallery of Flora and Basement.*—Egyptian Collection, Terra-cotta Collection, Prehistoric Collection (from Cuma, Salerno, etc.).

The rooms and corridor at the northern end of this wing are filled with torsos and fragments of decorative and coloured marbles. The corridor is called the *Gallery of Diana of Ephesus*, after the well-preserved statue of the many-breasted mother there (6278). Statues of Serapis (975), Anubis (981), and Isis (9370, 9372).

The West Wing.—Turning to the left from the main entrance out of the Central Hall, we find ourselves in the *Corridor of Bronzes from Herculaneum*, a list of which is given on p. 179. This corridor contains the bronze horses' heads from equestrian statues, the bronze horse from Nero's chariot (4904), and statues of matrons and citizens who had held municipal office at Herculaneum. At the end Tiberius (5615); Claudius (nude) (5593); Augustus (5595); equestrian statue of (?) Nero, from Pompeii (5635); (?) Perseus (126,170). [After Lysippus]; Cæcilius Jucundus (110,663). [A speaking likeness of the banker of Pompeii (*see* p. 203).]

At the end of this gallery is the *Gallery of the Emperors*. This and the four rooms opening out of it are filled with busts and statues of the Roman Imperial family, of which (?) Agrippina (6029); Antinous (6030); Antoninus Pius (6031); Caracalla (6033); Julius Cæsar (6038); Marcellus and Livia (6041, 6044); Matidia (6032), are the most notable.

From the Hall of the Emperors we enter (1) the *Hall of the Great Bronzes. Room I.*—Bronzes from Pompeii. Round the sides of the room: Python erect to strike (4898); Hounds worrying a boar (4899); Lion springing (4897); Goat (4903); Bull (4890); Gull (4891); Stag (4902); Serpent (4901); Fisherman with rod and creel, intently watching his line (4994). The walls are decorated with frescoes. On a pedestal in the centre of the room, statuette of *Dionysus Listening* (number (5003) gone). [Formerly called Narcissus, but the goatskin flung over the left shoulder and ivy wreath identify the God. He is standing listening to the distant cry, perhaps of the Bacchanals on Cithæron's heights, calling Io, Bacche! His weight is thrown on the right leg, the left thrown slightly forward. The feet are encased in elaborate *cothurni*. His head is bent forward and down in an attitude of listening, an attitude confirmed by the extended right hand and raised forefinger. The outline of the body and legs forms an exquisitely sinuous double curve, which constitutes the chief charm of this delightful creation. The limbs are slender, though perhaps unduly heavy below the knee. The modelling of the back of the head and left shoulder is not altogether satisfying.] On table confronting it (i) Drunken Silenus (5001). [A staggering, intoxicated figure, with left hand raised above the head to hold a lamp or vase.] (ii) Faun with wine-skin (111,495). [He is pouring wine from a goat-skin held in his left arm into a vessel (lost) in his left hand; his lips parted and face aglow with an expression of vinous delight and rapturous anticipation. He wears a wreath of fir twigs and has pointed ears and a long tail.] (iii) Dancing Faun (5002, number gone). [An original Greek work, and surely the very perfection of life and grace and gaiety. Without a touch of vulgarity or a hint of self-consciousness the artist has portrayed the very spirit of the wild, inspired faun dancing to the sound of Bacchanalian cymbals, right foot advanced, arms upraised in rhythmic movement. Beautiful from every standpoint, it is perhaps most beautiful when viewed from behind on its left quarter.] Cupid carrying a dolphin (111,701); Cupid with a duck (5000).

Room II.—Apollo Citharista (5630) from Pompeii. [His right hand held a cithara. There is a plectrum in the left. Copy from original of time of Phidias.] Winged Victory (4997).

[Half held in the air by outspread wings, her toe rests upon a modern globe. The very incarnation of the fleeting goddess.] Apollo with lyre and plectrum (5613). Venus Anadyomene (4998). [Copy from fourth-century original.] Statuette of an Ephebus (125,348). [An original Greek statuette of late fifth century, from Pompeii, converted into a lampholder.] Ephebus, The Boy Victor. [Found at Pompeii in 1926, *see* Chap. VIII. A Greek masterpiece of singular grace and beauty of the age of Phidias. Arms restored. Life size. This statue also had been converted, Prof. Mauri thinks, into a lichnoporus, or light-bearer. It fulfils the searching test from which only the greatest masterpieces emerge successfully, it is equally beautiful in every aspect and from every point of view. Some traces of original gilding remain. It has been suggested that the *Ephebus* here portrayed is Pantarkes, an Elian youth of extraordinary beauty, whom we know to have been victor in the Boy's Games in 436 B.C. The suggestion does not admit of proof at present. But it is, at any rate, a very happy and satisfying one, artistically. For not only are the limbs beautifully modelled and the body perfectly proportioned, but the muscles over the hips, along the back and upon the well-developed chest, point to a trained athlete. They are features of a youth whose athletic training has not permitted the development of muscle to obscure the natural grace or to stiffen the spring and elasticity of his lithe, boyish limbs. There is here nothing of the effeminacy which crept into later art. On the other hand, there is nothing of the stiffness and austerity of an earlier period. The anatomy of the adolescent figure is indicated to perfection. It is wholly free from the heaviness of the fully developed male athlete exemplified in the *Doryphoros*. The suggestion of a portrait of the Boy Victor is confirmed by the pose of the arms. The left hangs by his side, but the right is extended. The half-closed fingers of a strong but well-made hand may be thought once to have grasped some offering which the boy is about to make, with a gesture as natural as it is charming. This gesture carries out and harmonises to perfection with the grace and pose of the whole form. With that curious, indefinable skill which is the hall-mark of Greek genius, the artist has managed to convey, as much by the whole, as by any particular detail, the natural modesty of a lad new to the triumphs of life. But, beautiful as is this lissom figure, beautiful as is the half-shy gesture of a boy offering, it may be, a sprig of laurel from the crown of his first victory in the Games at the shrine of some deity, it is the head, the poise of the head, with its perfect Greek features and hair, which more than any other detail contributes to make this newly recovered statue one of the lovely, unforgettable things in the world.]

Room III.—Bronzes from Herculaneum. Mercury resting (5625). [Copy of a motive of the school of Lysippus. Hermes seated on a rock, his right hand resting on it; in his left hand a fragment of a caduceus. Wings strapped on the feet. The messenger of the gods has just alighted after a flight, which he is about to resume. His left leg, slender like that of a runner, is drawn up, and the right extended and resting on the heel, an attitude natural to an athlete after exertion. Yet he will soon be on his way again, for his winged left foot is on tiptoe for the flight. His features wear a faint expression of fatigue; you can see that he is partly supporting his weight on the right hand. The whole body, not merely one or two details of it, gives an expression of momentary weariness from which it is rapidly recovering with the elasticity of a youthful athlete. A lovely and perfect thing, faultless in every detail, from the glorious, godlike head of him to the tips of his light and lissom limbs.] Next to him the Sleeping Faun (5624). Five Dancers or Water-carriers (5604, etc.), and copies of Greek heads and busts of amazing beauty (enumerated in Chap. VII.), notably the Head of Doryphoros (4885), [Copy from Polycleitus], and Bust of an ideal type (Dionysoplaton) (5618); Sappho (4896).

Room IV.—Two Boys preparing to Wrestle (5626, 5627). [From Herculaneum.] Wild Sow (4893). Two Gazelles (4886–88); Drunken Faun (5628). [Sprawling in drunken jollity, his left elbow resting on a wine-skin, he is snapping the fingers of his upraised right hand.] Other heads and busts from Herculaneum, notably the vivid portraits of Seneca (5616) and (?) Heracleitus (5623); Scipio Africanus (5634). In the S.W. corner of this wing, at the end of the Gallery of the Emperors, is the *Sala d'Iside*, where are collected the objects found in the Temple of Isis at Pompeii (*see* Chap. VIII.), notably the Dionysus-Osiris (6312), Aphrodite Anadyomene, arranging her hair (6298), and the exquisitely beautiful archaistic statuette of Isis, painted and gilded, and holding a sistrum in her right hand and the ANKH in her left. Her robe is carved with extraordinary delicacy (976). Mural paintings from the Temple on the walls. Lamps of charming lotos design. Sacrificial knife, etc.

Adjoining this room, the *Room of the Pompeian Temples*, containing notably the bronze statues of Apollo and Artemis, shooting (5629, 4895), and Hermaphrodite (marble, 6352). Room of Inscriptions, N.E. Gallery.

Entresol.—On staircase, Colossal statue of Zeus (8266). [Copy of fifth-century original.] *East Wing* (*r.*), Wall paintings, chiefly from Pompeii, Herculaneum, and Stabiæ. The *Gabinetto Pornografico* at the end of Room V. is now closed to the public. *West Wing* (*l.*)—Wall paintings and Mosaics from Pompeii. In *Room V.* is the largest and one of the finest ancient mosaic pictures, Alexander and Darius at the Battle of Issus (10,020). [Portrait of Alexander, probably authentic.] As to the wall paintings, which I have not space to enumerate, the visitor will be as much amazed at their state of preservation as at the frequent charm and grace of the designs, *e.g.*, Women playing with knuckle-bones (9562); Perseus rescuing Andromeda (8998), etc. (*see* Chap. VIII.).

First Floor, *East Wing*.—Small Bronzes from Pompeii, Herculaneum, etc. Domestic utensils and ornaments of great variety and interest, and wall paintings from Pompeii. The lovely Flora is set up here. A spiral staircase leads up from Room I. to the *Second Floor*. *Room I.*—Terra-cotta ware. *Room II.*—Alabaster and glass. Vase of Blue Glass (13,521). [Found at Pompeii and rivalling the Portland Vase. Vintage scenes amid a network of vines.] *Room III.*—In the next room, gold ornaments and the "Tassa Farnese," a cup of Sardonyx (27, 611). [A wonderful cameo of Alexandrian workmanship of first century A.D. On the outside is carved an ægis with Medusa head; within, Egyptian agricultural scenes. This cup was broken by a disgruntled employé in 1925, but has been mended.] This room is succeeded by rooms of silver objects and arms, engraved gems, coins (90,000), and figured vases. Two vases from Canosa (i) Funeral figure of Patroclus (3254), and (ii) the Darius Vase (3253), showing King Darius enthroned. Cumæ collections (Stevens, etc.).

The East Wing of the *Second Floor* contains the *Picture Gallery*. Rooms and pictures are at present being rearranged and renovated. One can only indicate *Room I.*—Tapestries, Battle of Pavia (1525), by Bernard van Orley, and Story of Perseus (Gobelin). Bronze Horse's Head (4887). [Formerly attributed to Donatello, now to third century B.C.] *Room II.*—Vases with Gorgon mask, etc. (10,810, 10,525). Bronze tabernacle of late sixteenth century (10,509). [From a sketch by Michelangelo.] *Rooms III.–V.*—Paintings, chiefly Neapolitan, sixteenth to seventeenth century, Andrea Sabatini da Salerno. [Probably a pupil of Cesare da Sesto.] Luca Giordano, Cavaliere, etc. In *Room III.*—Bronze bust of Dante (10,516). *Room VI.*—Umbrian and Lombard schools. Caravaggio, Christ bearing His Cross (83,809); Luini, B., Madonna and Child (83,998);

C. da Sesto (83,878); Sodoma, Resurrection (84,166). *Room VII.*—Bolognese school, Caracci, Lanfranco, etc. Domenichino, Guardian Angel (84,013); Guido Reni, St Matthew (84,152); Atalanta and Hippomenes (84,030); Vanity offering a jewel to Modesty (84,130); Farnese Casket (15,507). *Room VIII.*—Italian schools, sixteenth and seventeenth centuries, Guido Reni, St John (84,094); Annibale Caracci, Pietà (83,984); Sofonisba Anguissola, Portrait of herself (84,092); Vasari, G., Justice (84,214); Francesco Torbido (Il Moro), Portrait of an Old Man. Signed (83,980); Bronze statuettes (i) Mercury running, by Giovanni da Bologna (10,782). [Full of the poetry of motion. A smaller replica of the Florentine bronze.] Hercules, sixteenth century (10,785, 10,520). *Room IX.*—Canaletto, Pannini, Mengs, Portrait of a Prince (83,818). Giovanni da Bologna, Bronze group, Rape of the Sabines, 1579 (10,524). *Room X.*—Italian schools, seventeenth and eighteenth centuries. *Room XI.*—Schools of Ferrara and Parma. Benvenuto Tisi (83,963, 83,939, 83,952). [In the manner of Dosso Dossi.] Dosso Dossi, Madonna and Child and St Jerome (83,915) etc. *Room XII.*—Correggio, Betrothal of St Catherine (83,972); Madonna and Child (83,969); St Anthony (131,060); Parmigianino (Francesco Mazzola), Portrait of Anthea (84,024 and others); Michelangelo, Anselmi, etc. *Room XIII.*—Titian, Danæ, Signed, 1545. [A wonderful symphony in gold and blue. Her hair, the colour of ripened wheat, falls about her shoulders like a scarf of golden thread, strays in long wisps about her side and is sprayed about her like a cloud of gold. It is the very counterpart of that cloud of litten gold in which the god is descending to her. Her blue eyes gaze upwards, half in fear, half in welcome to the deity. The colour scheme is carried out by the Cupid on the right.] Titian, Magdalene (84,019). Signed. [Badly repainted.] Titian, Charles V. (84,594). [Badly restored.] Titian, Cardinal Alexander Farnese (83,919). Titian, Cardinal Pietro Bembo (83,983). Palma Vecchio, Holy Conversation (*c.* 1515). [St John, St Jerome, and St Catherine implore the Madonna's intercession. Badly restored, but a very beautiful painting.] Titian, Pope Paul III. (83,920). [Badly restored.] Titian, Pier Luigi Farnese (83,924). [He carries a Field Marshal's baton.] Titian, Paul III. with his nephews, Alessandro and Ottavio Farnese (83,921). [Marvellous portrait of the faded, cunning, but tenacious old man scolding his nephew.] Titian, Paul III. (83,974). Titian, Philip II. (83,957). [A series of masterpieces.] Paolo Veronese, Pool of Bethesda (83,977). *Room XIV.*—Raphael Sanzio, Cardinal Alessandro Farnese, Paul III.

(84,004). Raphael, Copies of Madonnas, etc. by (83,779, 83,783, 83,791, 84,002). Raphael, Madonna and Child (84,005). [The Madonna del Divino Amore. Partly at least by a pupil (?) Giulio Romano, *cf.* No. 83,988, Madonna with a cat, by him.] *Room XV.*—Tuscan and Venetian school. Simone Martini, Christ Blessing. Andrea Mantegna, St Euphemia (83,946). [Spoiled by restoration.] Botticelli, Madonna and Child led by two Angels (84,193). Lorenzo Lotto, Bishop of Treviso (84,487); Madonna and Child (83,956). Signed, 1503. [Note the landscape background and play of light in the drapery of this pupil of Giovanni Bellini.] Transfiguration (83,990). [Signed. A fine early work, with beautiful landscape.] Antonio da Solario (Lo Zingaro), Madonna and Child (131,059). Signed. [Landscape visible through window.] Alessandro Moretto, Ecce Homo (83,932). [A fine work by the Brescian master.] *Room XVI.*—Neapolitan school. Francesco de Mura, Francesco Solimena, Sebastiano Conca, Giuseppe Bonito, etc. *Room XVII.*—Ditto. Giuseppe Ribera (St Jerome (83,980, 83,979, etc.), Massimo Stanzioni, Andrea Vaccaro, and Luca Giordano. Pietro Cavallini, Judith with head of Holofernes, St Cæcilia, Prodigal Son, Lazarus, Death of St Joseph, Crucifixion. [Over-restored and varnished, but showing the effective, if exaggerated, use of chiaroscuro and dramatic appeal.] *Room XVIII.*—Salvatore Rosa, Micco Spadaro, etc. *Room XIX.*—Rembrandt, by himself (84,508) (? copy). Van Dyck, Crucifixion (84,527). Van Cellen, Portrait (84,501). Velasquez. The Drinker (84,048). [This dramatic vintage scene, painted *in tempera*, with wonderful portrait studies, is a copy of that at Madrid.] *Rooms XX.–XXI.*—Foreign schools (chiefly Dutch and Flemish). *Room XXII.*—Pieter Brueghel (84,486), The Hermit; and The Blind leading the Blind (84,490). [The leader falling into the ditch. An admirable interpretation of the parable.] Others of Dutch and German schools. *Rooms XXIII. and XXIV.*—Tapestries and small bronzes.

APPENDIX III

NOTES ON PLACES OF INTEREST NEAR NAPLES

For *Posilipo* and *Baia*, *see* Chaps. III. and IV.
For *Vesuvius*, *Herculaneum*, and *Pompeii*, *see* Chaps. VII. and VIII.
Beyond *Pompeii*, *Castellamare*, *Vico Equense*, *Sorrento*, *Amalfi* (Cathedral, 1204), *Ravello*, *Salerno* (Cathedral built by Roger Guiscard, 1076).

These little towns have a charm and beauty all their own. The coast road provides perhaps the most magnificent drive in all Italy.

Pæstum (*Pesto*) can easily be done in a day by train from Naples (Stazione Centrale, 58 miles Dep. 7.35 a.m., through carriage) via Torre del Greco, Nocera, Vietri, Salerno (35 miles), and Battipáglia. *Arrives* at Pesto 10.39 a.m. Restaurant at Railway Station. *Return* 2.25 p.m. *Arrive* Naples 5.50 p.m. Fare 67.50 l., 2nd class. Entrance, 5 l.

Approaching Vietri we gain a lovely view of the prosperous little town of Salerno, with its harbour below to the left, and, on the right, of a section of that beautiful coast of curving promontories and tiny bays which form the entrancing surroundings of Amalfi. Between Salerno and Battipáglia the land is rich, but after that we pass into the desolate plain of Pæstum (Piano di Pesto), where herds of buffalo roam over malaria-stricken fields. It is bordered by the sea on one side, and on the other by a range of limestone hills, with glens not unlike parts of Scotland. Some attempt is now being made to reclaim this district from the ruinous pest of malaria which has devastated all this coast and driven the few remaining inhabitants up into the hills for refuge from the fields in which they work by day.

Malaria and the Saracens, who plundered it in 871 A.D., were responsible for the ruin of Pæstum, the remains of whose temples now rise in lonely grandeur looking out to sea, across the remains of ancient walls and silent streets.

Poseidonia was the name of the city of Neptune which the Greeks from Sybaris founded as a trading station in the sixth century B.C., and which became known as Pæstum in Roman days. It must have been a flourishing little town, if we may judge from the remains, which, though few in number, render it still one of the wonder spots of the world. Amongst roughly cultivated fields, strewn with debris of ancient buildings, and surrounded by coarse grass and scrub, the city, once so famous for its roses and violets, moulders in solitude and silence. The walls—approached through a field close to the station—were about three miles in circumference, with four gates and eight towers, and are built of square blocks of travertine. Erect and isolated, facing the Samnite Hills on the one side and the sea on the other, stand three temples. Passing through the Porta della Sirena or Eastern Gate, on our left we see the Temple of Poseidon (Neptune), and the so-called Basilica, and, on the right, remains of a Roman amphitheatre and Portico, and the so-called Temple of Ceres. Robert Guiscard used the deserted city as a quarry of marble for his buildings and churches at Benevento, Salerno and Amalfi. That these three temples were left is due to the fact that they were built, not of marble, but of such heavy masses of stone. If the Temple of Poseidon were not so superb in its majesty, infinite beauty of proportion, exquisite colouring of golden-brown stone, and grandeur and simplicity of design, we should admire and marvel more at the rather earlier type of Greek temple in the so-called "Basilica," and the intermediate type of the "Temple of Ceres," or at the foundations of the old houses and streets surrounding them. As it is, this magnificent Temple of the fifth century A.D. absorbs one's attention. It ranks with the Temple of Theseus at Athens, and the Temple of Concordia at Girgenti as one of the three best preserved monuments of the Doric order in existence.

Raised on a stylobate of three steps, it presents rows of thirty-six fluted columns, six at either end and twelve on each side. The fluting at the bases is worn as if by the action of the sea. The *cella* within is supported by sixteen columns, above which two rows of smaller columns carried the roof. This point commands marvellous vistas of the Tyrrhenian sea and the Samnite Hills.

The Temple of Demeter and Persephone, called the Basilica, dated from before 550 B.C. It has fifty fluted columns with heavy flat echinus and entasis. A third row of columns divides the building longitudinally, indicating the worship of dual divinities. The so-called Temple of Ceres is similar in construction to the Temple of Poseidon, but half the size.

These places deserve a book in themselves. I cannot do more

INDEX

D.

E.

F.

T.

Printed by Turnbull & Spears
at Edinburgh in Great Britain